THE
PROFESSORS

THE
PROFESSORS

WHO THEY ARE, WHAT THEY
DO, WHAT THEY REALLY
WANT AND WHAT
THEY NEED

HERBERT LIVESEY

CHARTERHOUSE ☐ NEW YORK

THE PROFESSORS

Library of Congress Cataloging in Publication Data

Livesey, Herbert B
  The professors.

  1. College teachers—United States. 2. College
teaching as a profession—United States. 3. United
States—Intellectual life. I. Title.
LB1778.L58   378.1'2'0973   74-25730
ISBN 0-88327-046-3

MANUFACTURED IN THE UNITED STATES OF AMERICA

For Barbara. Forever.

CHAPTER 1

Once, a group of undergraduates at Miami University (the one in Ohio) stood teasing and laughing by Thobe's Fountain on Old Slant Walk. The hair was poodle-cut, ponytailed, or crew; the skirts were mid-calf, the pants chino and buckled in the back; the shoes were ballet slippers or white bucks. Eisenhower was in his second term, his second recession, and nearing his second heart attack. Beer busts, blanket parties, and panty raids were common diversions. The Alpha chapter of Sigma Chi had just held its annual Watermelon Bust, the highlight of which was the selection of a reluctant *Miss* Watermelon Bust. The sexual revolution and the feminist movement were ten years away. Jim Bohan and the rest of us were young.

Jim was of a whimsical turn of mind. Assuring himself of the attention of the five girls in the group around him, he began slowly unzipping his fly—to their growing and only partially feigned horror. He reached inside, pulled something out, and cried, "Surprise! New shirt!" The girls, of course, squealed. Then he tucked his shirttail back.

Dr. James Bohan, lecturer in logic and epistemology, is rather more sedate now. He looks about the same, if a trifle thicker of jowl and middle. The black hair is still all there, combed as it was fifteen years ago. He slouches in his chair,

1

chin on chest, and pushes what might be the same black-framed glasses back on his nose. After five years of graduate study at the University of Washington, years more teaching philosophy at Wichita State and the University of Tennessee at Chattanooga, after the army, marriage to Mary Busey from Miami, and two sons, Jim has come to Hayward, California. His appointment at the State College is tentative, term-to-term. He might make $12,000 this year if he's reappointed each of the next two quarters. The newspaper on the coffee table announces that street-sweepers across the bay in San Francisco henceforth will be paid a minimum of $13,000 a year.

"If you have a Ph.D. in chemistry these days—or philosophy—you might as *well* go sweep streets. These are very dark days for professors. There's an enormous spirit of disenchantment. And I'm only one of a very large number of people who are disenchanted. The nineteen sixties made an awful lot of promises to people in the academic profession which haven't been kept. There's an enormous gap between what you're trained to do in graduate school—the kinds of things that attract you to get degrees—and what you wind up doing most of your work week at the university. People who get a Ph.D. were trained to think of themselves as eventually getting on a faculty which would reward them for research. The standard story was that even though you didn't make much money, you had prestige and you had time.

"But! The gag is, the vast majority of jobs available in the country are not in such departments, and the programs themselves are cutting back. And there's a breed of person in the professoriate . . . well . . . to take an example from my own discipline, the best of all possible worlds for him would be not to have to teach philosophy. For him, teaching philosophy is a pain in the ass. The idea is to be able to *philosophize*. Namely, read, write, and talk philosophy with other philosophers. That's what he wants to do. Having to go in and water

2

down stuff to a bunch of undergraduates—most of whom don't give a damn anyway—that is the drudge. And this is why you have a lot of lousy teachers."

Whether because of self-interest or professional altruism or overproduction of scholars, the expectation gap widens. The hopes of Bohan's youth seem unlikely to be fulfilled.

"Lousy money . . . anti-intellectualism . . ." He shakes his head in dismay and frustration. "In the early Sixties, with Kennedy and good old Jackie in the White House beating the drums for culture and the arts, it seemed like the creation of a mini-renaissance . . . Well . . . those days are gone. This country has always had an abiding fear of the egghead. It's extremely difficult to figure out why. The people felt he was a threat to their religion. But also, there is the notion that the academician doesn't have to make any actual decisions, that all he has to do is sit and think, that his thinking on a given policy matter isn't tempered by having to live with what he thinks is the right thing to do.

"Since we've been in California, I've really felt the presence of the governor as a genuine person. You could live in the state of Tennessee quite a while and never know who the governor was . . . or care. But *Reagan!*" He shakes his head again, leaves his obvious feelings unsaid. "Especially in education. His anti-intellectualism and his insensitivity to the kind of a thing a university is have really hurt. He's hurt us, but he's hurt places like Berkeley even more."

Faculty salaries at the public colleges and universities in California have been frozen for two years now, and the Carnegie Corporation has listed the University of California at Berkeley as in "serious financial difficulty" for the second time during that period. But most people and organizations these days are affected by the state of the economy. If professors have been caught in the crunch—well, what else is new? That can't be all there is to Bohan's unhappiness. And after all, Bohan is an unremarkable, average sort of professor. He's not

3

tenured, but tenure before forty is not common. He has published, but he hasn't written a precocious opus riveting the attention of his colleagues—books like the philosophical *Age of Jackson* by an Arthur Schlesinger, Jr. not yet twenty-five or *Language in Thought and Action* by an S. I. Hayakawa barely thirty years old. That's for the *wunderkinds* of academia, putting together a combination of brilliance, luck, and timing. Bohan is brighter than most people, but so are most professors. He is lacking in driving ambition, but so are most professors. He is underpaid, but so are many professors.

Despite all this, most professors aren't dissatisfied. Behind the grousing about money and bureaucrats and anti-intellectualism are people apparently content with their chosen lot. In a report entitled *Work in America*, produced in 1973 by an HEW task force, professors at urban and church-related colleges and universities were judged to be among the happiest workers in the United States. Although only 43 percent of all the white-collar workers and 24 percent of those in blue-collar jobs in the cross-section surveyed would choose the same vocation if they could begin again, 93 percent of the urban university professors said they would opt for their present careers. Of those working at church-related institutions, 77 percent expressed the same satisfaction. In between were listed non-academic mathematicians, physicists, biologists, chemists, lawyers, and Washington journalists. (Not surprisingly, unskilled auto workers took up the last position, with only 16 percent satisfied.) The same survey further noted that two-thirds of all college teachers would use the extra two hours in a 26-hour day in work-related activity. Yet only one out of four lawyers and one out of twenty other workers would do the same.

Bohan, nevertheless, is unhappy. Why? The reasons range from his own dissatisfaction with the profession to seeing forty just ahead without hope of significant improvement in his circumstances. It's also mid-life slump, the end of the first half of his allotted years. The good ones.

Bohan looks around the cramped room. He didn't have a car, so he had to find the apartment by riding buses. It costs $210 each month. They haven't been here long enough to put a clothes bar in the closet. The walls need paint. He goes to the kitchen and pours another Scotch. Thinking.

"General unhappiness," he resumes, "is a gap between expectation and achievement. If a person's expectations are kept sufficiently low, he's likely to be happy. Most people's expectations—mine—were for things being a little better than they've turned out. In some cases, a *lot* better. The other thing is leisure time. More and more people find themselves with more and more time on their hands, and they don't know what to do with it."

A professor has more leisure time than most, hasn't he?

"No more than he used to. A professor's leisure remains more or less constant. I'm thinking of people who aren't academicians. A shorter work week, three-day weekends. Professionals, semi-professionals, lots of them fudge a way in which they can knock off on Friday or Friday noon to Monday noon. They work like hell and get an ulcer in between, but. . . ."

But a professor has that leisure all the time, hasn't he?

"The trouble is, it's difficult to decide how hard professors have to work. You've got to be a self-starter, you've got to be self-motivating. Also, it's very difficult to correlate the amount of time you put in with success—promotion, salary increase. . . . At a research-oriented university where they literally say 'publish or perish,' you can get a little better fix on yourself. You take a job, you know you have to teach two classes *and* you better damn well come up with a publication or two by Christmas, or you're out. And some publications are easy to come by, and some are very, very hard.

5

"In philosophy, getting published is relatively hard. Getting a paper accepted to be read at a philosophy conference, for example, is as hard as publishing. Also, it's difficult to publish in a respectable journal. It really is. On the other hand, a chemist goes into a lab, he's got a lab assistant who sets up the experiment, who does most of the work, and draws up some graphs of most of the results. And there's a Southwestern Chemical Society meeting, including the states of Oklahoma, Arkansas, and north Texas. They have a little get-together, O.K.? And everybody hands in their research of the last couple of months. It's accepted for publication automatically. Now, how do you compare that to a guy who has a substantial piece of original research in a major field like, say, history? Some deans are stupid. They say, 'This chemist did this, this historian did that.' Shit, there's no comparison at all. Night and day. So, what counts as a publication? There is no answer."

So publish or perish is one of the evils of the system, isn't it?

"I'm not sure. There's a tendency for a large number of Ph.D.'s to go home, shut their books, turn on the TV, and relax. To a certain extent, that's what the publish-or-perish business is all about. It's designed to ensure you're not doing that. Conversely, if you're in that publish-or-perish situation, the demands on your time are really extensive. If you want to be really good, you want to know as much as there is to know, be able to make a contribution, and it's a helluva lot of work. It isn't something you can do and have done. The work always remains. And, of course, it *can* be publish *and* perish."

If it looks like he will stay in philosophy, Bohan will finish his half-a-book. As soon as it's accepted, he'll "go in and hit the dean on the head with it, scream and holler and dance around" for a raise in salary.

But he isn't at all sure he'll stay. Whether he's employed four months hence depends upon budget cuts, enrollment dips or increases, the loss or retention of other faculty, and, perhaps, the whim of his superiors.

Bohan concedes—or chooses to believe—that he is not a typical professor, whether in terms of temperament, in range of interests, or in total commitment. Academic people are, to his mind, almost religious about their calling, devout about their subjects. The profession is dominated by first-generation college graduates, new members of the middle-class who took the traditional teacher–preacher–social worker path up from the blue collar ranks. For them, to be a college professor is a wondrous escape from the lifelong tedium of lunch pails and the scrimping of their fathers. It fosters self-satisfaction, not a little smugness, and, in many, a conviction of surpassing personal and professional worth.

If most professors have fulfilled their expectations, Jim Bohan has not. It has never been clear to him, he says, why professors should live in circumstances dramatically below others of similar success in other fields. He believes that professorial salaries run as much as 25 percent below what they should be to meet reasonable expenses, even discounting the fact that professors have more time for themselves and that they are not in profit-making businesses. The happiest professors are those who have something to supplement their incomes: lecturing, writing, consulting, supplemental research grants, even clandestine teaching jobs at other colleges. Bohan doesn't have any of these things going for him, but he's working on it.

"I have business opportunities here, with a land developer." He whips out a full-color prospectus featuring vistas of windswept northern California seacoast and artfully angular condominium clusters. "My main difficulty is that I don't have any background in business and I don't know the right people in the Bay Area. But now I'm here, and within a year I can make up for a lot of that. By that time, I may be in a position to get work with a commercial real estate firm in San Francisco. Eventually, that's really what I want to do. It isn't just that there's more money. It's more challenging intellectually than residential real estate. You sell one house . . . it's almost like selling cars. When you sell office buildings, manage and lease property, every deal is a little different. It's really kinda interesting."

He's not sure he has the inclination or determination for hustling, but he feels that he's convinced the people he'll work with that he does. Not that he doesn't have qualms.

"I've just had peeks now, little tastes of the business world. In certain ways, it's just as bad as we all thought it was, but in others, it's really a refreshing improvement over the academic world, most aspects of which just bore the hell out of me. Here it's lethargic, and the people are rather boring. Of course, the good ones are the greatest people in the world, but. . . . In any event, no matter what they may do for me here, I'm going to continue doing the real estate work. Because, no matter what the college may pay me, it's not going to be enough."

If money is the basic motive for dipping his toe in the streams of commerce, it is not the only one. Mobility is supposed to be a major benefit of the academic profession. After all, there are colleges everywhere. A professor can, presumably, choose the geographical area he prefers, or try several. Status isn't everything, either. For many professors, a position at the smoggy Riverside campus of the University of California, for example, is less desirable than one at presumably less prestigious San Francisco State, in the heart of everyone's favorite city. But reality intrudes. Stars of the professoriate can take their pick of locations bucolic or cosmopolitan. Except for good planning and lucky breaks, the others—the majority—settle. Who wants to go to Wichita?

"Wichita State isn't that bad! Wichita's medium, even a dream job! No, listen! They have guys from Harvard and Yale, Ph.D.'s, stabbing each other to get that job. That's how bad things are!"

With that withering dismissal of choice of location as a

virtue of the profession, Bohan moves easily to academic politics and what he and many others view as excessive concern with the achievement of status within the institution.

"I made a very bad mistake going from Wichita State to Tennessee. It looked like it was going to be a better deal, but it turned out to be much, much worse. And it wasn't the money, which was about the same. I was working for a guy who was a charlatan. He was a phoney. He'd been passing himself off as a Ph.D. in philosophy at Vanderbilt, where I knew some people. I discovered this quite incidentally. This guy was basically a preacher. He married 'em and buried 'em. And this was his mentality, fundamentally. The philosophy–religion gap is enormous, but it's quite common for people in religion to cloak themselves in the mantle of philosophy to make themselves look academically respectable. It's a pathetic situation, because there are some people in religion who *are* respectable.

"But most of them aren't. It's a fact. He was totally incompetent in philosophy. He paraphrased secondary sources in the classroom, for example. And his students knew. Once, he was quoting a logical positivist, and one of his students asked which logical positivist said that? And he said, 'Oh, I don't know. One of them said it. That's what they used to say.' This is what I consider to be gross incompetence. Yet he was an associate professor with tenure and widely respected on the campus. Well, that's a comment about the campus and about the administration, that a man like that can succeed."

Bohan lets loose a short burst of rueful laughter. " 'That's what they used to say!' " Then he tells how he left the Chattanooga campus—or was pushed out—and accepted the eleventh-hour lecturing job at Hayward State.

"That was true for me in my circumstance, not necessarily true for everybody. But for guys in their late twenties, early thirties starting out today, it's bleak, dismal. There's no room at the top, there's no money, there're no jobs. There aren't going to *be* any jobs. And while the Ph.D. production rate has leveled, and even begun to drop off somewhat, it still far exceeds demand."

True enough. The Ph.D. Glut, as it became known when belatedly recognized in 1970, is still facing would-be professors, and is likely to continue. In 1959, the number of doctorates awarded totaled 9,829. Ten years later, the annual figure was nearly 30,000. By then, the number of people holding Ph.D.'s reached almost 290,000 and it is over 350,000 now.

Dr. Alan Cartter, a senior research fellow with the Carnegie Commission on Higher Education, tried to warn the academic community of the oversupply during the boom years of the mid-Sixties. Now he says that the worst is yet to come. With popular acceptance of birth control devices, then of sterilization and legalized abortion, the college-age segment of the population is shrinking and will go into sharp decline well before 1980. Further, the percentage of the pool of high-school graduates going on to college has dipped from estimates as high as 75 percent in the pre-Woodstock era to 49 percent in 1973. Potential students look for alternatives, discover the earth and trees and simpler pleasures. Young people who would have been unquestioning English majors a few years earlier are now picking berries in Maine or apprenticing themselves to crafts unions or just pumping gas. When constructing ferro-cement boats or blacksmithing pales for the impractically uncommitted among them, they will return to traditional avenues of achievement. But not all of them, not any longer. Although the college-going rate will stabilize, it will not return soon to the inflated levels of 1965.

As if to seal the coffin, federal grants for graduate research and for financial aid are drying up, and the states and corporations are following suit. In a speech to the Committee for Corporate Support of American Universities, the chairman of the Board of the Hewlett-Packard Corporation horrified university presidents and development officers by speaking out against unrestricted gifts by corporations to colleges. "The case for a corporation giving unrestricted funds to a private university can no longer be supported," said David Packard. He went on to suggest a future policy of not very enlightened corporate self-interest, dispensing funds to institutions which did not provide haven for radicals or anti-establishment professors or ideas detrimental to the efficacy of the free enterprise system. At about the same time, the planning office of HEW recommended a 40 percent reduction in aid by 1977 to previously sacrosanct medical and dental schools. The justification was the possibility that at current production levels, the nation might have "too many" doctors, dentists, and nurses by 1985. The Ford Foundation announced that it intended to reduce its grants to universities for other than carefully delineated special projects; New York State withdrew its special Regents grants to doctoral students; and the Woodrow Wilson graduate fellowships were cancelled.

But although some states have attempted to freeze the production of Ph.D.'s by denying approval for new doctoral programs and insisting upon re-evaluation and coordination of existing programs, pressures to continue and even expand graduate study are still felt. Oddly, these demands are primarily internal, coming from faculties and misguided or bullied administrators.

Universities go to considerable effort to attract talented professors: they offer money, benefits, housing, reduced class loads, and little committee work. They offer graduate students to grade the professors' papers, assist in the laboratories, and serve as acolytes. And graduate students are challenging and rewarding to teach. This makes professors happy and happy professors settle down.

So universities on the make initiate and develop graduate programs and damn the consequences. Bohan talks about one such place, a flourishing Midwestern degree farm.

"They put out a dozen philosophy Ph.D.'s a year." He makes a face. "It's a third-rate program, a bunch of crap, and their product is lousy. And it shows. Their graduates get the absolute bottom of jobs. This kind of thing floods the market. It means that each department chairman who has an opening has a stack of résumés this high. The general estimate of the number of people *needing* jobs—not the same as applicants for jobs—is running seven, maybe as high as ten to one.

"How did this happen? Mismanagement. The Sixties saw a period where expansion caused its own expansion. Graduate departments put out more Ph.D.'s, each of whom wants to join a graduate department himself to put out more Ph.D.'s. So, if you can't get to the mountain, you bring it to *you*. What happened was, these people took jobs at institutions that didn't have doctoral programs. Enough of them got together and they said 'Hey, we want one!' Then a few of them got some publications and convinced a dean it was okay. The enrollment was going up, the money was there, so suddenly you had new Ph.D. programs cropping up all over the place. In 1964, there were forty-eight Ph.D. programs in philosophy. In 1971, the number had almost doubled. We don't have even an M.A. program here at Hayward, but some of the faculty want one. Trouble is, we don't need one. The last thing this country needs is another M.A. program. What the hell do you do with an M.A. in philosophy?"

Or, it might be added, in English, history, or French? Not long ago, a master's degree was satisfactory for a faculty position at one of the burgeoning public two-year colleges which were absorbing much of the increase in college enrollments. But then those swelling numbers of Ph.D.'s started to crowd out job applicants with mere M.A.'s even at two-year colleges and at third-rate four-year institutions. In college teaching, any credential less than a doctorate is all but worthless.

To Bohan's list of low pay, unreasonable publication

university position was limited to east of the Mississippi. Other professors rankled at the restriction, but it suited Crandell just fine.

Still, he and his family have driven down roots in the lush green suburban countryside. He was just elected trustee of the local school board, to add to his posts as secretary-treasurer of the country club and board of directors of the University Club. His wife, the former Mary Ann Stromberg, is president of the League of Women Voters chapter, director of the College Aid Fund, and member of the Social Concern Committee of their Presbyterian church. Mary Ann teaches breadmaking at the library, they both weave on a loom in the family room, and they and their three children play nine musical instruments among them. And now he has made perhaps the ultimate commitment. He has bought another, larger house a few blocks away—shifting thereby from the town's upper middle-class to plain upper—at a price hovering just below $100,000. Not something the average professor would ever hope to undertake.

"That locks the barn door. If I ever dabbled with the thought of sneaking back to the classroom, it's gone now."

Their new house is English Tudor, generously constructed for the large families and household staffs that preceded the Depression and income taxes. In the wine cellar, one of the labels on an empty shelf reads "absinthe," and an auxiliary generator stands ready for service in the event of one of the area's periodic blackouts. The Crandells are not selling their former house. A United Nations diplomat is renting it for $800 a month.

It's a long way from Iowa.

Their first home was a trailer. It was the silversided 23–foot model, he remembers, with portholes, a davenport, a sink, and a bed. Ted and Mary Ann had been brought together by their mothers and a mutual hatred of Scrabble. Mary Ann, blonde and pale as the immigrant Scandinavian farmers who settled

Missouri and the Dakotas, grew up in the "greater Canoba metropolitan area." Ted, who claims his Indian-head-nickel profile is the result of ancestral interbreeding, was raised in Vermillion, South Dakota, an even greater metropolis. They set up housekeeping in the trailer while Ted served out the last months of his army hitch at Fort Sheridan, Illinois. Mary Ann taught elementary school.

One January morning, the trailer caught fire when a short occurred in the electrical tape heating the exposed plumbing. It burned down to the axles. They moved into the second floor of a nearby farmhouse. After his discharge in June 1955, Ted joined his wife in the Willow Lake school district. He taught music at a salary of $4,000 per year. Mary Ann made $2,800, "since she was only a woman." The superintendent of schools left to become an executive with a tractor company not long after. When the school board looked around for a replacement, they came upon Crandell, and, for reasons he still cannot fathom, gave him the job.

He decided he liked administration, so he went back to college to learn how to do it. Once he had his Master's, he found a position as instructor in higher education and field assistant for the Bureau of Field Services at the University of Missouri. The $3,000 stipend was regression, but Mary Ann found another teaching job at a $400 increase over Willow Lake. Both entered further study, Ted for his doctorate, Mary Ann for her B.A. (At the time, her two years of college were sufficient for a teaching license. Now a Master's is required just for permanent certification.) With the trailer insurance money, they bought a small white frame house for $10,500. Mary Ann had her first child—by then-unfashionable natural childbirth—two days before she graduated *summa cum laude* from the university. Now Ted accepted an assistant professorship at City College of New York. They sold the house for a resounding $1,000 profit. The new job paid $9,000. That was followed after two years by an associate professorship at the

University of Iowa, at $12,000. (There are two ways to get promoted, he says—one is on merit, the other is by changing jobs.)

Five years later, he was drawing $18,000, having developed an on-campus agency for educational information exchange. Partly in connection with that sideline, he was called one day by a headhunter for Booz Allen, Hamilton, management consultants. They were seeking candidates for an executive position with a computer organization, and did he have any candidates among his graduate students? He viewed the placement of his students as part of his function, so he was pleased to recommend a number of candidates. In time-honored tradition, however, the recruiter had merely been fishing, and Ted was asked if *he* might be interested. He was. One month after his promotion to full professor, he returned to New Jersey, the computer firm, and, eventually, the $100,000 house.

All this financial history has a point. When Ted Crandell is asked why he left the professoriate, he smiles and rubs his thumb and forefinger together. Money is why—not enough before, the realization of the American Dream now. It is the bottom-line reason he shares with Jim Bohan and probably every other unhappy professor. But that doesn't explain it fully. Unlike Bohan, Crandell was well on his way to marked success in his profession. He had been awarded tenure in the relatively short period of five years and was, at thirty-seven, a full professor, a level many never achieve and few reach that young.

(The Association of University Professors tabulated rank at 1,244 institutions, employing 267,587 faculty—about 56 percent of all college and university faculties in the country. Of these, 38,530 held the rank of instructor; 93,600 were assistant professors; 64,547 were associate professors, and 66,563 were full professors. Lecturers, a title used to denote temporary faculty, were the remaining 4,347. Although no comprehen-

17

sive figures are available, estimates contained in AAUP literature suggest that the average age of instructors is a little over twenty-seven, of assistant professors nearly thirty, of associates thirty-four. Full professors, however, have an average age of 51.)

Apart from money, Crandell's motivations are unclear, and he doesn't make it easy to discover them. He encases his responses to inquiries in breezy irony, an apparent device to avoid unseemly self-aggrandizement or injury to others. His conversational style is bland on wry, his tone mellow, his infrequent opinions unabrasive. What did his father do? "He cried a lot." (And was the clerk of the federal court for the district of South Dakota for most of his life.) What did he play in the 1948 Rose Bowl? "The snare drum." What was Vermillion like? "A little cul-de-sac along the river into which all the heat of the nation pours every summer." Why wasn't he sent to Korea when he was in the army? "The Fifth Army Band needed a second oboist. Also, I was chicken. Fortunately, the army still had scruples then, and I'd never had basic training. They couldn't send someone to Korea who had never fired an M-1." What was his first impression of the East? "I didn't care for it. Do you know everyone claimed I had a Midwestern accent?"

And he wasn't driven *from* education, he was attracted *to* another opportunity.

After a while, though, he mentions that he left one of his college jobs because he had been appointed chairman of that institution's team preparing for accreditation review.

"I couldn't find anybody to take responsibility for the self-evaluation of the administration. So I did it. For several years thereafter, it was known as the Crandell Report. It merely said that the Office of the Dean needed 'help in communication.' Y'know, when everything's lousy and nobody does anything and everything's bad, you call that a 'communication problem.' After I submitted my report, I submitted my resignation."

So money wasn't the only reason he left college teaching? "No. I was interested in the possibilities of change. The resources of education were wanting, and I found another source of economic wherewithal to make change happen for education—called the investing public of America. Actually, I saw no real difference in disposable income the first few years, what with higher costs and taxes here. I still object to $20 lunches and paying $2.00 for a hamburger. In any event, I think what I'm doing is important. I don't know whether it's gratifying. . . . As a teacher, as an administrator, as a college professor, I felt we had to do something about the way education is handled. I tried to do it in that variety of ways, but the only way to do it is where there's enough capital to make a difference."

Asked finally whether he might go back to college teaching, he muses for several long moments.

"If I could go back to professing, to teach, to deal with problems of intellectual curiosity, to work with students on those topics . . . sure, that would be delightful. But I would have to deal with academic politics, with manipulation and operation, and I'd just as soon do it in the industrial sphere. It's the same problem, only they pay better. If I could construct a situation in which I were in a teaching–learning relationship with others—and keep it there—without the overhead of politics and the ladder-climbing of ruthless individuals who are willing to sacrifice educational concepts for personal gain, that would be a very desirable position. But. . . ."

He shrugs, fills his glass, and adjusts the volume on his quadraphonic sound system.

"Did I tell you about my Master's thesis? It was called 'A Study of Immigration and Emigration of Teachers of South Dakota Between 1952 and 1956,' and the reasons thereto pertaining. An article based on the thesis was published in the *South Dakota Teachers' Association Journal*. It was distributed widely and its title was 'The Grass Is Greener.' The reason all of the teachers left South Dakota was to get more money, and the reason they all *came* to South Dakota was to get more money. And to get better television reception."

CHAPTER 2

For some time, the American college professor has been the most pampered professional in our society. Despite the grievances of often dubious legitimacy touched upon by Jim Bohan and Ted Crandell, no other occupational group can match the accumulated compensations, both economic and psychic, of the professoriate. Only in private do professors concede this reality. Understandably. Large segments of the public have been persuaded that academics are the browbeaten underclass of the educated vocations, harassed by despotic administrators, harpooned by reactionary businessmen, suppressed by totalitarian politicians, abused by student idealogues, and ground down by the shackles of near-poverty. But as militant faculty unionist David Brody said from the deck of his spacious California home overlooking the lights of the San Francisco Bay area:

"When I was a kid in Elizabeth, New Jersey, I never thought I'd ever have it this good."

He and his colleagues are not about to go around saying such things aloud. Because they want more.

What they already have is impressive. Take money. In 1958, the average college professor made $6,015 per *academic* year, while the typical salaried professional and technical worker in the U.S. made only $5,300 for a *calendar* year. That difference favors the professor by a sizable 13 percent. In 1970, the gap widened to 22 percent, with median salaries for academics at $11,745 and for all salaried professionals and technical workers at $9,600. During that period, salaries for professors improved at a rate of 5.5 percent each year, compared to 4.8 percent for total salaried professionals.

During the lean years (for everyone) of wage-controlled 1970 to 1972, the professorial median rose to $12,932, then jumped again by 5.6 percent in 1973.

These are not unfair comparisons. The term "salaried professional and technical workers" includes architects, accountants, engineers, pharmacists, public school teachers, even physicians and dentists who are not self-employed. Formal training for such positions requires as much time as for the professoriate, or nearly so. Obviously, if *all* workers—farmers, plumbers, sanitation men—are added to the equation, professional compensation appears even more generous. National per capita income in 1971 was $4,156.

Of course, professors do not permit themselves to be compared to clerks and ditch diggers, with good reason. They've made substantial financial investments in themselves, deferring gratification to arm themselves with the credentials necessary to obtain their jobs. No, they would have their incomes matched against the traditional professions—law and medicine, perhaps engineering and architecture. This is what Jim Bohan is saying when he can't understand the unfavorable difference in compensation between academics and "other professionals." It is as imprecise as comparing professors to seamstresses.

True, the average salaried physician made $12,919 in 1970 and his self-employed colleague $24,727. But the commitments in energy and dollars and the sacrifices in working hours and discretionary time of physicians relative to those of professors are startling in contrast. Beginning with education: At mid-seventies prices, an M.D. degree program, excluding undergraduate study, runs from $8,000 to $16,000, plus living expenses for four years. For a Ph.D., increasingly the basic credential for college teaching (but not mandatory in all fields), tuition can be as much as $10,500 or as little as $3,000 for the necessary three years. Adding in $3,000 a year in living expenses for both the medical student and the hopeful professor, the M.D. costs as much as $28,000; the Ph.D. no more than $19,500 and as little as $12,000 if he or she attends a low-cost public institution. Throw in $14,000 to $25,000 for the bachelor's degree each must obtain, and the M.D. can push $55,000 in total expense, but the Ph.D. puts in significantly less—about $45,000.

Further, financial aid is more widely available to academic doctoral candidates than to medical students, and while full- or part-time employment is virtually out of the question for medical students, it is common for Ph.D. candidates for whom study is less demanding and more flexible.

After graduation, the new physician can expect three or more years of apprenticeship; the Ph.D. can begin his or her career immediately. The financial barriers don't end there for the physician. If he or she sets up private practice, basic equipment will start at $50,000, but more is common. There is office rent to pay, salaries to nurses and receptionists, drugs, billing services.

The Ph.D. has no such expenses. And that is a clear fallacy when professors equate themselves with other members of the traditional professions. Professors are, by definition, salaried employees. They do not have the option of independent practice, but neither must they take the risk of enormous capital expenditure. When matched with other wage earning technical and professional personnel, their median salary is much greater.

That is not the end of it. An engineer with ten years' experience making $15,000 a year feels the equivalent of an associate professor with the same background and salary. But he is wrong, for the engineer has nothing resembling the leisure and flexibility of the professor. Assuming that the engineer is employed by a generous concern offering him an annual four weeks' vacation and thirteen paid holidays, he can expect 230 working days each year.

Consider, however, the professor's obligations. For the same salary, he must report to the typical campus no more than *120* days of each calendar year. At a college or university operating on the conventional semester system, faculty members begin work at the start of the second week in September and finish by the end of May. In between, they have two weeks' vacation at Christmas, a week between semesters in January, one to two weeks in March or April, four days to a week at Thanksgiving. And even that is not all. Most courses are scheduled to meet in two sessions, about two hours each, twice a week; most professors teach no more than three courses a semester. Even if they teach four—more would be unthinkable!—that totals sixteen classroom hours each week; the Association of University Professors recommends no more than nine. With favorable scheduling, even sixteen hours can be accomplished in two days, but certainly no more than four. Woe betide the professor who suggests more to his colleagues, such as one-hour classes five days a week in each course.

Given this superficial evidence of the professor's eight-month year, four-day week, and four-hour day, the engineer cited can understandably think himself grossly overworked. The point having been made, however, it must be conceded that this generalization is simply drawn and incomplete. Defenders of the professoriate cite numerous extra duties. Professors in some fields, for example, must put in many more classroom hours. A painting instructor often conducts studio courses requiring eight hours each and every week. But then, outside preparation consumes less time. And the reverse is also true. At many prestigious and/or affluent institutions, faculty frequently teach only two courses a semester, meaning no more than eight hours behind the lectern each week. Variations include alternating responsibility for two courses one semester with three courses the next, or teaching one or two courses with "released time" for the guidance of five to ten graduate students engaged in independent study.

A professor's responsibility admittedly does not end with classroom lectures, and it is nearly impossible to establish parameters on extracurricular professorial working hours. Those lectures must be prepared. The associate professor outlined above can be assumed to have sufficient experience to be able to conduct classes without extended prior preparation. If conscientious, he might spend five to ten hours a week in revising his notes *and* keeping up with current literature in his field. At the outside, that expands his workweek to twenty-five hours. Then he is expected to spend time in student advisement. Although much of this is accomplished while packing his materials at period change, add a generous five hours a week (remembering the far from inaccurate stereotype of professorial office hours as "between 1:15 and 1:45 on Mondays and alternate Wednesdays except in the event of rain and January and May").

There are organizational meetings. Professors are fairly diligent about departmental get-togethers once or twice a month, much less so about those conducted for larger units of their institutions. As testimony, deans complain repeatedly about the difficulty of achieving the 25 percent attendance required for a quorum at divisional faculty meetings. To be sure, some professors—the same few, usually—are sufficiently dedicated to serve as representatives to the faculty senate or as members of curriculum committees or as coordinators of the endless teas and non-credit seminars that colleges feel are broadening experiences. They are exceptions. Most professors are too busy. They have research in critical stages, they say. Or their publishers are nagging about deadlines. Or their sabbaticals start next month and they have to clean things up before they go. Say thirty-two hours a week altogether—when working.

"Publish or perish" now rears its head—the most ambiguous of all professorial duties. Leaving aside for the moment the inequities of the system, the mandate to produce published results of original thought and research is a device intended to insure that academics use their ample discretionary time toward appropriate scholarly ends. Apart from whatever contribution may be made to a given body of knowledge, it is assumed that publishing will sustain individual intellectual initiative, thereby enhancing a professor's worth to his discipline and reflecting favorably upon his department and institution. It is rarely contended that publishing his work will make him a better teacher. That is something else again.

In practice, publishing is necessary to a professor to (1) be promoted; (2) obtain tenure; and (3) get a better job. Once all three objectives have been achieved, little material incentive to publish remains. But these are legitimate personal goals, and, when well-met, the results profit institutions, especially those universities dependent for financial support upon their reputations for research.

This institutional need is often the major justification for the bountiful dispensation of unrestricted hours and weeks and months of free time bestowed upon professors and accepted by them as their due. From noble origins, the practice of time incentives in behalf of scholarship has hardened into a structure in which academic ideals are buried beneath the mechanics of distribution. Professors expect all that time because their predecessors had it, not because they want the opportunity to make contributions to knowledge—and colleges and departments impose the tests of quantity of published work because no one wants to evaluate quality. Since the institutions have forgotten why they wanted the research done, the professors forget why they wanted to do it, so an inadequate measurement of professional worth is counterbalanced by a desensitized appreciation of professional responsibility.

Even given these duties—classroom teaching, lecture preparation, advisement, writing, research—the inescapable conclusion remains that college professors are usually underworked and frequently overpaid. Yet they insist just the opposite.

Were that the worst charge to be leveled against the professoriate, no one but those who must listen to whining protestations of poverty and repression would turn a hair. It is in the American tradition to get as much as can be squeezed from a stone, and then demand more. A contempt for reality is no more a trait exclusive to college professors than it is to Teamsters. Perhaps the most consistently vituperative faculty union in the country is the one representing teachers at the City University of New York. The Professional Staff Congress there fills the pages of *The New York Times* and academic journals with charges of administrative malfeasance and skullduggery and claims of unbearable working conditions.

The CUNY faculty is, however, the best paid in the country. The *median* compensation for *all* faculty ranks at City College in 1974 was $26,208! At the University's graduate center, the figure for the same year was $32,031, and even at the lowest status level, average compensation for teachers at Manhattan Community College was $21,656. All this for the usual 120-day working year and the freedom to complain without end, and with relative safety, about the intransigence and venality of the administration, the state legislature, and society at large.

That is the heart of the contention that the academic is of the most favored of professions. Freedom. No other worker enjoys it to the same degree or in as many dimensions. Being a professor means nearly half of every year free to read, to study, to travel, to idle, to be with one's family. It means the extended opportunity to earn still more money through lecturing, consulting, writing, editing, even teaching. It means being able

27

to call the boss a fool and worse, without being fired. It means a degree of job security known by few other occupations. It means the periodic disengagement and retreat from life-shortening pressures to consider alternatives, to immerse oneself in those mysteries found most intriguing, to think, to spin out dreams.

In a broader sense, it means the freedom to speak vigorously on any issue with little fear of economic reprisal. Needless to say, this freedom is not absolute. Retaliatory measures are available. Nevertheless, superimposed upon the protection of civil law is the tradition of academic freedom, with the organizations and sanctions to buttress it.

The doctrine of academic freedom insists that any faculty member of an institution of higher education must be permitted to espouse any position—social, political, sexual, spiritual, intellectual—on any issue, however noxious those views might be to other members of the institution and the community. Attempted violations by trustees or administrators occur, to be sure. But that successful acts of retribution are widely reported proves the strength of the tradition, not the contrary. If an outspoken Marxist were terminated from employment with ITT it would not be regarded as particularly newsworthy. But when avowed Communist Angela Davis was dismissed at UCLA, it was front-page copy, for it was the exception to the rule. The American Association of University Professors, watchdog of the profession, has never had more than two percent of the nation's colleges and universities on its censure list for violations of academic freedom, and the bulk of those institutions were and are educational backwaters. Yet self-proclaimed atheists, Communists, homosexuals, racial supremacists, and apostles of virtually every form of sociopolitical deviation abound in the professoriate.

Few of those concerned with higher education believe this should be otherwise. The attitudes of often conservative trustees and alumni are more remarkable for their public expressions of tolerance than for their private grumblings of distaste. This is not meant to imply that freedom of expression is not the object of assault, nor that it does not require vigilance and protection. That's what tenure is all about.

In theory, tenure is a shield for duly protected professors against dismissal for any reason . . . except in cases of moral turpitude. There is the immediately apparent rub—the question of interpretation. Obviously, the loophole has been abused, as in the famous case of the University of Illinois professor who was fired because he suggested that free love wasn't a bad idea. Quaint as that furor seems now, it was the watermark which subsequently established that "moral turpitude" was not what a professor said, but what he did. In the upheavals of the Sixties, professors who not only proposed the destruction of their institutions but took active part in "trashing" raids found little support from the majority of their colleagues when they were subsequently disciplined.

Up to that admittedly ambiguous edge between vocal promotion and physical action, however, tenured professors are, in the main, safe from unusual punishment. Beyond the question of interpretation of the actions protected by tenure is a fact less commonly understood: tenure does not extend to all members of the academy. Administrators, as example, do not possess tenure unless they happen also to be professors. More important, no more than half of all college faculties are so protected.

At most colleges, faculty positions are divided into four categories: professor, associate professor, assistant professor, and instructor. As a rule, only the top two grades rate tenure. Instructors and assistant professors work on a specific contract basis or on the understanding that they must be granted tenure within a certain period of years or face dismissal. Typically, that means a probationary period of from five to ten years, although a Ford Foundation commission found in 1973 that one quarter of all colleges had terms shorter than five years. At some colleges denial of tenure at the end of that period means automatic dismissal. More often, it is a signal that the assistant professor might be wise to seek employment elsewhere. When granted, tenure amounts to a lifetime contract, barring, of course, "moral turpitude" or the financial exigency of an institution forced to cut faculty, and that cause is by no means fully accepted as adequate reason for termination.

Once again, though, a practice founded in idealism flounders in application. Those untenured souls judged by their more-than-peers to be oddballs or malcontents can be denied the ultimate security as readily as those obviously inept or slothful. Naturally, this fosters caution and me-tooism on the part of those not yet anointed. They play the game, respect their elders, avoid confrontation, add weight to their *vitae* with whatever they can get published (some include their letters to newspapers), and generally avoid roiling the waters until the final approval is granted. After that they can say as much and do as little as they wish.

And here is the point: The recommendation and, on most campuses, the actual awarding of tenure is made *by professors*, not, as commonly assumed, by know-nothing vice-presidents or reactionary deans. Even when administrators do have right of final approval of tenure, they are loath to contravene faculty wishes. The anguish sure to follow simply isn't worth it.

The same people who determine the changeable requirements for the achievement of tenure—the faculty—perpetuate the evils of the system. Designed to protect academic freedom, the tenure system is instead its principal violator. The guarantees of due process are held only by tenured faculty, yet those most likely to need them are not covered. Other things being equal, the young instructor or assistant professor is more likely to be the radical, the activist, the militant, the unorthodox teacher, the least patient with form and convention. The older, more conservative professor holds the keys to the club, and is easily offended.

Senior faculty use the promise of future security both to dampen unwanted deviation from scholarly dogma by junior faculty and to protect themselves from established but maverick professors seeking to join their departments. Martin Duberman, the brilliant and controversial historian profiled in Chapter 8, was approached once by a representative of the history department at NYU who had heard of Duberman's unhappiness at Princeton. If hired, he would have received automatic tenure in the rank he had already achieved. Duberman was interviewed twice, once by a committee of faculty and once by a panel of graduate students. He never heard from the department again.

A professor close to the discussions about Duberman was reluctant to discuss the matter. No, it wasn't the money. An endowed chair was vacant, with a substantial salary for an appropriately distinguished occupant, and Duberman was admittedly well-regarded as a scholar. No, it certainly wasn't that Duberman was a self-proclaimed homosexual. A university in the middle of New York's bohemian Greenwich Village wasn't going to be concerned about that sort of thing. It was just that Duberman was judged "too far-out." The faculty didn't want to be stuck with a tenured newcomer they couldn't control. The graduate students went along.

The graduate students usually do. They have begun the hurdles of doctoral study, however antiquated and muffling to creativity, because those are the rules and they must have the Ph.D. Once they are able to locate positions—if they are—they fill their untenured limbo with scrambles for article publication year after year, even month after month. The results are often trivial, tortuously conceived to demonstrate originality. But they will have, by the lights of their elders, endeavored to "advance the knowledge of their disciplines."

Having set upon this career course in the first place because, as often as not, they were good at school work (as much a skill as the knack for selling cars but identifiable earlier in life), they are people likely to embrace both caution and devotion to accepted truths as the primary virtues. Imagination is rarely a facet of the professorial personality. When ventured, innovation is suspect, and is commonly subjected to labored discussion which it cannot survive. Witness (as in Chapter 9) the experiences of those foolhardy enough to propose educational alternatives within traditional institutions. The system can hardly be expected to do other than defend the status quo.

These considerations—time, money, freedom, tenure—are central to the lives of faculty members. They moderate every professorial response to challenges from within the college and university and from the often hostile world beyond the ivied walls. Those reactions are critical, for college professors are among the most influential people in our society. Yet considering the tons of paper consumed every day to record their observations in essays, textbooks, monographs, lectures, magazines, trade books, newspapers, and the reports of foundation and governmental commissions, remarkably little is understood about the impact they have on our lives and just what kinds of people they are.

Professors talk—endlessly—about other people. With the possible exception of journalists, no other occupational group stands quite so ready to tell the rest of us what we are doing wrong. But, given the relentlessly tedious obfuscation masquerading as objectivity which characterizes the professorial prose style, their infrequent self-evaluations rarely enlighten.

There are, according to the U.S. Office of Education, 603,000 professors working at 2,606 American colleges and universities with a total enrollment of 8,116,000 degree-seeking students. Individually and collectively, they have helped shape our foreign policies, develop radar, identify our sexual proclivities, create our literature, adorn our museums, explore ancient civilizations, run our conglomerates, route our traffic, defend our civil liberties, and build our bombs. They have trained our doctors, agronomists, accountants, lawyers, physical therapists, actors, dieticians, sculptors, politicians, filmmakers, dentists, generals, curators, priests, floriculturists, nurses, forest rangers, secretaries, architects, hoteliers, morticians, enologists, school teachers, engineers, cotton growers, cops, brewers, editors, and smoke jumpers.

Hundreds of professors are as honored as Arthur Schlesinger, Jr., or as notorious as Angela Davis. Thousands are well known in the more limited circles of their own specialties. Tens of thousands, noted only at their own colleges, are equally capable, though they may have little flair for self-promotion or may have chosen specialties of slight popular interest. But even the least able of the professoriate, on the most obscure campuses, have the opportunity over their careers to shape the lives of thousands of human beings. They merit close examination if only because they are paid, or spend in behalf of students or research, over $31,500,000,000 a year, nearly half of it in tax money. Whether at Stanford or Rosemont, Antioch College or Bob Jones University, junior college or medical school, private or public institution, the rest of us are paying them to do what they do.

Generalizations about a group as large as the American professoriate are precarious. As a point of departure, however, the academic Everyman is white, male, fortyish, and married. A 1973 study by the American Council on Education offered more specifics, some of them contrasting sharply with long-held stereotypes.

¶ It was reported that 60 percent of the respondents in the survey regarded themselves as religious, contrary to the assumption of many that the campuses are peopled by atheists.

¶ The fathers of 42.7 percent did not finish high school.

¶ Only 20 percent of those reporting were women and

just 2.9 percent were Black, but only 33.6 percent of the total group felt there should be preferential hiring for female and/or minority professors.

¶ With the slowing of expansion of enrollments and facilities, fewer young people have entered the profession in the early Seventies, the reverse of the situation a decade earlier at the start of the boom in higher education. Now, 58.7 percent of the faculties are forty years old or over, up 4.3 percent in just three years.

¶ Faculties in different levels of institutions differ widely in the amount of time they spend teaching. At the research-oriented universities, only 17.2 percent spent more than twelve hours a week in the classroom. At four-year colleges, it was 27.6 percent, and at two-year schools, where the pressure to publish is weakest, it was 72.6 percent. As most students are enrolled at four-year and graduate institutions, it is a riveting statistic that four of every five of those professors teach less than twelve hours a week.

¶ Conversely, at the university level, only 43.2 percent claimed to devote more than eight hours a week to research and writing unrelated to lecture preparation. The proportion dropped to 23.1 percent at four-year colleges, leaving the impression that the teacher at a four-year liberal arts college feels he has met his obligations with a twenty-hour work week.

¶ And, least suprisingly, 69.8 percent felt that respect for their profession had fallen over the last decade.

It is even possible to outline professorial ideology with some precision. The ACE study found that 44 percent of its respondents counted themselves conservatives. Seymour Lipset and Everett Ladd, themselves academics, broke this percentage down still further in a report in *Change* magazine in 1971. They found that social science professors were consistently left–liberal, and teachers of agriculture were most commonly conservative. Reading from left to right, the progression went from professors in the humanities to those in law, fine arts, science, medicine, business, engineering, nursing, and home economics. Lipset and Ladd also found that professors in the liberal arts are less likely to be religious than those in the creative arts and the sciences.

The resultant composite of a gentlemen of leisure and modest scholarship, middle-aged, middle income, and middle-of-the-road, is a singularly undramatic figure. But within those bland outlines are Daniel Moynihan, Noam Chomsky, John Kenneth Galbraith, George Wald, John Barth, Walter Rostow, and John Roche. Hubert Humphrey, Barbara Ward, Henry Kissinger, Margaret Mead, George McGovern, and Timothy Leary have been professors. Thomas Wolfe, Enrico Fermi, Woodrow Wilson, Samuel Morse, and Hans Hoffman were professors. It is logical, therefore, to lead from the general to the specific.

The professors introduced in the following pages cannot be contained within statistical parameters. They are, in the main, achievers. Most are senior in their profession and have reached levels of respect and authority that the majority of their fellows never will. Widely published, skilled in classroom or boardroom, innovative in problem solving, daring to risk, these men and women are exemplars rather than representatives. They are also more articulate than most, even in an occupation that theoretically demands lucidity.

There is a measure of balance, nevertheless. These professors work at small colleges and megaversities which are rural and urban, church-related and nonsectarian, elite and uncelebrated. They are mostly men, but only one out of five professors in the nation is a woman. Only one is Black, but that, too, reflects the racial composition of the total. The majority are employed at institutions in the Northeast and the Far West, but more than sixty percent of all college students are enrolled in those regions.

To some degree, the chapters that follow emphasize the

roles these particular men and women have chosen for themselves *beyond* their academic disciplines. The nature of the profession requires that college faculty possess expertise in fields outside the jobs for which they are presumably paid—teaching and research. A professor of art, for example, must be artist as well as teacher; a professor of law must be a qualified attorney. The breadth of knowledge and accomplishment—and power—of the faculty of a single university is a resource of staggering and largely unappreciated dimensions. If nothing else, the most superficial examination reveals that many professors both do *and* teach, George Bernard Shaw notwithstanding.

But Eugene Santomasso is of that rarest professorial breed. He teaches, and that's all he really wants to do.

CHAPTER 3

Santomasso is late. His long legs accelerate their easy stride, swallowing great gulps of the plaza stretching before Butler Library. He sweeps past the famed sundial and diagonally up and across the expanse of stairs that flattens momentarily for the statue of Alma Mater and two flanking fountains. Perhaps images of surging mobs of young people shaking their fists and roaring their rage flicker through his mind, for it was here that Columbia became the symbol of what newspapers chose to call "campus unrest." Such things never leave the mind, but that Columbia was five years ago. Gene Santomasso has a class at three, a student to meet, and slides to select.

He veers left on the brick path alongside the library, past the boxy engineering building. Black children from the ghetto beyond the wrought-iron gates stroll past and scramble over the marble bench donated by a forgotten class of loyalists. A fat girl in tight jeans plays with two poodles on a patch of grass bordered by low cropped hedges, keeping an eye out for the security guards. Santomasso turns down an alleyway to a stone pile of forgettable design, erected at the turn of the century to house instruction in the humanities. A greenhouse tops the building, the arts again surmounted by the sciences.

His fourth floor office is cool and dim. A tiny air conditioner hums competently from its place at the top of the twelve-foot-high window. Santomasso sighs in gratitude for this shelter from the mid-July Manhattan humidity, although he appears unaffected by the heat. He doesn't smoke, seldom drinks, and doesn't sweat. He has the narrow-chested, angular body of a distance runner at an age when most men are turning blubbery. In freshly-laundered dark blue polo shirt, wide-cuffed chambray pants, and Fred Braun sandals, his show of relief at his escape from the heat merely seems intended to reassure others of his commonality with their discomfort. This quality of open-hearted sharing is basic to his personality and critical to his skill in the classroom. And there is consensus among his colleagues and students that Eugene Santomasso is *the* most effective teacher at Columbia. "He makes dead things come to life" is the way it's said, so often it might be a bronze tablet passed from sophomore to freshman.

Later, his slides for today's discussion selected and his advisee advised, Santomasso, disdaining the elevator, trots up two flights of stairs to his classroom. He punches another air conditioner into operation and pulls down the shades. The room is square and high-ceilinged, with cream-colored plaster walls and varnished gumwood mouldings. The stained brown linoleum floor probably dates from the erection of the building in 1888. Two oak tables are pushed together in the center of the room. An assortment of sturdy chairs rings the table and borders the walls. On three of the walls, large inept copies of Raphael tapestry cartoons hang in elaborate gilt frames. On the fourth, two painted plywood panels, butted together and stretching nearly to the ceiling, serve as a projection screen. At the opposite end of the room, a lectern supports two ancient black projectors with accordion pleats. Two smaller, more contemporary machines occupy the space between. Santo-masso busies himself with these, sorting his slides as his class files in.

The students are mostly women, half of them sleekly upper East Side, in slithery synthetic-silk shirtdresses, color-coordinated sun glasses perched carefully atop their heads. The rest of the young women and the men are scrupulously unadorned and without artifice. Hair (except for one wildly extravagant Izzy, the Jewish Afro) is drawn back and tied at the nape of the neck. Colored tank shirts and jeans are their costume. There is little conversation. Summer session courses are languidly businesslike, a process of degree-credit accumulation. Few of these students seem to know any others. Anyway, they would rather be by the ocean.

To make the outlook for a stimulating exchange of ideas even less sanguine, this is an art history class. Those who have plodded doggedly through such texts as Helen Gardner's *Art Through the Ages* or have drowsed in a classroom darkened to show reproductions of bovine Madonnas and punctured St. Sebastians will understand the prospect.

Santomasso strolls easily to the front of the room, before the screen. He makes a few preliminary announcements about class papers and next week's field trip to the Metropolitan Museum. He speaks so softly that his words are swallowed by the whirr of the air conditioner. The students lean forward to hear him. Having drawn their concentration, and satisfied himself that there are no questions—he erupts!

He whirls to the blackboard at the side of the screen. His voice suddenly strengthens to an easily audible pitch as he rapidly scrawls MANNERISM *c. 1515–20* in large white letters, the chalk slamming against the board.

"Now! We're studying Michelangelo. We've looked at his early works, and now there comes a radical change which is indicative of his affection for . . ."

He whirls again, strides to the door, snaps off the lights, and moves quickly to the projector.

". . . that kind of distortion known as . . ."

He shoves two slides into place, and the screen fills with the images of Michelangelo's magnificent tombs for Giuliano and Lorenzo de Medici.

". . . Mannerism!"

39

Carefully adjusting the focus, he nearly runs back to the screen and faces his class, hands on hips.

"Mannerism is an anti-High Renaissance movement . . . *against* that world of perfect order of which Michelangelo had been, in his earlier years, a leading exponent. And this—" his arm flies out to indicate the photographs—"is one of his greatest efforts, realizing the seeds of this Mannerist movement which existed in his earlier work."

Santomasso races back to the projector, slaps two more slides in place. They are an exterior shot of the Medici Chapel in Florence and its floor plan. He hurriedly points out the nave, transept, the cloister, and two sacristies, for this is a repetition of ground covered at the last class. The floor plan is replaced by an interior, and by now he is back in front of the screen. He pauses, touches his moustache, as he does when he is about to ask a question.

"What strikes you about the nave?"

The students stare intently at the screen, not so much to seek an answer as to avoid being called upon to give one. Santomasso doesn't let them off the hook. He waits. Finally, the boy with the Izzy hairdo mumbles a reply. Santomasso accepts it, repeats it, elaborates.

"Yes. Notice how the architect Brunelleschi works out the plan. It's almost like looking into the projection of a Renaissance painting. The repetition of arches, the vaults in the ceiling, even the central axis of the dark line in the floor."

Then he is at the projector again, and the tombs of Giuliano and Lorenzo are back on the screen. Each figure is in a niche above the two symbolic tombs, and the allegorical figures of Twilight and Dawn and Night and Day lie back-to-back across the tops, at right angles to the central figures above. Leaning over the projector, Santomasso's face is taut with concentration as he focuses the machine and determines his next points. Now he markedly slows the pace he has established, strolling easily to the front of the room.

"Now as you look at these tombs," he murmurs just loud enough to be heard, "what would you say is traditional about their organization? Obviously, he wants to place emphasis on the central figures, the two brothers. He also, though, wants to visually connect the tombs *and* the figures on the tombs to the architecture, which is his. The relationship is all very carefully calculated—he marked off the background wall where those divisions fall, he marked off the position of the four allegorical figures, and the tomb itself, all in balance with the main figures. How did he accomplish this? What shows he was *really* concerned with this alignment? And in what traditional ways?"

Silence again. But now a few of the students are seeking an answer. A hand starts to rise, but drops away. Santomasso folds his arms, strokes his moustache. Another student takes the plunge.

"I think he does it in a number of ways . . . the allegorical figures face toward Lorenzo and Giuliano, their knees point up . . . and . . . their bodies form a kind of arrow going that way . . . and . . . the niche emphasizes it. . . ." Her voice fades.

"Yes. And what else?" Three hands go up. "François?"

"He separates the Night and Day figures."

"Right. You mean that, first of all, he gets a niche. Then he *fills* the niche. Yet right below it, he creates a void." Santomasso is at the screen, squaring the space between the two figures with his hands, then arching back, hands still in place, to look over his shoulder at the class. He freezes in that position until he sees a nod or two among the students. "So notice what he's doing. He's dealing with a traditional left–right–horizontal composition. *Very* traditional. A kind of triangle relationship with the most important figure at the apex of the triangle. But! He's leading us *toward* the figure, and he's also pulling us *away* from it. *Tension!*" He moves his hands toward each other, as if trying to squeeze an invisible beach

41

ball. His body seems to strain at the effort, then the hands spring away like magnetic toy Scotties.

He continues, gathering momentum as the first hour of the class passes. He pushes with his arms when he says "push," sweeps his arms when illustrating the flow of stone limbs or fabric, makes tiny tight circles with his fingers when pointing out detail. Hand gestures soon are moving arms which soon move shoulders and his whole body starts to flow with those movements. But still the energy is kept in check. Or, more precisely, held in reserve. The flurry of movement at the start of the class was to rivet the students' attention, wrench them into the task at hand. Then he decelerated, coasting while they were fresh and required no unusual stimulus.

By the time the midpoint of the session is reached, he is back to the plateau of the early moments, whirling, trotting, gliding. He has established Michelangelo's transition from the early, classically inspired *David*, with its unblemished purity of line, through *Moses* and *Pietà*, to the Medici Tombs, where conventional composition has become a backdrop for the contorted figures of Night and Day, Twilight and Dawn. These are not sublime demigods, but anguished humanity. Marble has become tortured flesh, yet still within the accepted framework of High Renaissance order.

Having carefully constructed this foundation, Santomasso is ready to plunge into the meat of the lesson. He has pulled his students along this far, but he knows he can lose them now. The first hour was easy. From here, their attention can dull, they can drift. He isn't going to let them.

He slaps new slides into the projector. The *Last Judgment* panel of Michaelangelo's Sistine Chapel fills the screen. Santomasso whips into high gear. The Roger Bannister body becomes Marcel Marceau, a pedagogical Nureyev. He assumes the postures of key figures of the hundreds filling the canvas. He lifts imaginary weights, he cowers, reaches, twists, lunges. A figure despairs, Santomasso despairs. Another is joyous, he does a little hop and yelp. Every movement underlines his words, carries the lecture along to the next logical point.

Santomasso is concentrating fully, and now so are they. Without exception, they lean forward, their faces strained with the intensity of the effort. They are almost physically drawn to him. So caught up are they in his arresting performance, they forget to take notes, and must scribble furiously to catch up. Santomasso doesn't observe the niceties of classroom methodology. He doesn't pause to permit them time for their note-taking. He doesn't digress to folksy anecdotes or wry sidelights or intellectual puns. He doesn't repeat key dates or events. Every word and action is directly to the point, with not an ounce of rhetorical flab.

He is asking more questions now—directly, and by leaving sentences uncompleted—for the students are bursting to participate in this event Santomasso has created. Although the class is only in its third session, he knows all their names. He makes a point of that, in all his classes.

"This is totally the imprint of Michelangelo here. There are the sibyls, the . . . who is this here? Hillary?"

"Catherine."

"Right. And here, in the folds of the flayed flesh hanging from the hand of St. Bartholomew, what do we see? François?"

"The face of Michelangelo."

"Yes! Aren't the details fabulous? Here, this figure is about to succumb to these forces pulling him down. His one eye shows through the fingers of the hand covering his face. That eye is haunting, despairing, yet it is one tiny detail in a panorama of hundreds of bodies. The smallest parts of this painting are the best parts. Harry?"

They are *asking* questions now. There is more give-and-take, although Santomasso still dominates when necessary, leading the discussion back on course. He is quieter, less frenetic, for the class is fully engaged. The first hour was foreplay, the next half-hour a race to climax, and they are

43

coming down together now, turning the experience over in their minds. They are almost touching.

Santomasso moves to paintings of true Mannerists, but they are secondary to Michelangelo, and he treats them casually. Their value is only to reinforce the primary concepts Santomasso has been building from the start of the class. He even permits himself a small joke about "Cupid grabbing Love's tit" in one painting, which causes some of the women in the room to fold their arms. Then he summarizes, wrapping today's package and tying the ribbon with a flourish.

"It is calculated chaos. They *want* the irresolution, a calculated irrationality. That's what they want. The mannerists don't want this perfectly fashioned High Renaissance world. Ambiguity, counterpoint, tension, that's the world they're creating."

The class ends. The lights go on. A few students linger. Santomasso's face, all sharp planes and edges in the half-darkness of the last two hours, now softens. There is warmth in the eyes, and openness. Although he suspects that these remaining students may simply be apple-polishing teacher, he listens carefully to their observations, and responds at length. He seems genuinely interested in what they have to say. He gives no impression of impatience as he replaces a projector lamp and stacks the slides. Finally, the last student leaves.

Back in his office, two students await him. One seems not to be in Santomasso's good graces at the moment. The professor smiles ruefully at him, something unspoken passes between them. The student averts his eyes. Santomasso is happy to see the other young man, and returns a paper the student had written with the unusual grade of A plus. Santomasso is warm and voluble about his gratification with the paper and the student grins and reddens with the pleasure of a wriggling puppy. The student is going to Russia the next day, and they make plans to meet when he returns. The other student slouches unhappily in his chair.

Santomasso ignores him. He sits at his desk, one of several in the room. Untenured professors don't get private offices, and Santomasso is untenured. He was a *cause célèbre* on the Columbia campus last Spring, when his department refused to promote him from assistant to associate professor, thereby denying him the tenure that automatically goes with the change.

His is the classic case of a professor who likes to teach and is good at it, and for whom research is an ungratifying chore. He has committed the sin of not "advancing himself within his discipline," of failing to "earn a name." No one in higher education suggests, least of all Gene Santomasso, that research should be relegated to the back rooms of academe. Teaching and research are the functions of the university. Neither can proceed indefinitely without the other. Most complaints rest with the imbalance in the importance granted either endeavor. Research can bring status, money, and students to a university. It is a profitable and marketable commodity. Good teaching is not, if only because it cannot be readily measured. Its only end product is graduates, and measurement of teaching skill is subjective, at best. It cannot be *proved* that students graduate because of—or in spite of—the teaching they have received, or that they are better citizens or human beings as a result. At least lists of published articles and books can fill pages and be tallied. Determining their quality is another matter, but at least there is *something*.

So professors who eschew research and are simply good teachers settle. They ply their trade in colleges too small or too poor to support research or at universities where simple longevity is rewarded. They settle. Or they keep moving.

Santomasso is moving. He has accepted a position at Brooklyn College, still without tenure, but at least for more money. ("Much in excess of $16,000" is all he'll admit.) He does not seem bitter. On the contrary, he almost toes the carpet and tugs at his forelock in gratitude for the student effort last Spring in his behalf. He smiles a row of dazzingly white teeth at the memory.

"It was fun! Great! I loved it, but I was also embarrassed. Couldn't show my face. Mixed feelings." He inclines his head at the woman across the room engaged in animated conversation with another graduate student. "Debby was instrumental in leading the whole thing. It came out in the college newspaper, then it became the 'Save Santomasso' kind of thing. They had meetings with the executive committee of my department to see whether something could be done to give me tenure, and they organized petitions all over campus, got a lot of names over a weekend. The students feel that teachers have just as much value as someone who publishes a great deal."

Unfortunately, student opinion doesn't count for much on the road to advancement in the academy. On those campuses where students can generate sufficient enthusiasm to complete the necessary questionnaires, much is made of the student evaluations of teaching effectiveness, mostly by the professors who are the subjects of the examination and are incensed by the presumption of their customarily obsequious flocks. Anonymous critiques aren't likely to be welcomed in any profession. But no cases of retardation of careers as a result of such compilations of undergraduate opinion have come to light. Students are the bothersome justifications for the existence of institutions of higher education, but professors are no more likely to be unduly concerned by their grievances, except in the cosmetic sense, than is the management of General Motors over the complaints of *their* customers.

In terms of personal advancement, Santomasso has committed every possible gaffe. He began by liking students and enjoying teaching. Obviously, he can never hope to amount to much. Although he is one of a minority of professors, that he is not unique is evidenced by the only partly tongue-in-cheek scenario presented by Pierre Van Den Berghe in his waspish

Academic Gamesmanship: How To Make a Ph.D. Pay (Abelard, 1970), written years before the demonstration in Santomasso's behalf:

> [There is] the young assistant professor who has not yet had the time to become bored with his subject and disgusted about his students' anti-intellectualism. Happily, this set of attitudes seldom survives five years of abrasive contacts with students, but, while it lasts, it can do considerable damage to a young professor's career. . . . With the neophyte's enthusiasm, many a young assistant professor polishes his lectures . . . and does his best to make them lively, dynamic, interesting, relevant to his students' life experiences. . . . He regards students as idealistic, progressive, identity-searching youths who look up to him as an elder brother leading them up the garden path of truth. . . . The danger of devoted teaching is [that] their enrollments grow alarmingly, and their offices are assaulted by hordes of unscrupulous young barbarians seeking recognition, attention, solutions to their love affairs, or loans of money. . . . Three to five years later, the no-longer-so-young assistant professor is politely shown the door of his university with a suggestion that his teaching talents would receive greater recognition in a more modest institution that specializes in the lavish dispensation of personal attention to students. His long-haired coterie of students may stage a little demonstration in his support in front of the dean's office and write a couple of letters to the student daily, but in the end he must pack his bags . . . bemoaning the ingratitude of his colleagues and embittered about the unrewarding character of academic life.

That Professor Van Den Berghe (loosing his barbs, incidentally, from the parapets of his own tenure) anticipated Santomasso's plight in advance is testimony to the pervasiveness of the academic truism that teaching has few rewards. As Santomasso moves from toney Columbia to proletarian Brook-

47

lyn, he professes no serious disappointment—openly. He hopes to return, although he probably will not, unless he dramatically alters his priorities. That doesn't seem likely.

Santomasso does not reject the value of research. He is currently attempting to bring his dissertation on German Expressionist architecture into shape for possible publication, and he has two articles underway. But he will not try to publish just because it's expected, and he won't let it interfere with his teaching. What does it mean if you don't pass on what you've learned in the classroom? Teaching does give him the greatest pleasure, and he works at it.

"My technique *is* theatrical, something of a performance. But hopefully with substance behind it. It's a way of dragging the kids along, getting them involved with the work. I once tried a more relaxed teaching manner and it just wasn't me. I'm trying to get the students to 'read' a work of art, to project into it completely, to liberate them. The way I do that is to make it a tableau. I act out the way people move in the picture to get the students to empathize with what is being done, always, though, coming back to why the artist did it, the context. 'Mannerism versus High Renaissance.' The search for new modes of visual presentation. And quoting from texts when I can. I ended today with a text from the Council of Trent tribunal. I want to give the class a sense of the way in which the period itself was thinking of these works. The kind of vocabulary *they* used, so it isn't just coming from me, it isn't just Broadway up there. The purpose of this course is to familiarize the students with trends and currents in Western art and the ideas behind them, but also how to see, to 'read' a work of art."

Santomasso admits to the devices. The conscious moments of repose are to change the tempo and to emphasize concepts. He gets the students to talk at key points by the use of what he calls "diametric comparisons." He did it twice in today's class, and he can recall both moments, for he planned it that way.

Further, he must pace himself in the presentation of the material, otherwise he is not able to sustain the necessary energy level. He finds it easier in a discussion format than in a lecture. When the class is talking, asking questions, he can relax a bit. That, too, has its pitfalls, however. Sometimes he finds his mind wandering when a response is being given, and he must ask the student to repeat. Juggling the slides and keeping the right pictures on the screen while listening to an answer is difficult, especially in a subject that requires very careful organization and exposition.

In his larger lectures, Santomasso has a student work the projector. The slides serve as his notes. Although he rewrites his lecture notes each summer and reads them over before each class, he works without them during the class itself. This frees him from mechanics, and the slides serve as his outline. (It's said by his students that the way to bring Santomasso to a confused halt is to "screw up his slides.")

The approach suits his personality and inclination. He did do some work in theater, it turns out. For seven years in a row, he was maître d' at a resort in upstate New York, where he did double duty as an actor in Friday night productions. His was always the Rex Harrison–Robert Preston talk-singing role, with a bit of acting and dancing. That was the way he put himself through graduate school, and the experience obviously helped shape his teaching style.

With all this—teaching three courses each semester and one in the summer, advising students, being with his family, his graduate study, and researching and writing his doctoral dissertation—he does not find it unusual that he did not receive the Ph.D. until this year. But that is why he teaches only undergraduates, and it is why he was not granted tenure. He looks to the bright side. Even after he goes to Brooklyn, he will continue as an adjunct professor at Columbia, teaching a modern architecture course in which he has a personal interest. He likes the university and its eagerly competent students and hopes to return fulltime. Although the elders of his department were not encouraging about his chances for tenure even at a future date, maybe he can change their minds. He's still young, and he should have some publications soon.

Gifted teachers are as rare as gifted scholars. One of the pervasive myths of higher education—perpetuated by professors—is that of the brilliance of academicians. Actually, there is no reason to suppose greater intellect or skill on the part of professors than there might be for any other professional group. One study places the median I.Q. at 128. Good, but unremarkable. Mediocrity bracketed by clumps of stupidity and dollops of brilliance is the more accurate representation. At the high end of the graph, the great teachers are outnumbered by scholars, if only because academic people blessed with requisite imagination and aptitude are bent in that direction by the weight of years of graduate study. Whatever latent talent there might be for the creative instruction of others is permitted to wither.

The reward for good teaching is more students to teach. Apart from the thinly disguised popularity contests in which students and alumni elect handfuls of "Great Teachers," with their plaques and certified checks for $1,000, professors who have chosen to hone only their skills as teachers can expect little more than testimonials at their retirement dinners. At first, they take on ever larger classes in more courses because they are gratified by the opportunity to instruct still more students. But even if they retain that enthusiasm, they realize too late that their willingness to teach receives little tribute from their colleagues except to the extent *they* are freed from the chore. After all, the resultant reduced classloads for others means they can get on to what really matters: research.

On the way from Santomasso's office, the visitor stops at the door of another classroom, for at the front of the room is a man known far beyond Morningside Heights. The face is familiar from television talk shows, the name seen on the covers of magazines and a dozen textbooks. From that moment until the end of the class a half-hour later, the man never moves from the window. Staring out at the plaza, hands in pockets, turning only occasionally to the class, he drones a lecture given perhaps a hundred times before. He does not joke or accept or ask questions. Swiveling once to make a point, he orders a student to stop chewing gum. Then he continues.

Outside, in the steamy dusk of Morningside Heights, the visitor is struck once again by a compelling physical aspect of the Columbia campus. In the spatial relationships of the buildings and the architectural detail of their façades, it very much resembles a reconstructed Roman forum.

CHAPTER 4

Since they are inclined to regard themselves as less fallible than other citizens, it would be reassuring if professors were heir to fewer human failings. It is not to be. Consistency, for one, is rarely a professorial virtue. Although the majority of professors wish that advancement were based upon teaching effectiveness rather than published research, they characteristically resist evaluation. Apart from denigrating compilations of student opinion of teaching skill, professors cling to the tradition that one does not violate a colleague's classroom. Since no one has come up with an alternative to consumer appraisal and/or peer review, it is hardly surprising that faculties have fallen back on lists of publications as the only available method by which to evaluate their colleagues. This is one reason for the elevation of the scholarly function over that of teaching.

There are others. Since no one is sure what makes a good teacher, efforts to convey the art to others are doomed at the outset. The result is that very few professors ever have teacher training, while every course they take, not to mention the doctoral dissertation itself, demands mastery of the research techniques, which are in turn the basic tools of scholarship. More significant, perhaps, is the fact that successful scholars bring money to their campuses in the form of grants, which can enhance the reputations of academic departments beyond their parent institutions, easing the way for further grant proposals, bringing more money and prestige . . . and so on.

Little wonder that capable scholars are cherished over competent teachers by everyone but students. Students hardly matter, for they are merely transients. The academy is defined as a "community of scholars." Although the description theoretically embraces students, their motives are in divergence from those of professors, for only a few of them have any intention of pursuing careers devoted to scholarly inquiry. This accounts, in turn, for the disdain of scholars for the crass vocationalism they peer down upon within their own institutions and at proliferating community colleges.

In the multi-layered hierarchies of the professoriate, the most desirable institutions for the scholar are those which demand the least of him as a teacher, those which offer the most sophisticated facilities in his specialty, and those which demonstrate their gratitude for his subsequent achievements by reducing his classroom load or eliminating it altogether. Those universities can be readily identified. Over 47 percent of public and private funds for research go to just 25 universities—out of over 2,500 institutions of higher education.

Even federal grants—which must be more egalitarian in distribution for political reasons—consistently favor with 68 to 75 percent of their annual bequests only one hundred institutions. With some shifting in position from year to year, the leading recipients are hardy perennials. In 1971, for example, the top twenty, in terms of total federal dollars received were: MIT, Minnesota, Michigan, Wisconsin, Washington, Stanford, Harvard, UCLA, Berkeley, Columbia, Howard, California at San Diego, Johns Hopkins, Illinois, Ohio State, Pennsylvania, Cornell, NYU, Yale, and Chicago. Some of these drop in the rankings, replaced by runnersup, but the group is fairly stable. The stakes for holding these positions are staggering. In that year, recipient universities divided up $3.48 billion. The institution at the top of the list, MIT, raked in $89,574,000. Even number fifty—the University of Arizona—accumulated $18 million.

Although the federal government is by far the most generous benefactor, there are others. The Foundation Center reports there are 5,454 private foundations in the nation with assets of $500,000 or more making grants each year of at least $25,000. The largest of these emphasize aid to education, although their largesse is extended to other types of organizations as well. The Carnegie Corporation distributed $12,544,754 in 185 grants in 1970 alone. The Ford Foundation made Carnegie seem a poor relation with $239,448,608 awarded in 1,730 grants the same year.

The projects for which these funds are approved run from the abstruse to the obvious. Either way, their descriptions can provoke both awe and ridicule. Columbia University, for example, recently received a $590,000 National Science Foundation grant for an eighteen-month study of management of refuse collection and disposal. A local newspaper chose to headline the story "A Scholarly Study of Garbage."

Legislators periodically and predictably trumpet their dismay at such expenditures of the common weal. Congressman John Conlan of Arizona is one of the more recent politicians to mine this vein. He has railed at federal funding of such projects as those concerning the bisexual behavior of Polish frogs, the smell of perspiration in Australian aborigines, and the blood groups of Zlotnika pigs. Whatever the eventual benefits of these efforts, the Congressman can be assured that he will reap the support of those already predisposed to the conspiracy-of-pointy-headed-pseudo-intellectuals version of current events. Conversely, he can anticipate the rebuttals of scholars noting, as one did, the discovery of the polio vaccine in the course of growing monkey kidney cells.

Certainly the scope of scholarly inquiry is mind-boggling, as well as bewilderingly recondite, even when sympathetically examined. New York University's report on sponsored research for 1971–1973 illustrates this diversity. Random examples of approved projects include:

¶ Transformational-Generative Approaches to the Diachronic Syntax of English and Related Languages

¶ An Investigation of the Placenta and Umbilical Cord of Untreated Diabetic Rats during the First, Second and Third Trimesters of Pregnancy

¶ Isolation and Characterization of Cytolysomes from Acetate-Deprived *Euglena gracilis*

¶ Prehistoric Cultural Interaction and Ecological Systems in Thirteenth Century Pueblo Society

¶ Architectura Numismatica: Monuments Represented on Ancient Coins

¶ An Experimental Investigation of the Turbulent Boundary Layer Undergoing Adverse Pressure Gradients

With such diversity, the potential for support of even the most remote of professorial curiosities seems boundless. Surely there are charlatans lurking among these incantations and doxologies, but they are decipherable only by those initiated to the academic priesthood. Boondogglers are nearly impossible to ferret out, for scholars understandably merge into phalanx at the tiniest hostile tremor from the barbarian public. They chant their liturgies of unfettered freedom of inquiry (for those privy to the catechism) and recite in chorus the painstaking process of approval of proposed projects.

The procedure *would* seem to reduce frivolity to a tolerable minimum. In outline, it goes like this:

A professor settles upon a particular line of inquiry he wishes to pursue, but decides it can't be done with existing funds, staff, or equipment. After checking the literature in the field and with colleagues to make sure the proposal is sufficiently original in concept not to conflict with other research underway, he or she discusses the project with the department chairman. With that approval, an appropriate agency is selected and a proposal written. This is something of an art, and most universities provide manuals in proposal-writing. The project must be original, but conventional in methodology. It is then passed by the chairman and perhaps a departmental committee to the institution's office for sponsored research. At least 300 universities have these, staffed with professionals whose fulltime duty is peddling faculty proposals to government agencies and private foundations. So important is the head of this office to the fiscal health of his university that his or her title is frequently on the vice-presidential level.

The recipient agency passes the submitted plan to a "study section"—ten to twenty specialists in the discipline involved, most of them professors. Thousands of academics and others serve in study sections on a consultant basis, drawing $75 to $150 a day, plus expenses. (Another professorial goody.) This group rules on the merits of the proposal, the competence of its initiator, and the soundness of the plan. For those it approves it assigns a numerical priority rating.

Advisory committees then consider the approved plans. In government agencies, these councils include a mix of specialist, government, and lay members. The National Institutes of Health, one of the largest funding agencies, has over 200 advisory groups with at least 2,200 members. Although these committees rarely question the scholarly judgements of the study sections, they may rearrange priorities in light of available funds and current agency fashions.

Criticisms of the system are plentiful. Some object to lack of strong administrative control, to the potential for conflict of interest for the academic who receives funds in one capacity and distributes them in another, to the concentration of research monies at a handful of select institutions. To all of this, most of the scholarly community replies that only their peers are capable of making these judgements. Of course, they invoke the catch-all of academic freedom. Anyway, they say, collective subjective judgements are preferable to bureaucratic assessments unresponsive to new channels of investigations.

Swirled in the stew are the possibilities of projects judged by the personalities of their initiators and their relationships with members of the study sections and the advisory councils, as well as approaches or subjects which are out of the mainstream of current fashion.

Until very recently, only the "hard" sciences could count on a steady flow of dollars from government coffers. The onset of relative peace and waning interest in the space program has shifted interest to the social sciences and even the humanities. Since 1970, for example, grants from the National Association for the Arts and Humanities have doubled—to over $140 million annually. As a result, many universities find that while their physics and engineering professors cry unaccustomed poverty, overall gifts and grants are increasing.

Apart from the presumably engaging opportunity to investigate a subject close to one's heart, the receipt of a grant has very distinct financial advantages for the professor who wins it. Normally, grants cover the cost of salary for two or three of the summer months, pro-rated on the basis of his compensation for the academic year. Thus a $20,000 a year professor would receive a tidy $4,400 to $6,600 bonus. Other "perks" may include a discretionary expense allocation, meaning the "principal investigator" need not go hat-in-hand to his department chairman for money to atend a convention, or funds for secretarial and laboratory assistance, often in short supply. (It is much more difficult to find a capable secretary than a competent medieval history teacher, which means professors customarily must share steno-typists. The grant can free them from that inconvenience.) And too, the university may well agree to reduce the recipient's teaching load (to nothing, in some cases) to permit greater attention to the project. It is in the institution's interest that the project be regarded as successful.

The inescapable conclusion is that scholar-professors are better paid and happier at their work than the great majority of their colleagues, who, in return, cordially dislike, or at least envy, them. They are free to explore their interests with greater freedom than their teaching colleagues, who must of necessity pick up the scholar's classroom duties. And students become assistants rather than contentious consumers.

Although the truly skilled teacher is an oddity, the pure scholar is found in not much greater quantity. Most professors *must* teach whether they're any good at it or not, whether they love it or loath it. Only a few have the choices of a Robert Braidwood.

If most professors are happy with their work, then Robert Braidwood can only be described as serene. Braidwood is an archaeologist at the Oriental Institute of the University of Chicago. Where Eugene Santomasso is the archetypal classroom teacher, Braidwood is very nearly the cliché scholar. He has not taught a formal class in over ten years, and has spent most of his university career at digs in the Middle East or in museums and laboratories classifying his inventories of artifacts. Both men follow the paths directed by their individual gifts. Neither has contempt for the skills represented by the other—quite the contrary. But both are exceptional at what they do, and there is need and room for both. What is most unusual is their singlemindedness.

There is a grim, cloistered aspect to the sprawling South Side campus of the University of Chicago, despite the many tree-shaded streets and quads. One of the nation's largest and meanest black ghettos threatens the university on three sides, backing it up against Lake Michigan on the eastern fourth flank. The prevailing architectural style is gray Gothic. The buildings all might have been built within the same year, and there seem to be too many to house the activities of only 12,000 students and faculty. The ambience is almost ecclesiastically solemn, a heavy portentousness that drives students and faculty alike scurrying along walkways and corridors as if in fear of being left behind. The pursuit of truth is an all-consuming business here, as it is not at most other colleges. There is little time or tolerance for frivolity. Chicago's Big Ten days are a distant and unlamented memory. A library now stands on the site of the old football stadium.

By most estimates, the University of Chicago is one of the very best in the country. It is a senior institution, enrolling more graduate than undergraduate students, and has the resources and intent to be hospitable to scholars and their explorations. Robert Braidwood has a comfortable niche within this scheme.

Braidwood is a tall man, erect despite his sixty-five years. His greeting is warm, his manner rustically informal. The seams in the craggy face are not the result of stress, but of years of squinting into the sun. In these clothes (plaid flannel shirt, grey work pants) his gangling narrow-shouldered body might more readily be at home in an alfalfa farm miles to the south. Surely he is not an urban man.

His office garret under an eave of the Oriental Institute overlooks the spires and towers thrusting above the treetops. The ends of the dim room slope over a semicircular window in one wall. The diffused April light spills over a long work table covered with brown wrapping-paper. The paper has been there a long time, fuzzed along the edges and marked by knife, glue, and pencil. Half-empty mucilage bottles stand about on the table amid a scattering of worn and well-used things. There are rulers, journals of learned societies, battered eyeglass cases, a variety of scissors and shears, notebooks, crumpled tissue paper, pencil stubs, a compass, and a scarred dispatch case. A plain oak desk sits off to one side, covered with duplicates of the same articles. It all looks like grandfather's attic.

Braidwood sits at one end of the work table and starts

gouging the residue from an ancient briar pipe. The knife he uses is Turkish, fashioned from an auto spring, enclosed in a shaft of ram horn. When he begins talking about his work, he must be reminded several times to gear down to the level of his novice visitor, for he makes the assumptions of knowledge characteristic of one absorbed many years in a particular field of study.

It is not immediately possible to pin down the specific field of inquiry in which Braidwood finds himself. He holds his doctorate in Oriental languages and literatures, and an appointment to the Anthropology department, but he is an archaeologist. More, he feels he is inaccurately described as a prehistorian, preferring the description "preliterate archaeologist." The cultures he has explored are a part of history, and lack only a written language or record. This finally delineated, he notes that the definition of archaeology with which he feels most comfortable is "the way of studying the ethnology of extinct people." He has chosen to work in the preliterate range of time—rather than in the more glamorous period of classical archaeology—because he has a greater feel for artifacts than for languages, especially ancient languages. This seems unlikely in light of his achievement, but he insists.

"I've never been good at languages," he says. "I've never been good at mathematics, or at grammar, or anything like that. I am more comfortable with visual impressions. I can remember motifs on pottery or the forms of flint artifacts, and can bring them out of the crannies of my mind and put them together with something else. And all our interpretations in preliterate history have to be made on the basis of the inventory of artifactual and non-artifactual materials."

The word "inventory" is to come up frequently. What does it mean as applied to archaeology?

"Think of a Sears Roebuck catalogue, like those up there." He motions at a shelf in a corner. "I use them for teaching, have since long before it became fashionable to reprint them.

It's a fine demonstration of what we do. How many students could I find right now who would know for sure what an ice pick is? It is not an artifact common in American households today. So *our* inventory is of the totality of a preserved and recovered artifactual yield from a given range of time in an ancient living site. And the inventory can be of both an artifactual and non-artifactual nature. The non-artifactual yield would include the bones of animals, the shells of snails, the impressions or carbonized bits of acorns and wheat and barley. Stuff like that. Things that weren't made by man, but were part of his normal daily use or diet or whatever. It's from this inventory that one attempts to make the interpretations and build the descriptions of the extinct culture he's dealing with."

Braidwood came to his particular specialty after working for other men in the Thirties and after what he describes as "the World War II interim in archaeological activity" in the Near East. He became intrigued with the origins of food production, how it was achieved, what were its consequences, and in particular, how it came about in the Southwestern Asian region. "After hundreds of millennia of predatory food gathering," he wondered, "how did men move on to the next stage of actually controlling their own food supply, and what were the sociocultural consequences of that major new stage in human history?" This range of time had barely been tapped in Southwest Asia, and Braidwood's project proposal happened to fire the imagination of certain people in a position to offer financial backing.

He and his wife Linda set off in the fall of 1947. Their luck was good. Normally, months would be spent in what is called "surface survey." This is a process of picking over and cataloging artifacts and other materials found on the ground over a potential site, and then trying to guess what might be underneath. In the Sears Roebuck analogy, is one standing in 1898 or 1924? This first time, though, Braidwood's friends in the office of the Director General of Antiquities in Iraq were able to focus their efforts on some specific mounds likely to prove profitable. The surface indications were compelling at two of these sites. By early 1948, excavations had begun at Matarrah, followed by a move to the site they chose to call Jarmo. This was in a wild, unpopulated valley east of Kirkūk, a mountainous region forming the northeastern border with Iran. The yield was gratifying, and the Braidwoods returned to Chicago with the conviction that Jarmo was worthy of an extended field program.

They were not able to return until 1950. Plans had to be drawn, field colleagues recruited, money found. The team selected had to offer a broad scope of competances. "To understand the origins of effective food production," Braidwood later wrote, "a firm grasp of the details of ancient environments, their climates, land forms, and the plants and animals which flourished in them would be necessary.

"I wouldn't dream of trusting my own judgement in the identification of a sheep bone or a pig bone," he says now. "Some of my colleagues have the notion that it is possible to teach a Ph.D. student enough about plants and animals to do his own field identifications. I don't think so. An archaeologist ought to learn about culture generally, and it's far better for the project if he does his best to get colleagues who are *really* prepared in the other areas. They must analyze botanical, zoological, and geomorphical matter. Pollenology has been a great thing with us recently—the establishment of climatic history by the recovery and analysis of pollen in lakes and bogs. You drop a cord in a hollow tube, bring it up, examine it microscopically. If you're lucky at all, it will have been laid down in stratified order. And you go down through time and find such-and-such a proportion of pine to such-and-such a proportion of birch, and birch to something else, then maybe birch will peter out and you will get just a cold tundral flora. This is why the archaeologist needs help. His job is culture more than nature, and he can't possibly be a jack-of-all-trades.

63

Enough evidence has come out of the ground so that it is impossible for any one human being to hold onto it all."

As evidence, Braidwood cites the people who accompanied him on his return to Jarmo and later expeditions. There were several zoologists, a Pleistocene geologist, an agronomist and plant geneticist, a limnologist, a microbotanist, a dental paleontologist, and a pollenologist. These, among others. There were usually graduate students in tow as well. Money came along from the National Science Foundation after the second field season.

"In the days before War One and until about 1935, the effective money-getter was the man who could fire up an individual millionaire. With the tightening tax structure you are less likely to open one individual spigot. The growth of the foundations has been a much healthier thing, because there was an awful lot of nonsense growing out of overselling to some millionaire's whim. Now I make a proposal to the National Science Foundation and supply them with thirty copies of it. A dozen of these are circulated to colleagues at other institutions. They serve as referees, and I better not have tried any tricks or they'll shoot it down.

"Once you have the grant, the next step is gearing up. This is simply a business of lists. Over the years, we've learned where you're likely to be able to buy shovels that don't break the first time they're used. And what kind of medicines to take, and what is available in the markets of Baghdad or Ankara. Then, the staff. You probably already know who you want, the senior people, anyway. Now, let's say you're going to a new region. If you're working in a fairly flat valley, as we were in 1959 in Iran, whenever you see a hump on the landscape it is probable that it is the remains of an ancient site. You do your survey in Autumn, when the dense vegetation is burned off by the local farmers and the grounds are fairly clean. You walk over the surface and begin picking up broken bits of pottery, flints and bricks and whatnot. Then if you know the sequence of your archaeological Sears and Roebuck, you can begin to make some guesses as to the contents of the mound. If you find the equivalent of horseshoes and sparkplugs and television tubes, you can begin to estimate what occupations were involved and how many times the mound was occupied. Now, depending upon the antiquities laws of the country, you can test. This means modest little holes, two meters square. If it's a low mound, you go right to the bottom, three or four meters deep. Hopefully, you find that you only have one period of time, the period you want."

There is a knock on the door and a small white-haired woman enters. She, too, is brown from years in the outdoors. Dr. Cheryl Otten, one of Braidwood's former field staff members. Braidwood towers over her, but Otten is in no way awed. They seem very much the people of Andrew Wyeth— sturdy and self-contained, private and cautiously giving. Dr. Otten takes a seat at the work table. As Braidwood continues describing the process of archaeological study, they reminisce about past digs. They have shared much together.

When the first visitor observes that Braidwood makes it sound as if artifacts are sprinkled all over the ground of Southwest Asia, he and Dr. Otten reply together, smiling, that that is truly the case. Otten is amused by American archaeologists on their first trip over there. "They get so thrilled over two or three little flints."

Life can be bleak on a "dig" far from even rudimentary civilization. Some of his sites have had all the charm of endless vistas of tennis courts, says Braidwood. Inevitably, the isolation and resultant closeness of staff and workers can ignite interpersonal difficulties, especially when stirred by the clash of cultures. European women can seem infuriatingly provocative to Arab men. For the sake of continued harmony, Braidwood has found himself acting the stiff-necked patriarch. He remembers having to dampen the ardor of a Turkish male student and a young Swedish woman. In the bazaars of Islam, it is common to see men walking hand-in-hand, but public displays of affections between men and women are inflammatory in the extreme.

More critical in the volatile region of the world in which Braidwood works is the necessity of remaining thoroughly apolitical. Even now, though Braidwood is not likely to return, he is cautious when expressing opinions about the people and governments of the area. Still, it is not possible to be blind to local conditions nor to avoid forming sympathies with host nationals.

"You feel sympathy and happiness when things are going well for the people you've been involved with. There are warm attachments. I have worked long in the Arab countries and have many happy memories of the people there with whom I've worked. I can't attempt to understand all the rights and wrongs of the Israeli–Arab thing, but because I know the Arabs well, I tend to favor the Arabs in the matter."

He regrets voicing even this mild opinion, and moves to firmer ground.

"Archaeologists anywhere in the world must walk a carefully neutral line. Mind you, I cut my teeth in 1930 when Iraq was a British mandate, and my next work was in Syria and Lebanon when they were French mandates. From the point of doing what one pleases archaeologically, those were great days. But it simply isn't realistic or moral to go on wishing for that kind of thing."

Archaeology is finicky, cramped work, and daily progress is measured in inches. But Braidwood seems to cherish every memory, every blistering day, every choking dust storm, every flooded site. He chuckles as he relates each incident of discomfort and border inconvenience. There was the time the top blew off the water tank in a howling dust storm and the water turned to the consistency of flour paste and they had to brush their teeth with Perrier water. There was the field assistant who turned out to have a Teflon heart valve and had to be transported to Ankara periodically for "servicing." There was the first trip out in '47, by unconverted Italian tramp steamer, battered Turkish Airlines DC-3, and camel through Athens, Istanbul, Beirut, Baghdad, and a Syrian cholera epidemic.

It was on that trip that he learned the virtues of having your children travel with you. At that time, his son Douglas was three and his daughter Gretel six. Linda Braidwood made them two fetching little book bags in which they carried their toys. Customs checks being the tiresomely drawn-out events they usually are in that part of the world, the Braidwoods learned to push their children ahead of them in the line. Douglas and Gretel opened their bags with pudgy hands to reveal their treasures, peering up with big eyes at the customs agents. The gruff officials would promptly melt and wave the entire family through. Having the children along assured an extra measure of care in selection of quarters and the preparation of food as well.

Both children loved the Arab countries, Braidwood says. When they accompanied their parents at field seasons, they were able to keep up their schooling with a home study system. Braidwood doesn't think the experience blighted their lives. Gretel married a graduate of Harvard Medical School. Douglas did graduate work in geography, and now, having completed a Navy hitch, hopes to find a career in the Middle East.

Linda Braidwood has been an integral part of Robert's professional life since they were married in 1937. Although her undergraduate degree was in merchandising, she subsequently took a master's in Near Eastern archeology at the Institute. She is the co-author of many of Braidwood's articles for scholarly journals.

"Linda is a very orderly person. I don't know how to run one of these expeditions, she does. She knows how the accounts are kept, what should be ordered, how the house is run. And she has, as well, very considerable expertise in the flint tool categories. We both cook meals. In the field, you do your best to get as good a cook as you can. Linda enjoys cooking, and by now she has a pretty good notion of what is possible. There's a great deal to simply seeing that everything is clean, that dishes are washed with scalding hot water. Good food means good morale, and well-prepared food means a healthy camp."

Braidwood had been in the field a number of times before he married Linda. But he had not come to that professional decision as one answering a calling. It just happened. He was born in Detroit in 1907. His father was a pharmacist. Although paleontology piqued Braidwood's interest in high school, in 1926 he entered the University of Michigan as an architecture major. After two years, he left to take a job in an office and as assistant to the architect on a building job. When he returned to Michigan in September 1929, the building business was not looking too promising as a career. His flagging interest and a basic ineptitude in integral calculus and what was called "French for Engineers" landed him solidly on academic probation. He was urged by his mathematics professor to consider alternative careers. He did, and within six months the university museum had sent him to Iraq as an artist and surveyor. Upon his return, he transferred to another division of the university, conquered literature and the arts, and was awarded his B.A. in 1932. This was immediately followed by an M.A. in 1933.

A Syrian expedition followed. Braidwood had been learning to clean skeletons at an Indian dig in southern Michigan, so he was added to the Oriental Institute's field staff as "a ghoul, first class." He got around to marrying Linda, whom he had met at Michigan, in 1937. After one more field season, the war came, and he returned to finish his Ph.D. and teach graduate students until its end. Then it all began again.

Now it is over, he thinks. If he were starting out right now, he imagines he'd look into the cultures of the New World. The Mayans, perhaps. Or Africa. And if China opens up . . .

As a professor concerned primarily with research throughout his adult life, Braidwood does not rankle at the persistent criticism of those who insist that professors must teach. He has done what he does best. And he *has* taught, although usually in an indirect, informal way. And too, the students who come to the institute as anthropology majors are concerned with more contemporary aspects of the field. It doesn't leave Braidwood with too many prospects to teach.

"When a good kid comes along, I help get him involved down in the laboratory. He marks flints to learn which end is up, and if he's good, he may be asked if he'd like the field. That's the way it works. In the last eight years or so, what teaching I do has been around this table with six or eight students. They read site reports and discuss them; they talk about methods. Things like that. For about twenty years, I was involved in a team-teaching outfit in the anthropology department. They were big courses, maybe as many as thirty-five students. That was fun. But I enjoyed the courses the most when they have been small—eight or ten students. They fit in the room and we can go down to the laboratory and the basement and look over stuff. And then it's not lecturing, it's conversational."

So he likes teaching, then?

"Yeah, I don't mind it."

Obviously, the field work has been the real pull. It was romantic and exciting. Now he's not sure he wants to do it anymore. They have a forty-acre farm in Indiana, from which he commutes when he must be at the Institute.

"It's not really good agricultural land, but we put in pine and Linda has a good-sized garden and I take care of the orchard. It's at a point now where it's damned pleasant. I find I'm getting a little grumpy when we go back and find that someone cutting the grass cut down one of my nice little apple

69

whips. If it happened that Southwest Asia should blow up, if money became scarce, I've got enough reports to finish . . . I wouldn't weep if we didn't have to go back. There's a lot to do on forty acres. The Jarmo material is pretty well committed to manuscript, the drawings made, but there's still a fair amount of editorial work. And I'd like to do a more general book . . . No, I wouldn't weep. A camel is a camel. But . . ."

Robert Braidwood is ready to stop, to gather and collate, to reflect. But he is still of robust good health and his eyes are clear. And there are still times he wakes up in the night and finds he has been dreaming in Arabic.

CHAPTER 5

Outside, on the strip of grass between the building just built and the one being pounded to rubble by the Rinaldi Demolition Corporation, two barechested young men sluice a Frisbee through the sodden September air. Inside, Harold Cross joins the lines of new freshmen filing into room 414 for the first meeting of Political Science .0001. A bored upper-classman collects Harold's green IBM class card as he enters. The amphitheater gleams, for it is the first class of the new year in a building dedicated only six days before.

At the lower end of the steeply sloping hall, the professor is adjusting his microphone at a large, marble-topped counter. Behind him is a bank of sliding blackboards. (They are green, actually.) The loudspeakers squawk briefly. Harold cannot see the professor's face, but then the closed circuit TV monitors spaced along the walls bounce into focus. The professor has a very large moustache and a receding chin.

There are more people in the room than in Harold's entire hometown of Dawson, Minnesota (pop. 1,766).

This is a real class in a particular university. But this is big-time education, and the class might be at any one of a hundred universities in California or Illinois or Massachusetts or Texas. Take away a few hundred warm bodies, and it might well be one of the several score teacher factories turned dignified when state politicians were looking to shoehorn a few more future taxpayers between some walls of ivy.

In the Ed Biz, you use what you have. Wealthy and loyal alumni aren't enough, nor are generous legislators, the Defense Department, the Ford Foundation, nor student tuition. It takes all those things, but much more—or much less outgo. One John Kenneth Galbraith can buy a whole economics department at a lesser college than Harvard. A Catholic college, for example, staffed in whole or in part by members of religious orders, often pays only bare subsistence to its teachers. That's one way for a college to survive. Another is superstars. Big-time professors bring more than intellectual achievement to a college. They bring clout and money.

They present problems, too. Distinguished scholars often permit themselves and their aurae to be associated with a college only under the condition that they are not troubled by students. Regular classes interfere with negotiations with publishers, fact-finding trips to Thailand, Senate hearings, lecture tours, and airline schedules. This is not overdrawn. In the righteous wrath visited upon Ronald Reagan in his pledge to bring Berkeley to heel, no professorial fury exceeded that which met his suggestion that tenured faculty teach more than five hours per week.

You use what you have. At nearly every university and many colleges, graduate students teach undergraduate students. The full professors gather themselves for two or three hopefully splendid lectures each week. The thirst of the hundreds of students who wish to drink at that font is presumably slaked. Then platoons of graduate teaching assistants take over in discussion groups and recitation periods. They must underline the theories, collect homework, pick apart the formulas, grade papers, generate enthusiasm where it does not exist, or sustain it where it does. They are the enlisted troops and noncoms to the field-grade professors, and the battalions of T.A.'s keep growing. The Big Ten universities usually have a thousand or more each, and even fair Harvard has nearly that many. In 1972, there were 109,027 of them at the 252 graduate schools producing all the nation's Ph.D.'s and most of its master's degrees. Since many colleges do not regard them officially as members of the faculty, it is impossible to know how many are included in statistics totaling 559,000 college teachers. At minimum, they represent nearly a fifth of all those who are directly responsible for the education of the millions of students in higher education.

They are called fellows, teaching assistants, or just T.A.'s. It is believed by many they are better at their jobs than full-fledged faculty. More likely, they are as good and as bad in roughly equal measure. In any event, most universities would collapse to fiscal powder without them.

As Harold Cross leaves room 414, he is handed copies of the required and suggested reading lists, the course outline, and his recitation room assignment. He is to spend two hours per week with Gay Baldinger, a Ph.D. candidate in political science and a teaching assistant for *Currents of American Political Thought* .0001.

Thread-thin, pale, Gay Baldinger doesn't look the part of fledgling professor. She wears faded jeans, a Levi jacket, and a black turtleneck. When she speaks, her slender hands move like sparrows thrust into a cage. Her voice is sometimes reedy, sometimes hoarse. But her students listen, and the interest rises and the bright ones plunge in, followed by those less certain. Gay's classes nearly always end in a babble, for her students have been engaged and intrigued.

Her senior advisor says that makes her atypical, that few T.A.'s are that skillful. Gay takes pride in her flair for teaching, and that is very much what she wants to do with her life. Which is not to say she doesn't chafe under the frustrations and frequent pettiness of the roadblocks she must hurdle on the way to her goal. The obstacles are not always flagged, and some even leap into the course after the runner has passed. That is, critical choices affecting future academic employment are often made before the professorial hopeful has even decided on that career. It has been observed, by educational theorist Logan Wilson and others, that a professor cannot rise above the level of the institution which awarded his or her doctorate. A Ph.D. from a low-middling graduate school such as, say, Louisiana State, will almost surely confine the possessor to colleges on the same status level. It is a near certainty he will never receive a call from Princeton.

To gain the opportunity to scramble up the ladder from T.A. to full professor, one must first have aspired to, and successfully negotiated, the highest possible graduate school in the prestige pecking order. Although college presidents are obliged to insist there is no such thing, any professor will reel off the roster of those schools deemed "best" in his discipline. The consensus top nineteen are (in no particular order): Harvard, California at Berkeley, Stanford, Wisconsin, Cal Tech, MIT, Columbia, Chicago, Michigan, Princeton, Yale, Johns Hopkins, Washington at Seattle, Northwestern, Indiana, Ohio State, Illinois, Cornell, and UCLA. Quibblers might add NYU, Pennsylvania, Iowa, Minnesota, Rochester, or North Carolina. Few others are seriously considered. Efforts to pin down academic opinion on these rankings are fairly frequent and under respectable auspices (the last two studies, in 1965 and 1970, were made with the sponsorship of the American Council on Education). Although predictable howls of dismay turn the air blue with publication of each such assessment, complaints are with detail, not the whole.

Those hoping to join the professoriate are, therefore, wise to seek their doctorates among these golden few if they would hope to have the greatest number of options when circulating their résumés. Doctorates of less-esteemed graduate schools will find doors closed to them. An estimated fifty percent of all college and university faculties have their Ph.D.'s from these few schools. Moreover, undergraduates of the same institutions have the best chance of admission to those graduate schools, followed by those from the flossier four-year colleges such as Amherst and Vassar. Graduates of colleges and universities perceived to be of lesser quality are nearly always squeezed out. Equity and individual achievement have nothing to do with it. A graduate department admissions committee will select every time a solid student from their own undergraduate division over an apparently brilliant student from a college they don't know.

That's the catch for the apprentice professor: His choice of an undergraduate college is nearly as critical as his graduate school—yet the typical doctoral student does not even make the decision to pursue the degree until nearly twenty-four years old, after receiving the master's and often still not committed to a professorial career. The bright student who ambles into the local state college for lack of anything better to do, then catches fire intellectually two years later, finds himself settling for an undistinguished graduate school whose modest image will ensure exile to that Siberia of two thousand colleges known to no one but their inmates and their alumni.

Gay Baldinger has met the preliminary challenges. They were easy. She was graduated from high school with a 98.6 grade average, scored over 750 (out of a possible 800) on both parts of the Scholastic Aptitude Test, and persuaded the admissions interviewers at four of the redoubtable Seven Sisters colleges that she possessed inventiveness and tenacity in excess of that demonstrated by the other five applicants for the same classroom seat. She graduated third in her class, then surmounted the admission standards and masculine skepticism of this, her present school and employer.

Now came the hard part. The requirements of advancement toward the doctorate are as forthright as fifty years of modification and amplification and clarification by department chairmen, program advisors, deans, and assorted administrators can make them. Meaning not very, but at least they're written down. Apart from an undergraduate record of "outstanding achievement," Gay needed 700–plus on the Graduate Record Examinations and a "demonstrated reading proficiency in French, German, or Russian or other language appropriate to the proposed field of study." She had all that. Then there were the approval of her master's topic thesis, designation of the thesis committee, acceptance of the thesis. (Some graduate schools throw in a faintly insulting English usage test at this juncture.) Before award of the A.M. (Gay's school chooses to retain the Latinate abbreviation), she had to pass a comprehensive exam in her entering language. Before admission to formal candidacy to the doctoral program, she had to pass a written preliminary examination to prove her worth for passage into the rarefied realm of the learned novitiate. Before the awarding of the degree, she will have to complete at least as many courses as for the master's, persuade a faculty member to become her dissertation advisor, at least two more to form her dissertation committee, pass another test in another language, complete a written "qualifying" exam on finishing her coursework, research and write the dissertation itself, then defend it in a verbal inquisition by five or more senior faculty members known as the "oral." Then she can have her piece of paper, once having paid to have the dissertation bound and microfilmed and consigned to oblivion in the stacks of the university library. If diligent, she'll accomplish all this in four years, but eight are not unusual. There's a good deal of backtracking. Advisors resign or leave for greener vistas. New mentors must be persuaded of the value of a dissertation topic already researched and justified to their predecessors. Requirements are altered, funds are reduced.

All that can be sorted out. Most of it is committed to paper, however abstrusely, in school catalogs, which are legally binding contracts between faculty and student. A determined young scholar can weave through that maze without setback.

Many, however, are impaled on the spears of internecine contention bristling unseen along every corridor. It's called "campus politics" by students and faculty alike, but precise description even in barest outline is impossible. At no point in her hoped-for career will Gay's perception and skillful manipulation of these rivalries be more important to her advancement, yet never will she be more ill-prepared to cope with them. She is only beginning to accept their existence.

"Nothing in my experience prepared me for the backstabbing and one-upmanship I've found here," she says. "Friends warned me, but I couldn't believe it might be more than the usual squabbling you get when you put two or more people in a room and present them with an objective to be attained. Oh, maybe the maneuverings would be more erudite, but nothing much more than debater's points. That's what *I* thought.

"I assumed I would face the usual difficulties of a woman entering a field dominated by men, and I had neither the equipment nor the inclination of others of my sex"—her lip curls—"to capitalize on the differences. Apart from that, I expected merely to have to prove I was more able than the others, at least to the degree necessary to succeed. I couldn't have been more wrong.

"A graduate student, to survive, let alone excel, has to play departmental politics like a violin. You learn very soon that you have to pick your enemies as carefully as your friends. That is to say, it's one thing to ally yourself with a person likely to do you good, we all do that in this kind of situation. But also, you must select those with whom to disagree, because those important to you must support your assessment. Which means of course, you must make certain where everyone stands before you dip your toe in the pool. Who hates whom, who's looking for a chairmanship, who are the behaviorists, who are not. Then who feels bypassed, who made associate by what means, even if anyone's sleeping with anyone else. Not

77

for blackmail or anything as gross as that, just so you don't put your foot in your mouth at the faculty tea, or more likely, the faculty cocktail party. Poli Sci professors booze a lot.

"And it's not confined to the faculty. You have to watch your back from the other students. Apart from the endless put-down games—the favorite pastime of academics—there's the little zapper dropped in the advisor's lap about how so-and-so side-stepped some critical research, or how someone else proposed an approach directly counter to that advisor's pet technique. . . . The possibilities are endless."

Mere T.A.'s rarely give voice to these grievances. Their appointments are usually reviewed each year, and they need the best recommendations they can get from their professors when they finally have their union card, the Ph.D. They wait until they're tenured.

Leonard Kriegel waited. Then he wrote a book, *Working Through: A Teacher's Journey in the Urban University*, in which he said:

> The quest for status at Columbia had been passed down from the faculty . . . and invaded the very beings of the students. Never before or since have I encountered anything comparable to the massive neuroticism of Furnald Hall. The majority of graduate students who lived there were so caught up in the game, so victimized by their desire for careers, so willing to preserve a place at any cost at the side of some academic eminence, that their lives became mere extensions of the dehumanization of the university. It always seemed necessary to impress senior faculty; the words measured, deliberated; the opportunities were spotted and the thrust home made as deftly as possible. Ability and style were one. There were recommendations to be secured, jobs to be discovered. . . . We emulated our models, working for the day when we, too, might claim professorial status for ourselves and might look at our students as we ourselves were looked at—worshippers at the shrine of making it.

So T.A.'s, those determined to join the fraternity, attach themselves to the "right" professors. This means selecting the person who not only has the appropriate specialty for the T.A.'s own interests, but who also has a following in the department and a largely unassailable position. The T.A. intent on making it by this route can produce a thoroughly demeaning picture of himself, especially as witnessed by an outsider not privy to the undercurrents and unspoken understandings at work. This kind of T.A.—and most are "this kind" to a degree—preens before his mentor, citing his test scores, his grades in other courses, the fellowship he thinks he'll win, the favorable comments made by other professors. He hangs on the professor's every word, grinning and panting with each revelation, emulating the mentor's notions of wit and insightful analysis. The displays of fawning camaraderie can be witnessed in the halls and offices and elevators of every major university. They are painfully embarrassing to watch.

"What are we supposed to do?" says Gay. "You don't get by on simple achievement here. These people are in a position to destroy your life with the cock of an eyebrow. So we suck around the big men as much as we have to while hanging on to whatever shreds of dignity are left to us. We volunteer for grubby jobs to get close to them, we bray like hyenas at their jokes, we engage them in scholarly arguments, always making sure they'll be able to administer the *coup de grace*. It's a game I'm just learning to play. I just hope I'm not a zombie at the end."

Indeed, what are they to do? They are, as Professor Kriegel writes, the "untitled in a land of titles." In a profession where the gathering of the raiments of status compensate for what its members persist in believing is modest compensation, the new kid on the block plays by rules established long before he arrived. Since no one will tell him what they are, his quickness of perception is critical to his survival. Most aren't quick enough: Of every ten who move toward the doctorate, only three make it.

Given those odds, why does Gay Baldinger persist?

"Because I love my subject. Because I want the freedom a professor has to pursue that subject. I'm mad about teaching, but if that wanes over the years, I'm equally enthusiastic about reading and research. Look, I've been going to school fifteen years now, and I'm lucky: I've known this is what I want to do with my life for at least eight of those years. If I have to put up with this crap to get there, so be it. At least I know I'll never do the same things to my own students."

Perhaps not. In the meantime, being a T.A. has its advantages. Baldinger must teach twice as many classes as the senior members of her department, for which she is paid only $3,500 and free tuition. But if all goes well, she will be able to leapfrog the customary first rank of instructor into an assistant professorship. Depending on the institution in which she lands that job, she could have tenure within as little as three years. A lifetime contract at age thirty can smooth many of the irritations of apprenticeship, even cause one to forget. Significant changes in the system therefore seem unlikely.

Gay Baldinger is atypical. She probably will finish the doctoral program. She made her career choice before she entered college. As previously noted, most T.A.'s don't reach that decision until they are well into their graduate study. Where Baldinger knew all along where she was headed, most T.A.'s seem to drift along, piling up credits and diplomas until inertia and the passage of time carry them into the decision of least resistance. They delay hard choices by continuing on to the next step because it's comfortable. Studying comes easily to them, and it's the only real skill many of them possess. This kind of person, fraught with ambivalence about the profession and his commitment to it, is more characteristic of the group than Baldinger.

Dick Chase is one. Dick is married, as are most male T.A.'s. He's also pushing thirty and it will be at least another year before he finishes his degree requirements. After his eleven o'clock class one Spring day, he sits by the man-made lagoon across from the Case-Western Reserve campus and eats carrot and celery sticks and a piece of spiced ham from a plastic bag. His companion on the bench wonders if his drawn-out academic career is a source of problems between him and his wife.

"I think any conflict probably centers around the fact it's getting to be a long time and I'm not done. She's anxious to start a family and I can understand that. I'm not saying she's wrong or anything. I really would *like* to be done, settling down, get started in something, rather than to be always just finishing."

Dick's wife Sue works, providing nearly three-fourths of their income of "about $11,000." Dick draws $3,600 a year plus his tuition, which appears to be average at large universities. This semester he's only teaching one class. His advisors are trying to make it easier for him to finish up.

"Maybe I should be working more around the house," he muses, munching. "I'm not really getting things done as fast as I . . . as *we* would like. Sometimes I'll do the dishes. I always make breakfast in the morning. She has to get off at a certain time, so I make breakfast and pack lunches." He waves a carrot. "We have uninspired lunches and breakfasts, I'll tell you. Then she cooks at night."

It *is* getting to be a long time. He's been a T.A. at Case-Western for five years now, both a victim and a creator of what Berelson called "The Ph.D. Stretchout." After graduating from Rensselaer Polytechnic Institute in 1964, he joined NASA at its Cleveland laboratory. Soon he was taking night courses at Case-Western, at NASA's expense. He met

Sue ("picked her up, actually") at the Young People's Social Club of the Lakewood Presbyterian Church. Once married, they decided he should go full-time and get it out of the way.

A sign over the door to the office Dick shares with six other teaching assistants reads "Santa Claus' Workshop—No One Over Five Admitted." Professor Hoffman has the inner office. He's "Santa Claus," the group's advisor. He parcels out allocations from a department grant to meet the stipends of the T.A.'s in his charge. There is a pinup of an extravagantly proportioned woman taped to the coat rack. She is promoting gas chromatographs. ("Before that, we used to have a Rigid Tool calendar. They had very scantily clad . . . well, they're not *young* ladies . . . but they're standing holding various . . . rigid tools.")

Dick is wary when talking about himself, but he suffers no compulsion about his work. He doesn't even know exactly how many credits he has toward the degree. The pressures to complete his research and dissertation are mostly external—from his advisor, the department faculty, and Sue's desire to continue her own study. But not from him. Dick is comfortable, if a little confused. He enjoys teaching, but doesn't want it as a career, he doesn't think. He likes research, but he's not sure where he'll go with it. Perhaps at a university, maybe on the outside.

Another T.A. in the group, Bob Springer, radiates energy and purpose. He has a four-year commitment to the air force, starting in June, so he has to "get in there and tap dials and tweak knobs and get out."

"Bob's a hustler," says Dick, pushing the glasses back on the nose too large for the thin face. "He's younger and knows where he's going. Anyway, lately the pressure has been to get out."

Pause. His fingers comb through his full head of salt-and-pepper hair. Then, somewhat defensively: "The other thing is, he's got a system that's a little bit easier to work under, in the sense that he can go in there and open it up and rip it apart with his hands. He doesn't have to worry about the cleanliness aspect. It's really an inhibition to always have to be careful what you touch and how you touch it."

Dick's thesis research involves the use of an ultra-high vacuum system. It's a difficult piece of equipment with which to work, because even fingerprints ruin the vacuum. Normally, the thesis proposal is a formal hurdle in the obstacle race of graduate study, but he became involved in the project in a characteristically casual manner.

"We sat down to decide on a reasonable topic. It sort of evolved into something a little different from the original proposal, but my advisor has a tendency to keep adding things on. All advisors do. He's not as bad as some, but people in my group tend to take a little long getting out as a result."

"Getting out" means completing a piece of research, or some critical portion of it, rather than graduation itself. The absolute cleanliness required in Dick's work slows it down, as do people.

"I get involved in peripheral things. When I got to the lab . . . it looks pretty messy now, but it was a lot worse when I came . . . I really pushed to get things cleaned up. We had a room completely redone, had a laminar flow hood installed to keep dust off things you're working on. The guy who used the equipment before me . . . which is another reason I often got discouraged, he took longer than anybody getting out . . . he ruled the lab like a despot. He was the oldest T.A. there, the old patriarch, around long before anyone else came. He pushed his seniority real hard. He felt he deserved everyone's respect and tried to make everyone kowtow to his line of thinking."

There is a pecking order even in the T.A. sub-group. Dick points to a large bottle of distilled water. His predecessor had made a sign with a flow-tip pen which set rigid and specific rules for the use of the contents of the bottle and their replenishment. Some members of the group had the disrespectful habit of using the water to make coffee or to clean their glasses.

Dick concedes inertia and an inclination to rationalize. The Case-Western campus is a soothing oasis. Part of the University Circle complex on the eastern edge of Cleveland, it incorporates the Museum of Art, the Institute of Music and the Cleveland Playhouse. The students are thoroughly easygoing, and observe the Midwestern habit of saying hello to strangers. There are the usual signs of allegiance to contemporary collegiate enthusiasms—stripped-down European racing bicycles are chained to every other lamp post, with motorcycles and scooters filling the gaps. The uniform is patched jeans and T-shirts, and knapsacks or canvas carrying bags are slung over shoulders. Sprayed graffiti decry national and local inequities and promote the frivolous. The lagoon still sees the annual Spring rite of fraternity pledges tossed into its dubious waters to the off-key strains of the SAE drinking song.

Dick is no swinger but a T.A. can't afford night life, anyway. Dick likes trees and birds, and he's converted Sue from a walker to a hiker. Summers, they hike in New England or Colorado. Sundays, they stroll the large parks on the edges of the city, and return to brunch cooked on their hibachi. He has only the mildest interest in foreign travel, although a walking tour of Switzerland appeals. With a VW, an apartment, and the income from which they save $100 a month, Dick Chase is hurrying nowhere.

And there is the teaching, clearly gratifying to him. With a charitable advisor, he has a light load of one discussion class per week this semester. More commonly, he teaches one course three times a week. Last semester, he taught Physics 3 for sophomore engineering majors. The lecture classes require more preparation, more care.

"The course was essentially electricity and magnetism. It's taught out of the same text each year, mainly because the material doesn't change. It's one of the neater sections of physics to teach, because it's pretty basic. The ideas were worked out long ago, and there's very little room for variability. So what you essentially do is start out with Maxwell's Equations (they describe electromagnetic radiation like light) and then go backwards, or you start out with each equation and build up to Maxwell's. Going backwards is good only if you have very bright students. Throw four equations to typical students who have never seen those four things before, and they throw up their hands and quit."

The other three semesters of the first two years of physics are less well set, mainly because new texts appear so often.

"The ideas about what you should give freshmen in physics vary depending upon . . . oh . . . political climate or people's changing ideas from one year to another. Partly it's the old argument about should you give students a good basic discussion of mechanics and rotating bodies, things sliding down inclined planes, stuff like that, or should you expose them to some real physics? Everyone in physics has to know about mechanics, but they don't do that all the time. That's not what a physicist does. So people say you give students a very distorted idea of physics when you introduce all this mechanics at the beginning and then tell them nothing else. The approach keeps oscillating, between trying to tell them what physics is all about and giving them the basics, between getting them excited and turning them off."

Although graduate schools of arts and science are theoretically professional schools for the education of college teachers and scholars, as are those in law and medicine, few offer any formal teacher training. No one seems to be able to explain this. It is one of the oddities of our educational system that legal certification of pre-school teachers requires that a quarter of undergraduate study be devoted to development of teaching skills, while the future university-level seminar leader is rarely expected to complete even one course relating to the work techniques of his vocation. They're just supposed to "pick it up." Dick Chase, and the physics department at Case-Western, are exceptions. In his second semester of graduate study, he took a required course in teacher training. Harvard once offered a voluntary course and was overjoyed to enroll one of every eighteen prospective college teachers. Dick says his was better than nothing.

"I was very impressed with the professor I worked under, as a matter of fact. He had redesigned P1 and P2 in order to give them a feel for modern physics as well as for mechanics and basic concepts. And he had a very lighthearted approach. He gave tests that I thought were amusing, though some of the students were mad at him for making light of a sacred institution—tests!"

He grimaces briefly, pats his beard in a rare sign of physical self-awareness. Once, he taught a make-up P3 class. It was a discouraging experience since so many of the students dropped out, despite his efforts. But Dick sees the problem, again, in externals:

"Most of the people who drop out don't do it because they're stupid but because they have emotional problems. Most are smart enough to get through. The admissions standards are pretty high."

Teachers are inclined to direct their attention to their best students. Although T.A.'s are conscious of the tendency, since they are recent consumers themselves, they are apt to fall into the same pattern. They are bright themselves and it's more gratifying to work with students who meet the challenges readily. Dick tries to fight it.

"It's harder to pick up students at the bottom of the class. I'm not sure how successful I am at reaching both levels, but you have to try. You have to be flexible enough to get the better students to come in and discuss things with you, but you also have to get the bad students to feel that they can come in and ask stupid questions. I have trouble with that.

"If I didn't like the teaching, I'd be annoyed that it slowed down my research. The difficulty is that when I'm teaching a course, I feel strongly that I'm responsible for twenty people, that I must make sure that I'm well-prepared when I walk into class, that I know what I'm talking about. It's tougher when I'm giving lectures. When I first started teaching, that's the thing I dreaded most. What if someone asked a question I didn't know the answer to? After a while, you *tell* them if you don't know, which is better than giving them some b.s. that 'well, it should be obvious because of this, that, and the other' when you don't know yourself. I can't do that anymore."

Dick is, basically, content. He does not lead a harassed life of penury, the frequent depiction of a T.A.'s existence. The pressures are there, the frustrations, the small injustices: he teaches sections of the same course as some full professors, and has spent as much time teaching and in preparation as they, but at a considerable pay differential. But Dick accepts these things with equanimity.

It's difficult to find T.A.'s who don't do just that. Certainly, T.A.'s were involved in disruptive political actions at almost every major campus that suffered upheavals in the Sixties. But they were no more likely to be the first to mount the barricades than any other members of the university community. Like most students and professors, T.A.'s were observers. They signed petitions, attended rallies, inveighed against the war machine, big business, the Establishment, the curriculum. . . . But who didn't? Even the president of Yale did that.

Gay Baldinger is more vocal, and she rocks the boat a little over women's rights, but that she requests anonymity is evidence that her fervor does not extend to behavior possibly destructive to either her present position or her future career. The T.A. is almost forced to turn inward. He is isolated from his colleagues—half-student, half-teacher. He can attend faculty meetings, but cannot vote. He's beyond adolescence, but not yet accepted as an adult. He is unlikely to be receiving parental financial support (often for the first time since birth)

87

and is dependent upon the stipend and perhaps a spouse's income. He is without job security, serving at the pleasure of the department chairman and without the shield of tenure that stiffens the fortitude of his older colleagues. And, though the T.A. is loathe to admit it, and resists the suggestion, he or she is pledged to an elite order . . . and wants in.

Ashley Corson Brown calls it co-optation, for he still thinks in the fashionable terms of fading campus ideology. Given knowledge of his undergraduate and early graduate years, one might assume his rejection of the nearly uniform acquiescence of his professional compatriots. Ashley was a classic campus activist. The administrators at Bowling Green State University knew him well. He sat in, marched, organized, confronted, threw rocks, mouthed conventional radical rhetoric.

He doesn't do those things anymore. And he tells a story about himself that foretold his subsequent disinclination to make the ultimate commitment, through violent action, to the life of political outlaw. He and a friend prowled the Ohio campus one night, intent upon selecting an offending building suitable for burning. None seemed sufficiently combustible, so they settled for painting "FUCK" on the door of the ROTC armory. Their zeal proved wanting in fiber.

"Ashley Corson Brown" is, in any event, a name that could hardly be less suitable for a hard-core revolutionary. It lacks the steely brevity of "Mark Rudd" or the threat of the faintly foreign (and therefore suspect) "Mario Savio." And "Free Ashley Corson Brown" seems an unlikely slogan to enflame partisan passion, he concedes. His former nickname of "Boomer"—awarded because of a deadly outside lay-up shot in his early teens—might have been more fitting, but it fell into disuse when he failed to surpass his present 5'7", nipping his value to the Walnut Hills High School basketball team.

So Ashley serves quietly and conscientiously as a history T.A. at New York University. As it happens, his name, which smacks of WASPish privilege and boarding schools, is the result of a corruption committed by a Galveston immigration official when Ashley's grandfather arrived from Schimsk. ("What's your name, fella?" "Bren." "B-R-O-W-N. First name?" "Mordechai." "Okay, Max. On your way.") "Max Brown" went to St. Louis, because that sounded better than Galveston. His son went to Cincinnati where he became a respected lawyer and sometime politician of state-wide prominence. Then came Ashley Corson.

After Bowling Green and a year of high school teaching, he became a T.A. at the University of Cincinnati. That was a feisty year, culminating in the Cambodia-Kent State debacle. He made his presence known. Newly conscious of the importance of institutional status to his future career, and possibly because he was no longer welcome at Cincinnati, he accepted an assistantship at NYU. Unlike Case-Western, where, according to Dick Chase, nearly all graduate students teach or assist in research, NYU does not rely heavily on T.A.'s to flesh out the faculty. The history department, one of the largest in the country, has only eight. But they extract maximum effort from the T.A.'s available. Ashley has four lecture-discussion sessions a week, as many as any T.A. is likely to be assigned.

He doesn't feel put upon, as it seems to him a reasonable load. Since three of the classes cover the same material, preparation is not time-consuming. He doubts that he spends more than six hours a week in contact, perhaps another two or three "keeping ahead of the students."

The morning classes meet on the third floor of a converted private house near the campus gates. The room barely holds an eight-foot conference table. It's freshly painted, airy, with good light. When nine students have arrived, Ashley hands out test papers, lights one of his ten daily Tiparillos, and leans back in his chair. This is the discussion meeting of freshman "Topics in American History." It concerns, today, the Negro

89

experience following Reconstruction. Ashley knows it cold. Marcus Garvey was the subject of his master's thesis, and Ashley has only one page of notes before him.

His technique is restrained—no air-slicing hand gestures, no pounding of the table, no pacing—but his voice takes on a dramatic form of which he seems only slightly aware. It swoops, it whispers, it leaps forward, then slows. He punctuates the flow of the material with near-shouts to renew attention and denote progress in chronological events.

"*OKAY!* This is an extraordinarily broad subject we're going to try to cover today. Let's start with a quick glance at Reconstruction. What sort of opportunities do you see for the nation in terms of resolving the racial question once and for all at the end of the Civil War?"

Silence. The students shuffle papers, look at the wall.

"See any kind of possibilities?" he nudges. Pointing to a volunteer, "Yes?"

"They could have straightened out the society so the races could have been, y'know, equal. Not separate and equal, but completely equal."

"Could you be more specific?"

"They could get rid of, y'know, give blacks the same rights as whites. Y'know, voting . . . suing . . . property rights, same facilities. Should have been more action by the federal government . . . y'know . . ."

Ashley is undismayed. "Yes. Certainly. When did the Southern states begin to be reformed?"

Silence. Six students drift in. The chairs around the table fill up. A latecomer chooses to sit on the radiator, a feat he sustains throughout the class. Another blows a necklace of six perfect smoke rings.

"*WELL!* It really doesn't begin until 1868 or so. The Federal troops are occupying the South. *So!* It's an unprecedented op-por-tun-ity to solve this problem, but in order for that political equality to be enforced, what kind of a base do you need for that?"

Coughs. More smoke rings.

He surrenders, continues. "We *talked* about this when we talked about the Populist movement. . . . Did it do any good to have *any* kind of radical movement, or even a liberal, reformist movement if the employers wanted to oppose it? What was *missing?* It was the economic base! Would it have been possible to construct an economic base for black people during the post–Civil War years? How could it have been done?"

He waits again, puffs the cigar, rocks back in his chair. *They* surrender.

"They could have confiscated some of the lands of the Confederates," says the girl who is to answer most of the questions to come, "and divided it among the persons who worked the lands."

Now the students lean forward. Relevance! Ashley can feel the click of interest. This is supposed to be a discussion group, but he knows the subject, so he indulges himself.

"*YES! Land reform!* That land should belong to those people who work it, not those who by historical accident happen to own it. The argument was presented by two guys, Thaddeus Stevens and Daniel Sumner. You should know who they are. Stevens was a congressman from Pennsylvania who has been portrayed by many historians as one of the arch-villains of history. He lent himself to the role. Physically, he was bent out of shape, he had a clubfoot, walked with a cane, was actually one of the ugliest men to set foot in Congress. He was the villain."

Murmuring, chuckles. Dutiful note-taking.

"But he was also very shrewd. He saw the possibilities in the situation in the South. *ONE!* The people who received the land would vote Republican! *TWO!* Simultaneously you take away the votes of the white Southerners! Obviously. They committed treason. That means a tremendous base for Republican power in the South. So what could he propose to maintain the advantage of the Republicans? Any ideas?"

None.

"Well, look, let's go back a few years. What was one of the major economic causes of the Civil War? What were the differences between the North and South which were virtually irreconcilable?"

This time, several students start to answer. Not that there is a sudden surge in participation. It ebbs and flows.

And so it goes. Ashley later tells of a black candidate for sheriff in a Mississippi community who ran for sheriff and committed suicide by shooting himself three times in the back. It is gratifying to these students' ideological perspectives, and they laugh knowingly.

After another discussion group, his work for the week done, Ashley goes to the cafeteria for lunch. He seems unmoved by his day. He isn't up, he isn't down. He has fulfilled an obligation. He finds teaching agreeable, but he is not thrilled. Asked the difference between his former students in Ohio and these, he says:

"Mainly, it's that these are world-weary New York sophisticates. They received a pretty well-rounded education and they don't seem to particularly want to know any more. The Ohio kids, on the other hand, were easy to rouse. They were only taught one side: 'Reconstruction was evil!' Attack their preconceptions . . . or at least their high school teachers' preconceptions . . . and you could stir up some give-and-take."

Ashley, however, admits that he no longer wants to be a professor. In that, he is perhaps the norm among T.A.'s. In 1972, there were 539,062 Ph.D. candidates enrolled in American graduate schools. Only 29,000 doctorates were awarded that year. Guessing that one-third were T.A.'s on the assumption they are more highly motivated, and extending the equation over the five years normally taken to complete the Ph.D., it is unlikely that more than 45 percent of the T.A.'s enrolled in 1972 will ever receive the doctorate. And, of these, many will not enter the professoriate. They leave because they cannot tolerate the games that must be played, because they have children, because their grants run out or are withdrawn, because they feel guilt at being supported by their spouses, because they falter at one of the academic hurdles, or just because they change their minds.

Now Ashley thinks he might go to law school next year, if he can get in. His undergraduate grades were "uneven," and law schools don't look at graduate grades. Also, he bombed on the LSAT, the Law School Aptitude Test, and everyone seems to want law school this year.

The new ambition is partly because of his admiration for his father, who, as an ACLU attorney, has defended both the Black Panthers and the Ku Klux Klan. But law is also a "useful" skill, and Ashley hasn't lost all his fervor to change the system. It was just submerged for a while, the temporary casualty of the impotence an intractable system imposes on malcontents.

In the meantime, Ashley finds his present circumstance tolerable enough. Susan found a full-time teaching job in February, and Ashley moonlights as a substitute at the nearby grammar school. Between them, they manage perhaps $12,000 a year, more than the Chases and at least adequate even in New York City. The apartment, technically a two-roomer, is a walk-up—and a "rip-off," at $185 a month—in the flawed but charming historical district of Brooklyn Heights. Ashley just took the landlord to small claims court and won $15. They have no car, no bicycles, no evident extravagances.

Susan is a touch taller than Ashley, dark, attractive. Her eyes glitter with self-assurance and a knowledge of her own competence. She politely offers cake and orange juice to a guest, but there is nothing of the dutiful hausfrau about her. She retires to the tiny bedroom to grade papers.

Ashley smiles easily and often. His steel-rimmed glasses are thick, the billow of hair around the base of his neck compensates for the strands pulled across the thinning forehead. He looks the part of a scholar . . . and speaks of his understanding of those he knows who plant bombs. He, too, feels isolation. They live thirty minutes by subway from the campus and are not part of what modest social life the university offers. He knows few people in New York and suffers the fish-nor-fowl syndrome of most T.A.'s in relation to other faculty and students. Although he rejects the idea, he fits the T.A. mold.

T.A.'s follow the usual academic political spectrum, but usually with a more leftward tilt. To his associates at Case-Western Reserve, Dick Chase is the office radical. To Gay Baldinger he'd be merely a shade pinker than Genghis Khan.

If agriculturists among the professoriate are the most religious, social scientists are the least. Gay and Ashley do not believe. But neither does Dick, despite the convention about finding God among the test tubes. Ashley and Susan *did* get married in a church to please her parents, and she converted to Judaism to please his. Only Gay is distinctly hostile to religion; the others are simply unconcerned.

They do not have much social life, nor do they care. Most T.A.'s don't. As one of Ashley's colleagues suggested, "T.A.'s carry on like dentists from Altoona at a Grand Rapids seminar on orthodontia." Gay and Ashley have smoked dope, but both saw it as debilitating to their clarity of thought politically, and a potential excuse to the authorities to throw them out of school. So they quit. Dick doesn't touch grass or liquor, and never has.

All are inclined to believe that they are better teachers than those under whom they studied, although they suffer doubts about their techniques ("How do you keep from boring twenty-two kids to death?") and the importance of it all. None feels their classroom duties to be excessive, and only Gay really feels alive when she is before her students. All three feel adequately compensated.

For those who persevere, for Gay and perhaps Dick, the next step after graduation may be the most harrowing of all. Diplomas and hats in hand, they must hurl themselves into the marketplace. In these years of The Glut, few can expect to find slots in any way resembling the glorious tacit promises of their years as graduate assistants. Having spent those years at some of the best universities in the country, they must now scramble for positions at colleges whose names they first saw on lists in placement offices.

There are a number of avenues to academic employment. Ideally, the graduate assistant is offered a position at the institution at which he or she has completed study. That spares one the anguish of the search. Most new Ph.D.'s, however, must look around. They send out résumés, ask favorite mentors to send letters of recommendation, visit older friends on other campuses, ferret out leads. Sooner or later, though, the would-be professor finds himself at a convention of an academic professional organization.

A convention of college professors is not appreciably different in form from a gathering of collapsible-tube manufacturers. While professors are not inclined to wear funny hats and brandish buzzer-canes at pretty girls, there is a great deal of backslapping, hooting, and drinking in the hotel lobbies, and giggling forays into the seamier neighborhoods of the host city. Scheduled meetings are no better attended than at most conventions for the universal reason that the delights of downtown Omaha are invariably more appealing than panel discussions on the future of the diacritical mark or Lincoln's doctor's association with General Burnside.

And, as at most conventions, there is the unparalleled

opportunity of establishing contacts and making one's availability more widely known to potential employers. Department chairmen conduct interviews, colleges and applicants swap *vitae*. Inevitably, the conventions are described as flesh markets. In truth, for the uninitiated, they are academic versions of the more voracious singles bars, with a whole new set of signals to be learned. The new Ph.D. recipient, convinced that few illusions remain, discovers new ones to be shattered.

The annual meeting of the Modern Languages Association is unquestionably the premier organizational embodiment of the academic conference-*cum*-jobmart. It is by no means the only such convention, simply the largest. In attendance each year are over ten thousand professors and supplicants. The distinctions merge. Professor A meets old friend B, who has an opening for a bright young person in his department. Prof. A has just the one. Prof. B is interested. Prof. A is happy because his reputation rests in part upon his success in placing his advisees. Prof. B is pleased because his friend works at a classier institution and he will draw favor for his ability to attract young scholars from more prestigious universities. Neither is looking for a job himself, but they have added to the pervasive aroma of mind-peddling.

For the applicants themselves, it is a humbling ordeal. They smile until afraid their jaws will lock, all the time attempting to strike a balance between approachable self-assurance and beguiling modesty. They are outsiders, warming themselves at the fringes of conversations between the stars and superstars, even the merely tenured, of their fields. Then they retreat to the refuge of their circle of faintly hysterical fellow hunters. They begin to understand that an instructorship in Chickasha, Oklahoma, could well be a plum.

Withal, the fledgling will gain entrance to the guild; despite the cries of underemployment, nearly 95 percent of the new

Ph.D.'s who want academic jobs find something, somewhere. If the new employer isn't all that might have been hoped . . . well, just wait for that first *real* book. Then he will be known, maybe even a star.

CHAPTER 6

Arthur Knight is a star, of a sort.

There is a word written in huge white cutout letters standing against the ridge hovering above Wilshire Boulevard, H*O*L*L*Y*W*O*O*D. Some of the letters topple from time to time, and there is talk about taking them all down once and for all. Distraught starlets fling themselves in suicidal despair from the O's and L's left standing. Usually, they just hurt themselves.

Long before Arthur Rosenheimer first saw the sign, he loved the films created in the hills and valleys within its view. Now he lives not far away, near the final curve of a street without sidewalks in the hills overlooking the city. Down below, under an achingly blue dome of sky edged brown where it meets the ground, Los Angeles scrabbles out into the desert and down to the sea. He knows the city now, no longer a boy from the horizonless East, and he knows the people who make the films he still loves. The boy who watched Chaplin and Lloyd at the Germantown Rialto Colonial is now begged—please!—to watch movies. As a favor to his friends. For money.

He is Arthur Knight now—film reviewer, essayist, lecturer, and professor. (He changed the name when he was starting to do all these things in earnest around 1948 and kept finding Rosenheimer misspelled and mispronounced. Eric Knight, author of *Lassie, Come Home* and *This Above All*, had a strong influence on Arthur as a young man and had died during World War II. Arthur took his name.) Knight seems a man thoroughly satisfied with his life, doing what he wants, as he wants: looking at films, meeting the people who make them, writing, teaching, talking film. At base, he is a teacher. That is the one thing he would be if forced to choose. But his status as a quotable reviewer living (as most do not) near the heart of the sickly but dogged American film industry inevitably adds another dimension to the customary academic lifestyle . . . even in Southern California.

Easterners can't take California seriously. It's for fun, a brief flirtation with fantasy before returning to Real Life. People from New York who actually go to live in Los Angeles are escapists, trapped in adolescent reverie. What reality can there be in a place where people are known to drown in rain puddles, where the ghettos look like pastel Tenaflys, and natural disasters aren't down-to-earth hurricanes and blizzards, but earthquakes? And *mudslides,* for heaven's sake? Grownups live in earnest in Detroit and Cleveland and Baltimore, kids live in Los Angeles and get patted on the head. It makes the kids defensive. They assert that where they are is the future. Kids always do that.

Extend all that—and every other partly accurate denigration of California—to those who work the citrus groves of academe, and then layer it over with the light regard of most academics for fields of specialization with a history of not even a century, and some outline of how film professors are viewed by their colleagues begins to take shape. *Real* intellectuals immerse themselves in dusty carrels and sweat out five-volume analyses of one-volume nineteenth-century novels. How can King Vidor be even remotely as worthy of study as King Henry VIII?

In the interlocking charts of status which govern relationships in the academic world, the study of film is inserted just above hog breeding. The hierarchy can be said to be in inverse proportion to the degree of utility in the world of work of the skills taught the student. In this barely acknowledged ranking, then, the study of the *products* of creative artists is deemed more worthy than the training of the artists themselves. Art history *über* studio painting. As one liberal arts dean was heard to say when asked to award transfer standing for music performance courses taken at another division of the same university: "What? Give credit for tooting a horn? In *our* musicology department? Don't be fatuous." With occasional institutional exceptions, the most prestigious subjects will be the humanities, followed by the data disciplines, trailed by the only grudgingly accepted social sciences (after all, sociology has only been around since Max Weber in the late nineteenth century). Sociology professors themselves have, however, a broad choice of lower castes to lord over. Among them are departments of teacher training, nursing, business administration, dramatic arts, speech therapy, forestry, and agronomy, all made more alarming by the fecundity of their vocational offshoots.

Yet apart from occasional grumbles about professor-critics who don't know how movies are made and about overpaid Ph.D.'s who can't tie their shoelaces, Arthur Knight shows no animosity for, and little awareness of, those who belittle the study of film as a wasteful frivolity. He doesn't even trouble to trot out the major-art-form-of-the-twentieth-century bromide. He likes film and he knows it is important. That is enough. Beyond that, he shares a quality evident among many of his colleagues—an almost childlike delight in his chosen work.

On the surface, Knight's lifestyle is comparable to that of any reasonably affluent professor who happens to live in California. That is, of course, a sub-species as much distinguished from its fellows as it is in any other occupational group. It is in the nature of the place to lend a breath of hedonism and luxury not enjoyed by equally paid compatriots in Larchmont or Council Bluffs. But the ways in which most professors choose to live lend themselves to ready if imprecise generalization. The accoutrements of their surroundings and the methods by which they transport themselves from home to work to supermarket vary little, and are very nearly uniform in the absence of the more common symbols of middle-class materialism. The successful introduction of small foreign cars in America undoubtedly owes a substantial debt to the American professoriate. Indeed, it is difficult to find a professor who does *not* drive a VW or Toyota or Volvo, which is, furthermore, inevitably battered, dusty, and at least five years old. Professors will not be concerned with appearances.

What is more, professors in the mass look amazingly alike. Visit any scholarly meeting and convention and be engulfed by fortyish men, at least half of whom wear facial hair and/or glasses. To describe a professor as stylishly dressed is a clear contradiction in terms. Perhaps as a result of conditioning in their years as underpaid teaching assistants, they wear clothes primarily to cover themselves, oblivious to such faddish niceties as fitted waists and four-inch-wide ties. The only visibly sizable expenditures in their homes is in the books. The result is an almost aggressive frumpiness characterizing the decor of professorial home and body, a perhaps unconscious reaffirmation of their claims of poverty. Theirs is a simple life, they seem to be saying, stripped of any trace of conspicuous acquisition. They walk when they might ride, bicycle when they might drive, backpack into the wilderness rather than loll on beaches or roll dice in casinos.

Behind the desired illusion is a penchant for less visible, but more rapidly consumable pleasures. They travel quite a bit, and over long periods of time, for months are available to them. They indulge the tastes acquired in those travels, as well as their knowledge of the onset of the white truffle season, the proper consistency of brie, the location of that marvelous tea shop off Oxford Street, the description of St. Emilion as the burgundy of Bordeaux. They cherish experience over things.

The directions to Arthur Knight's house might be those to Ralph Williams' car lot. . . . Harbor Freeway to Hollywood Freeway to Gower to the Beechwood cutoff then right on Cheremoya to Hollyridge Road. Hollyridge twists, narrows, cuts back, twists again. Here in the hills over the city, the houses are close but private, in a manner never mastered in Scarsdale. The horn must be pressed at each switchback, for a driver can't see around the terraced gardens and stuccoed houses. No one is walking. That may even be an infraction of municipal regulations. No lawns, really, just masses of flowers and ivy spilling over the curbs, wound through with paths and steps cut from the rock and sand.

Knight's house is much like the others, not larger, not smaller. It's white, with an orange-tiled roof, and multistoried to cling to the side of the hill. A visitor goes down steep stairs to a cool porch landing hung with plants. A voice calls up from two stories below. The members of the household consult from rooms away to determine who will answer the door. No one appears for several moments.

Then Knight is there, calm, pleasant, if somewhat distracted, fresh from a telephone conversation. Inside, the house has arches and tiny landings and little staircases and white rough-textured walls hung with paintings of little distinction and substantial ambition—great chunks of New York cityscape and Los Angeles at night and costume layouts for movies.

And red. The shag rug is red, the sofa and chairs are red, the telephone is red. Knight brings the instrument into the living room and plugs it into a convenient jack. He is expecting some calls—about once every five minutes, as it turns out.

He settles into a scarlet velvet easy chair, offers a drink, coffee, tea. He is fifty-seven, and looks it, but in a placid, unworn way. The gray hair is full, brushed back. He wears a peppery mustache, faded plaid shirt, sneakers, and chinos held in place around an ample middle with a sash-knotted necktie. It might be a gardening outfit, but the plantings as well as the paintings are his wife's province.

As he sucks a pipe to life, the phone rings. He talks briefly, with long listening pauses, mentioning a faintly familiar name. Then he returns to his chair, starts working on the pipe again. He cautions that the calls may be heavy this afternoon. He's trying to set up an interview with Clint Eastwood for *Playboy* magazine.

"That was [he names a famous producer]. The producers here (puff) have more time than anybody and they think nothing of calling up and staying on the telephone for half an hour. He wanted to know whether I'd seen the new Lindsay Anderson film. If I'd encouraged him, I know he would read me the whole three columns in the trades this morning, because he's done that. But (*puff*) it's just a matter of filling up their day, I suppose, making them feel they've accomplished something."

It is said not unkindly, but as an observation. With few exceptions, he is not scornful about the ways other people conduct themselves. He disagrees, he is disappointed, but he rarely condemns. He obviously doesn't have the instinct for the jugular like some film critics—John Simon, for example, whom Knight describes as "a pompous ass and a mean, mean man." That's as acid-tongued as Knight gets, orally. He saves his best for print.

Ring. It's Clint Eastwood's agent. Clint would like to speak to Arthur tomorrow, at Clint's place in Carmel. Can Arthur make it? There is talk about plane and car connections. A soft breeze through the jalousied windows carries a sudden *braaap!* from a motorcycle down on the freeway. Odd, but there are no other sounds of traffic. Marian Knight's garden is extravagantly luxuriant with flaming poinsettia and other unbelievably lush flowers. And birdsong! It sounds as if a flock of canaries stoned on Hartz Mountain cannabis have taken shelter in the Knight's mimosa. Hanging up, Knight sees his visitor's wonder at fruit trees in the backyard. Lemons, and oranges big as melons. The oranges aren't really very good, he says. A hummingbird whirrs silently by and something larger and gaudier pauses to coo near the windowsill. It is not at all like Philadelphia.

Arthur Rosenheimer was born there. Knight's grandparents had brought their six children to America in 1900. His grandmother died the day they landed. The grandfather couldn't face a new country without his wife, so he went back to Germany, leaving his children with a cousin who raised them. Apparently they never saw their father again. They all worked to put the bright one through Bryn Mawr. She became a teacher; Arthur's father went into advertising; a brother into the insurance business. The third brother—the artistic one— ended up as a managing director of the Buffalo Symphony. In 1929, Arthur wrote a film column for his junior high school magazine. The first film he ever reviewed was *Disraeli* with George Arliss. His family moved to New York shortly thereafter and he entered City College.

Arthur's father prospered, moderately, during the Twenties. He was important to Arthur, whose voice lowers when he talks about him.

"He was a very cultivated man. He loved music, took me to concerts. He could quote long passages from Goethe and that sort of thing. After he lost his dough a lot of the life went out of him. One of the worst things I've ever seen was this man who used to read, who wrote a bit . . . he spent most of the time until he died listening to the radio and playing solitaire."

Pause. Now the voice hardens. "It . . . it always left a very sad feeling for me about him and I resented my mother because I thought she acted very badly. I know that money problems were very big so far as she was concerned but it's an emasculating thing when a woman takes over control of the purse strings, which she did. It . . . it made a very . . . it left a very unpleasant feeling for me about my mother."

While he was still at City College, he took a job in the film library at the Museum of Modern Art. The recognition of film as a legitimate art form was still tentative. The University of Southern California had a film program, as did New York University, but there were few others. Knight took a workshop course with Lewis Jacobs, talking about the "rise of the American film." He'd had to go into part-time night classes. Then the war. He was a first lieutenant with an infantry machine-gun platoon in France. In October of 1944 at the Belfort Gap, a tree-burst from a German .88 showered shrapnel into his body.

"I was evacuated down to Naples and came out on limited assignment. I still had a good deal of shrapnel in me, the wounds not quite healed, but one day I got a pass and took a truck to Naples. I looked around to see what film installations were there. I looked into Special Services, Red Cross, and the Signal Corps. Special Services was cutting back and the Red Cross only used enlisted men. But the 263rd Film Equipment Exchange of the Signal Corps had an opening. They needed an officer so as soon as I was in a replacement depot—the 'repple depple'—I took a truck up to Caserta to see the Signal major. I told him my qualifications in the museum and pointed out they needed an officer. He requisitioned me out. It really was the brightest thing I ever did in my life, because otherwise they would have followed my Form 20 and sent me off to some colored trucking battalion up in Leghorn. I finished up as the operations officer for the whole PBS."

That was 1945, and although the Italian film industry was getting started again, Knight didn't have any real contact with it.

"The one great revelation for me was when I was still in the

106

hospital and they sent me to Sorrento for a recuperation week. I wandered into a movie house where they were showing an Italian film called *Ossessione*. It was Visconti's first film [1942] and really the beginning of Italian neo-realism. Rossellini's *Open City* came three years after that. Most of the Italian films we'd seen back in the Thirties were just adaptations of grand operas. You tend to generalize from a single film, so I wrote back: 'We've been all wrong about the Italian movies. They're great filmmakers!' But then back in Naples we weren't allowed to go into the Italian movie houses, in Leghorn I was too busy, and in Florence I spent most of my time at the opera."

In 1946 he returned to his work at MOMA (The Museum of Modern Art) in New York. Then he moved to the Dramatic Workshop, which had just effected a divorce from the New School for Social Research. Mainly, they offered courses to returning G.I.'s, and Knight headed the film and television section. As the G.I. Bill of Rights and ex-G.I.'s began to peter out, so did the workshop. He switched to a full-time instructorship at City College, in Hans Richter's film department. He continued to freelance as a writer and lecturer, and taught courses at the New School, Hunter, Columbia, and Sarah Lawrence, among others. The position at City College left time—and the salary left the necessity—to pursue other sources of income.

He started his column for *Saturday Review* in 1949 (and was still writing it when the magazine folded in 1973). In 1956, he wrote *The Liveliest Art*, a history of the movies. Still in print, it has become a standard text for proliferating university and college film programs twenty years later. Despite his lack of conventional professorial credentials (he never went beyond his B.A. at City), he was offered a professorship at the University of Southern California. On the ride to the airport, he looked back at Manhattan and suddenly realized how happy he was to be leaving.

Not that the adjustment to Los Angeles was swift. He allows that it was two years before he could deal with the wholly different California lifestyle. But his interests and professional activities meshed perfectly here. Directors and stars and composers and editors are here. They visit his classes because they like to talk about their work—and because he is an influential reviewer. His conversation is casually sprinkled with the names of the most famous people in the industry and with those of craftsmen known mainly by colleagues and buffs. It is not name-dropping, for these are friends and acquaintances, or at least people he must inevitably know. The glamour of knowing them faded quickly as they became real. In any event, Knight is not a braggart. He speaks, for example, of having written "a couple" of documentary scripts, though the number is over fifty.

And now he is on the red telephone again. He asks "Roger" how "Ann-Margaret" is, alluding to the latter's recent fall from the scaffolding of a night club set. Awed by such third-hand brushes with celebrity, the visitor is told that Ann-Margaret was here a few weeks ago. A charming, shy little thing, very quiet. Ann-Margaret sat right here! In this chair! Oh, yes, so did Clint. Knight smiles. His first-time students are always excited at the start of a course when, say, Bob Evans from Paramount is scheduled to visit, but that infatuation with fame fades with familiarity.

"These are cinema majors, and they're mainly interested in what they can learn from these people. Anyway, I give them a rather stern orientation talk at the beginning of the semester. I say that 'the guests' are coming down to the class to give what they know. They're invited because they have a *lot* to give and if there are any ego trips involved, it's going to be *their* ego trips, not yours! Most of the students understand that."

There are problems from time to time. There was a non-cinema major who once asked Burt Lancaster if that was his real name and another who got personal about Evans' former wife, Ali MacGraw. But Knight now restricts the course to serious film students, and dilettantes are not welcome.

The human resources of Los Angeles are obviously priceless to a professor of film. Although Knight concedes "pretty good" status to film programs at UCLA, Northwestern, NYU, and Boston University, he firmly believes that his department surpasses all others. He has a case. The faculty is composed primarily of practicing professionals, not people who drew cartoons for Disney one summer over thirty years ago and who have been teaching animation ever since. He runs through a list of his colleagues—film editor Mel Sloan, novelist and script-writer Irv Blacker, makeup artist Bill Tuttle, producer Sol Lesser. Not all are career professors, but Knight is not persuaded that that is critical. A favorite example is Jerry Lewis, who taught a production class at USC and turned out to be a very serious and engaging teacher.

There have been others. Stanley Kramer talking about the period from the age of the almighty studios to independent production; directors Vincent Sherman and Peter Bogdano-vitch. And Clint Eastwood. Knight had doubts about him.

"I figured he'd be a 'yup' and 'nope' kind of fellow. Yet, because student interest in the Sergio Leone films was very high at the time, I thought it would at least be interesting to hear him talk about other filmmakers. When he came down to the school, I was amazed to find how easy he was to talk to, how informative he was. He set up a marvelous rapport with the class. After the class was over, I asked if he'd like to come down here to the house and talk with some of the students. He did, and that session went on until about four in the morning. The next week I told my editor at *Playboy* about it and he said they'd been trying to get an interview with Eastwood for the past three years. They told me to try, and he said yes."

Again, the phone interrupts. It's Clint. Again, Knight is talking to him as if he was just another human being, and not the top box-office draw in the entire world. Travel arrangements are adjusted, visiting hours modified, the interview schedule finalized. Knight wants this one to go well. For one thing, there's the money: *Playboy* pays about $5,000 for one of its featured interviews. But too, he has only done one other for *Playboy*, despite his status as a regular contributor. He had what he thought was eight marvelous hours of tape with Alfred Hitchcock, who went on the Dick Cavett Show a week later and used all the same material. An abbreviated version of the interview wound up in *OUI*, the lustier but less substantial younger brother of *Playboy*.

This unseemly fraternization with show busines people *and* a clear affection for "theatrical" films *and* writing for *Playboy* has brought Knight under fire from some of his fellow academicians as well as other critics and reviewers. Apart from a passing slap at USC's telecommunications department—"it's a ludicrous department that carries more weight only because it has three Ph.D.'s"—the disapprobation doesn't seem to trouble him. His *History of Sex in the Cinema* has outrun Hefner's *Playboy Philosophy* by six installments, with semi-annual updates planned. (Yes, Knight has visited Hef and his Barbie doll at the Playboy mansion, too—thinks Hef's the sweetest millionaire he ever met.)

In all this, he epitomizes that kind of professor who uses his position in the university to move into the larger world. One result is the contempt of colleagues, one of whom said sneeringly of Knight: "He's *not* a critic, he's not even a journalist. Even in his chosen field, he's regarded as a lightweight. To any legitimate scholar, he's nothing more than a popularizer." That is perhaps the most brutal condemnation of all. If a scholar of the most sincere intent of any faculty realizes, through circumstance or dumb luck, a popular success with a book or essay, he is sure to experience immediate attack from members of his profession. General acceptance of a published piece is regarded as proof of its superficiality and casts a reflection on the unfortunate scholar's entire body of work. Erich Segal is the best known instance. Until *Love Story* and his chats with Johnny Carson, Segal was regarded as a skilled teacher and a young scholar of already realized promise. His commercial success (and, admittedly, the way he sought and coped with it) cast a pall on his academic career that may never fade.

Nevertheless, many professors market their skills beyond their campuses. Depending upon how they choose to make themselves available, they can enhance or do damage to their reputations, and, not incidentally, supplement their incomes from a few hundred dollars a year into the thousands and even tens of thousands.

Physicists solicit grants from research institutes which bring the professors two or three extra months' salary a year. Law professors accept cases. Medical and dental school faculty maintain private practices. Businesses seek out psychologists and management specialists on campuses to lend prestige to their endeavors and to display before the stockholders. Faculty in every discipline write textbooks, often the most lucrative of all publications since demand can be sustained over ten or twenty years.

There are lectures on other campuses and before community groups. One of Gay Baldinger's advisors recently made a two-day tour of five colleges in western Massachusetts. He's not all that well-known, so his fee per lecture was a modest $350 plus expenses. Two days work equaled $1,750, clear. Academic superstars draw $1,000 for an off-campus appearance, sometimes more. There is consulting: The ten to twenty members of the study sections reviewing grant proposals for such agencies as the National Science Foundation receive $75 to $150 or more per day, for perhaps ten to twenty days a year. That can be as much as $3,000 a year. Plus expenses.

None of this is meant to suggest that all professors are doubling and tripling their salaries with outside work. Some do, the vast majority don't. The opportunities are there, nonetheless. Arthur Knight can be assumed to take full advantage of them. His *Playboy* articles alone might well match his USC salary although he won't talk about it. If Knight is troubled by the criticism, he doesn't show it. After all, he's written two books, hundreds of reviews and articles, and the motion picture entries of the Encyclopedia Britannica and the Crowell-Collier encyclopedia. Not many scholars with doctorates can match that, he reasons.

Knight is talking about the distinction between a critic and a reviewer. "A reviewer works from the immediate film experience and comes into print assuming that nobody else has seen the film. He has to give some idea what the film is all about, as well as his analysis. Whereas a critic, it seems to me, is more likely concerned with the broader aspects of films. He'll find a group of films that he can analyze for a specific theme or which represent a director's style. He makes the assumption that the reader has already seen the picture and doesn't have to have the plot recounted."

Knight is optimistic about the future of movies. There will be more diversity, greater specialization, perhaps similar to the route magazines have taken. The "art" houses were an early example, sexploitation theaters more recent. Knight points to the success of the reissued Cinerama films and sees signs of development of large presentation houses where "spectacular" films can be shown for a year or more.

"The nature of films is going to be affected by the technology through which they're presented. You wouldn't do an *Airport* on your 17″ TV screen. You'd do something far more intimate. I've been surprised at the number of pictures I've seen that were made for the big screen but look ever so much better on a little screen. George Cukor's *Gaslight*, as example, was played very much in closeup and looks much better on the tube.

"And technology is going to open the gate wide for

graduating film students. We're so used to thinking of film in terms of the major studios, but you have television, educationals, documentaries, training films, commercials. There are so many angles to the film at this point that our students don't have much trouble placing themselves. About 80 percent of our graduates find work in the field, and that's about as good as you'll find from law schools or medical schools.

"One thing I'm very pleased about at our school is that they don't let the students start filmmaking in the freshman year. They have to wait until they're at least juniors before they can start any production courses. We feel at USC that until a filmmaker has something to talk about, you're just giving him technique, and we feel we should never be a trade school. We should be a school which enables the students to express themselves filmicly. This system, I think is producing better filmmakers than the schools that are simply accenting the technical part of the job, of the craft."

Knight's professorial duties are not markedly reduced in deference to his celebrity. Others of similar reputation in their fields might insist on fewer classroom demands upon their time—perhaps a cosy seminar or two with five or six disciples. Knight apparently wouldn't want such an arrangement, even if he could get it. He teaches three separate courses with three separate preparations required. One is a film criticism seminar for about 15 seniors and graduates; the film history class has 70 students; and the third class has 120 students. Each meets only once a week, for four hours each. Such a schedule would send some senior professors into trauma, but Knight also meets his extracurricular obligations. That means about ten hours a week advising students and attending faculty meetings, although he does avoid committees. In addition, he encourages students to come to his home frequently.

Places like USC are targets of the standard "rabbit warren" criticism directed at any college with an average class size of more than ten. Knight insists that contact with students is not all that difficult to achieve. After the first few sessions, he claims, there are certain faces in the audience who become quickly familiar—they have their hands up and ask the bright questions. Those are the people he invites to his home. He gets to know *them,* at least, and to that extent, the system works. To get the reading and grading of papers done, he has one T.A. and, toward the end of each semester, two additional graduate readers. It's an impossibility for him to read *all* the papers—although he looks over about a third. So he has an understanding with his classes that if any students disagree with grades the readers give them, Knight will consider appeals.

In exchange, he has the security of tenure, a salary which can be assumed to exceed $25,000 for a nine-month year, close contact with the people for whom films are made, and ample opportunity to moonlight with his writing and lecturing. And he has the time to pursue his particular cause, combating censorship.

Given his academic affiliation, he is a natural for lawyers seeking expert witnesses for the defense of films accused of violating someone's sense of decency. He estimates that he has appeared in behalf of at least sixteen such films, the most notorious being *Deep Throat.*

"I would much rather make the stand against censorship on the basis of *Last Tango in Paris* than *Deep Throat.* It just happens that *Throat* was the one that came into the courts. I know very well the way the courts work. If a precedent is established on the basis of *Deep Throat,* it can also be used to cut the throat of a *Last Tango.*

"Actually, I'm much more concerned about the pornography of violence than the pornography of sex. You can only go so far in the depicting of sexual activity and that limit has about been reached. The violence, however, keeps increasing in very definite increments. Something that shocked us a few years ago, like *The Wild Bunch,* is simply a platform from which other films have become even more explicit and ugly in their increased violence, discovering new ways of showing it.

"Peckinpah showed *The Wild Bunch* to one of my classes in what he considered its final form. As these great goops of blood made their huge circles across the entire screen, the class began to laugh. It was so excessive it was funny. At that point, the film was recut, so that instead of letting you see the whole trajectory of blood from a severed artery going across the entire screen, they cut within the frame so that you saw the blood begin, then cut short.

"The filmmakers themselves must accept responsibility. They have brought this repression on themselves."

What happens now? Where does film content go from here?

Professor Arthur Knight is pulling on his pipe again, looking about his room in thought. There are backgammon sets under glass, plants and flowers in colored pots, rock and mineral samples heaped in cases, antique cribbage boards. The gaudy bird comes back to coo for a moment. His pipe lit, the professor decides:

"The bestiality is yet to come."

CHAPTER 7

"POWER" is scrawled on the blackboard in foot-high letters. Underneath are the words "Resources, Number, Organization." The professor's voice, deep, with an edge to it that would sound just right in a Mutual Funds commercial, bounces off the high ceiling and pea-green cinder block walls. He sits behind a metal and formica desk, dwarfing it. There is one book before him covering a few sheets of yellow legal paper with scribbled notes. He will refer to neither throughout the class.

"Power is vested in those who control the resources. Or maybe it's the other way around. Maybe what we're really saying is that in order to make the Establishment *the Establishment*, resources are put in their control."

He rises, moves around to the front of the desk. His class is seated in chairs arranged in an untidy semicircle. They are attentive, for they are educational administrators in fact or in aspiration. This is a basic graduate course intended to weed out those who, in the eyes of the faculty, are without aptitude for administration. Their professor this quiet Saturday morning is Leon Ovsiew. He sits on the desk, twists his left leg up onto his right thigh.

"It is important to keep bearing in mind," he continues, "that the economic model of power is not the one that fits the education model, or the government model. The parallels are not absolute, they're only analogous. In education, the control of resources is only partially vested in those who are in public school or university administrative positions. The school board and administrator do have 'control' of monies. But one has only to look at Philadelphia to realize how little that may mean."

He is referring to the then-current technical bankruptcy of the public school system, and the attendant complication of a months-long teachers' strike. Professor Ovsiew (pronounced "Ahv-see") uses his voice well, and his gestures are dramatic, if employed with economy. Confident and avuncular in manner, his presence is complicated by large glasses ground in a half-mooned bifocaled pattern that give him, from certain angles, the aspect of a malevolent owl. The middle of his face is broad, narrowing to sloping forehead and to pointed chin. There are white wisps of hair on top and a closely-clipped goatee; the forward-thrusting shape of his head is accentuated by the prow of his nose. His physical appearance underlines Ovsiew's lusty self-regard and his willingness to do battle in just cause.

Leon Ovsiew must be a sturdy friend, a relentless enemy. Possessed of a powerful ego, he tries to be gentle with the more fragile psyches of others. He listens carefully to the contributions of his students and responds with care. Even his most waspish pronouncements sting less than they might, for they are uttered in complete honesty and without apparent calculation of advantage. All of which, combined with an exquisite sense of equity, made him an almost unwillingly dominant figure in the faculty union movement at Temple University in the Winter of 1972.

"Without numbers," he is saying, "there is no power source. But suppose you were to imagine twenty thousand administrators and four students. The notion that students might have power is ridiculous. The whole union movement is predicated on the power that comes from numbers. Remember the Haymarket Riot, a watershed in labor history. The mere symbolism of masses of strikers walking, displaying their numbers, and being shot by police of a . . . certain kind . . . [he is given to irony] was a visible expression of the latent power numbers have, if deployed in a certain way. There is no question that there are enough students in any college to destroy that institution. The only thing that keeps them from doing so is that they don't *want* to."

And enough professors to do the same thing, but they don't want to, either. Professorial caution, and, often, apathy to unionization is crumbling under the example of their public school colleagues, but slowly. Those who choose to enter the profession are, in the main, loners, or at least, nonjoiners. The scholarly life is a solitary one. Among older faculty people, the traditional concept of shared responsibility for administrative decisions is still believed. If that collective power has become increasingly theoretical with the emergence of Big Education, more settled—and tenured—professors remain convinced that gathering up the reins of latent authority continues to be a possibility.

If they cared to do so.

Leon Ovsiew cares to. He is, on the surface, an unlikely candidate for the role of militant unionist. As a teacher of educational administration, he might seem more inclined than most to sympathize with an educational management confronted by a faculty that is both partner and adversary. But at Temple, he is vigorously blunt in support of the American Federation of Teachers' local which seeks recognition there, an organization conceded to be the most aggressive of the three contenders. When then-president Paul R. Anderson is quoted as questioning the viability of the partner-adversary relationship, Ovsiew replies that Anderson is "authoritarian by nature."

Ovsiew doesn't like Anderson. On more than one occasion, he has called the President "a liar." But that is not particularly relevant to his union activism. ("It's like saying you only need a union when you have a bad boss. That's not what unionism is all about. Unionism works best when you have a boss you like.") Nor does his own income seem to be a factor. Dr. Ovsiew professes no particular interest in money. Certainly that is a critical issue to most faculty unionists, whatever the idealistic protestations of some. But with an annual salary of "around $34,000" (for the academic year and one six-week summer session), not only is he compensated far above the national mean of $13,813 for all college teachers, but substantially above the standard for those who reach the highest category of full professor, $18,916. And this does not include admittedly amorphous "fringe benefits" or the income produced by his university-sanctioned consulting work and writings. Nor, finally, does he claim to be overworked. He has nine contact hours per week and, after all these years, he doesn't need as much time as he once did for preparation. He does advise a small number of students, but he is cutting back on the number of university and divisional committees on which he serves.

Ovsiew's primary personal motivation is, apparently, the service of justice. The word comes up often in his conversations and lectures. To make a point, he talks about it in his class:

". . . what people are really saying about institutions in our society is that we want them to do what they're supposed to do. We call that 'accountability.' But what we *really* want is that they demonstrate *capability*. I want a court system that produces something called justice. Now, I might be a darned fool for believing a silly thing like that, but that's what I want. I don't want them to be accountable to me . . ." The class titters. They suspect he'd like just that. "Ah, maybe I do, but that's a small thing. . . . What I *really* want is a system that produces *justice!* What I *really* want is a school system that produces a *learned* student!

"Unfortunately, by using the wrong word—'accountability'

—a lot of people are failing to perceive what we're talking about. I don't really want an administrator to be accountable to me, not in the last analysis. Think about that for a minute. That's not *really* what you want. What you really want is for the organization he represents to do its job. That's capability." He veers back to the lesson item at hand. "And the systems approach says that capability can only be exercised at the highest levels when people have a functional view of their roles rather than confusing their roles with prerogatives, status, authority, and a lot of other things which don't advance the capability of the organization."

He stands suddenly, picks up the book, slams it on the desk. The bell rang several minutes ago.

"That's why 'coordination' has a different meaning than in the phrase 'directional control.' " The point, a reference to previous discussion, is lost in the shuffle of feet, books, and note pads of people released from this tiny segment of their educational treadmill. There are leaves to rake before the first snow, errands at the hardware store and cleaners, the last TV football game. They are poised for exit. The professor smiles. He is always conscious of his loquaciousness—after the fact—and is a little embarrassed by the realization that he has gone on too long.

"I fear I have kept you longer than the law allows. Thank you."

There is the traditional exchange with one or two of the more eager students—the format of the next term paper, the length of the next quiz. How does he reconcile his fervor for unionism with the teaching of education administration? Might not his sympathies lie in the opposite direction?

"Curiously enough, I see no great conflict in that." He is moving down the utilitarian halls to his office. His strides seem effortless, despite the inadequate sandpiper legs propelling his barrel-chested, barrel-bellied torso, but the student with him hurries to keep up. "First of all, I pretend to no objectivity. I

121

have not very much use for objectivity, as a matter of fact. I have a great deal of respect for integrity . . . for responsibility, accountability . . . but I don't believe in objectivity."

His office is small, but it is his alone. Not so long ago, college professors despaired of ever achieving such privacy. The norm was a desk shared with one or two other teachers in a room filled with other desks. There is not much of personality to Dr. Ovsiew's office—the usual wall of books, a kite-like Mexican wall-hanging of multi-colored yarns stretched in a geometric pattern. On his desk, a modest jumble of papers, a pipe rack, and an ashtray with the legend "It's hard to be humble when you'r [sic] so great."

Stoking a pipe, he rolls back in his chair. The big voice fills the cell-like room.

"I can be objective about the number of coins I have in my pocket . . . although even that's difficult, because there's a certain amount of value judgement and wish-attitude which colors even my counting. I can't help feeling sad when there are too few. My emotion is that total objectivity is an impossible concept.

"But I believe in integrity! If I count the coins in my pocket and they total four, I *must* say that that number is four. I may allow myself to say that there are four but I wish there were nine, but I can't falsify the facts. Objectivity in teaching a social science is a very complicated concept. I think I teach educational administration with integrity. But that's in part founded on my notion of what educational administration ought to be. The 'Ought Prerogative' is very strong in any social science. I can present facts, but I have to say what these facts mean.

"Now today, in class, I was saying to them, 'Take that directional-control thing with a grain of salt.' But, 'Watch out,' I'm saying to them, 'because authority isn't the name of the game any more.' That much is a fact, at least as I perceive it. Integrity."

A conversation with Leon Ovsiew flows without prompting. The ideas he expresses, and the way he presents them, have the solidity of long-held conviction, of arguments examined and discarded, or accepted and mortared into place. Ovsiew suffers no intellectual turmoil, not any more. His capacity for moral outrage is enormous, and he is quick in reaction to perceived injustice because he doesn't have to look around for a philosophical foundation upon which to stand. He concedes that he hasn't had a truly original thought in ten years, but isn't apologetic about that fact. Anguish over alternatives is for people not yet fully formed.

The opinions tumble out. Ovsiew on Ovsiew: "I have never knowingly withheld a statement because I was afraid of its consequences. I have more often erred by saying things that didn't need to be said, which were unduly provocative or conflict-inducing.

"I don't want to be a dean. I probably lack ambition. I have no desire to move and shake, which is what an administrator really ought to have. Partly it's a matter of ego, believing that you can cope with the problems. In some ways—although my ego is not by any means deficient—there are things I feel very limited by.

"I don't have much doubt about the acuity of my intellect. I think I'm about as smart as anyone around. I've no doubts about that. But there are some things I have grave doubts about . . . such as my ability to work within the constraints of the ordinary organization.

"No one has ever accused me of subterfuge or shrewdness or canniness. There isn't anyone who doesn't know where I stand on an issue . . . if *I* know where I stand on an issue. It's not the way to get to be known as a good guy or get friends. But if those aren't the objectives—and they aren't, for me—it works pretty well in getting respect. I *do* have respect, and a lot of credibility. Almost too damned much, 'cause I get tabbed for every goddamned duty that comes along. They keep wanting to get me on committees and I have to keep fighting them off.

"No one can successfully say about me, 'I wonder what he means?' Everyone knows what I mean . . . which doesn't get me love. . . ."

On Ovsiew being co-opted: "That's routinely tried. Maybe not necessarily with malice. The vice-president said to me, 'Y'know, Leon, there are not too many people on the administration who like you, but there isn't anyone who won't listen to you.' That's all I've ever wanted. I haven't even been the object of an effort to be co-opted for many years now."

On other people being co-opted: "I can name names of people who have been co-opted and have been screwed as a result. We had a fellow one time who was chairman of the committee for the selection of the president who sold out the faculty. It's a provable fact. He sold out the faculty. He's since dropped out of sight. He has been ostracized. He sold out for a very clear objective: he wanted to be the dean of the School of Communications. When it got right down to it, the administration couldn't deliver. The faculty wouldn't let 'em. These things are, of course, not rare in universities."

On virtue: "I am instinctively contentious. I make a virtue out of it. I think the world is in a helluva lot more danger of going to Hell in a basket from the good guys in it than the bad guys. The good guys—the guys who won't stand up for principle, the guys who won't fight, the guys who avoid conflict. I'd rather engage in conflict with a view toward higher resolution. I *believe* in that. I think it's good for organizations, good for society. I distrust the people who are looking to be loved all the time. I don't like them. Can't stand them . . . I'm very sincere about that."

On epitaphs: "If there's anything I want them to write on my tombstone, it's 'He was a man of principle.' However stubborn, however wrongheaded, however much a bastard, by God!"—fist slams table—"He believed in his principles! Even

124

if they were dumb principles . . . hopefully, they're not. But by God!" Thump! "I don't want anyone to say about me that I acceded to anything I didn't believe in."

On his good qualities: "I'm an articulate, verbal man. I can hold my own in any conflict situation. I've never given up on a fight when I thought there was any way to win. I'll compromise, I'll trade off, I'm a pragmatic person. But by God!" *Thump!* "I won't *give* up! If I think somebody's wrong, I don't give a good goddamn if he thinks I'm nice or not."

On his bad qualities: "A lot of what I say may seem self-serving."

Predictably, Professor Ovsiew has strong views on faculty unionization. Four weeks earlier, the initial election for a collective bargaining representative took place. On the ballot were Ovsiew's AFT, the American Association of University Professors, a local branch of the National Education Association, and "none of the above." It was clear that the AFT would get the largest vote, so the AAUP and NEA groups directed their efforts toward denying the AFT a majority and coming in second themselves.

The Temple faculty, as at most colleges, was apprehensive about control by national organizations, so each group emphasized its autonomy. AFT was simply "a federation of independent local organizations." The local AAUP chapter publicly refused assistance from their national headquarters (without noting that the headquarters had little aid to offer). The NEA group claimed to be receiving only financial and logistical support (without specifying what other kind they might extend).

Professors arc, in the main, cautious, even timid. The militant AFT stance attracted younger faculty, but spooked most of the others. Concurrent AFT strikes at the Philadelphia Community College and in the public schools stirred their fears of a strike-happy union.

Nevertheless, the AFT came in first, followed by the AAUP. A run-off election was set for early December. Now, before the vote, Ovsiew is confident of victory. He claims never to have worked so hard for anything in his life. He had resisted active participation at first, but characteristically found the challenge impossible to resist. There were two major reasons:

"The AAUP would be a disaster for us. They don't know a goddamn thing about collective negotiations. They're gonna mess up the goddamn thing, and there's gonna be adversary stuff until they drive everybody up the wall. They are incompetent, in my view.

"But it's important symbolically, too. A university is made up of three constituencies: faculty, students, administrators. And those three learn how to work together or the whole enterprise is less successful."

The union was a device to intensify communication between those groups, in Ovsiew's mind. So he served as a member of the Executive Committee of AFT, as spokesman, and as gray eminence. "A couple of people came to me and said, 'Look. We're willing to do all the leg work, all the hard work. But we need somebody who knows this university, knows the political process, understands the administration, has the kind of acquaintanceship across the broad range of faculty that you do.' All of which was just true enough that they weren't lying.

"Certainly there were others on the campus with similar expertise. But . . . it's very hard for me to turn down the sincere request of a colleague. You see, the two co-chairmen are very young guys. Both fine people, done a really fine job. But they *do* lack experience and a certain amount of insight."

Leon Ovsiew served. On December 7, the AAUP beat his AFT by nearly two to one.

* * *

126

It is tempting, at this point in the history of American higher education, to compare the components of authority in a college or university to the industrial-trade-union equation: the administrator as manager, the professor as laborer, the student as consumer. Certainly, a redistribution of power is taking place. The student rebellions of the Sixties have mellowed into formal representation on academic councils and committees and assemblies concerned with issues of identifiable importance to students. Following that lead, thousands of college teachers on over two hundred campuses have chosen, as their historical partnership role has eroded, to reassert their prerogatives through collective bargaining.

But to reduce the relationship to this tripartite simplicity is to ignore reality. For one thing, power within academe never was either equally shared *or* absolute. The most autocratic university president, for example, still must answer to alumni, boards of governors, large donors, and to politicians. And just as that president must sometimes contend with runaway boards, the liberal arts dean can be reduced to a figurehead by faculty chairmen more successful than he at fund raising and by tenured professors with endowed chairs and independent turns of mind. Witness the academic department elevated to "institute" status, housed in a separate facility more sumptuous than that used by all the remaining departments put together, and complete with individual telephone exchange and switchboard. Observe the disgruntled star professor of a small but prestigious department who leaves in a highly verbal blue funk trailing a string of able and adoring junior faculty members. Power cannot be lastingly legislated.

The industrial-business model of governance doesn't tolerate ambiguity. For many reasons, the emerging educational version doesn't permit rigidity: Students have demonstrated, as on-site consumers, their willingness to throw themselves on the gears of institutional machinery as buyers of soapsuds and

Chevrolets have not and probably cannot. Their acquiescence can no longer be relied upon. While many professors see collective bargaining as a means to reassert or regain their role in governance, they have no intention of surrendering prerogatives already held. Collective bargaining is to be layered over, not substituted for existing rights and privileges.

At Temple, the faculty wants to retain its senate, which gives it participatory rights in the selection of administrators, the setting of curricula, the establishment of admissions and academic standards, and examination of general policy. Unionists at Temple say their faculty senate is ineffective.

The academic senate of the University of California at Berkeley is conceded to be strong—even to the point of trying to create a satellite collective bargaining unit—and has similar rights.

But activists at both campuses agree that union representation will strengthen their respective senates. They're not giving up anything.

The success of the AAUP at Temple and other colleges highlights other conflicts. More militant unionists claim that the AAUP has no real experience at collective bargaining, that the organization offers itself in that capacity only because it is pressured by the AFT, NEA, and others. Staff members at national AAUP headquarters do not deny the accusation. They seek the bargaining role reluctantly, and then only when local circumstances make it necessary. The staid AAUP is an unlikely candidate for traditional unionism. It undertakes no aggressive promulgation of the collective bargaining function, and is not about to counsel strikes. It has no strike fund. Inquiries on the stance of the AAUP toward collective bargaining are referred to a statement drawn in *1940!* As a tax-exempt organization, it avoids the taint of lobbying. Its annual operating budget hovers around $1,500,000, just about adequate to produce a newsletter and periodic journal, an annual survey of professorial compensation, and fulfill a watchdog role on the transgressions of institutions in the area of academic freedom.

"We've never been militant in what one could call the economic area," confirms Tom Truss, an associate secretary for national AAUP. A lank-haired Southerner of middle years, precise diction, and decidedly professorial mien, he may well exemplify the conservative inclinations of his employer organization. His answers to questions follow almost unbearably attenuated pauses, and are cautious, meticulously measured. From time to time, he has the disconcerting habit of offering a re-phrasing of his answer to the next-to-last question in response to the last one. Just as professors are inclined to identify with other professionals rather than with laborers, so does Truss associate the AAUP with a sympathy for the traditional collegiality of professor and administrator.

"There's quite a big difference between the academic sector and the industrial sector. In the industrial sector there is profit-making, and when a new contract is negotiated at GM, there may or may not be a price hike. In the traditional labor-management bargaining process, money plays a fairly strong role. 'The company has a lot of money, and we want to get some of it.' Whereas in education, there is only a certain amount of money in the pie. The issue, then, is not so much the quantity of money, but the way it is distributed. The emphasis is on the priorities for the money . . . whether the distribution of funds is determined through collective bargaining or through a faculty committee on the budget. . . . Well . . . we haven't had the circumstance with us long enough to have any opinions one way or the other."

It is difficult to imagine Walter Reuther so tolerant of management or so uncertain of his organization's desires. But the issues for a Reuther or a Chavez were more clear cut, and the maintenance of dogma or academic unionism is complicated further at state-related or -supported universities.

Temple is a private university with state financial support.

129

The National Labor Relations Board ruled it a public institution for collective bargaining purposes. The professors are therefore public employees, their right to unionize guaranteed by Act 195. This act stipulates that public employers must bargain on wages, hours, and conditions of employment, but not on matters of managerial policy, including budget, programs, structure, and selection of personnel. Strictly interpreted, this act, and similar ones in other states, would surely stiffen the labor-management character of the controversy. The faculty would lose its participatory function, except as the administration chooses to invite them to continue. University administrators are more likely, however, to resist unionization than enforcement of such laws. Their fear of the economic whipsaw of individual units bargaining separately within the institution is greater than of the continued limitation of their power to administer through faculty participation.

An observer who feels compelled to draw parallels with other forms of governance and the distribution of power, given these and other complexities, might be more precise in relating the American university to the British parliamentary model. There is the prime minister: college president and his cabinet; the loyal opposition: faculty; the house of lords: alumni and donors; the monarchy: board of governors; the constituents: students. And there is a permanent civil service in the middle managers (a group that quietly keeps the whole structure functioning), and clerical and maintenance people (themselves often unionized). All six component groups function within marked limitations; none can move freely without the cooperation of the others; none has full control. And, in the last analysis, few would wish to alter that balance.

That this is so is partly demonstrated by the demands of faculty unionists on other campuses. Rarely are their demands unique to an individual institution; almost never do they wish to abolish the existing system. Distinctions are made in terms of local emphasis, not radical departure.

* * *

David Brody is a case in point. A history professor at the
University of California at Davis, he, like Leon Ovsiew,
supports the AFT. But he does not do so blindly: "I have no
particular loyalty to the AFT as an organization. They're
mostly involved with elementary and secondary school activities. We're supported by them, but they don't really understand our problems. We're not wedded to them. All of us take
pride in our independence. Our affiliation with AFT is just a
first step."

Nor does he wish to destroy the University: "We adhere to
the University, we want to protect it. The University is in a
very vulnerable position. The administration and the University's friends are not enough. There's a power system within
this state, and we want to operate within it. It's pathetic how
ignorant people are of what a university does. We want to
have our input, to defend the University, and we can't do it
without organization."

David Brody and Leon Ovsiew have never met, nor have
they heard of each other. They work and live at opposite ends
of the country, in unrelated academic fields. But they share
many of the same motivations, the same reluctances, the same
convictions about themselves and their relationships with their
colleagues and to their universities.

Both feel they are amply paid, although Brody makes
$19,500, much less per year than Ovsiew. Brody is fourteen
years younger. Neither feels overworked. Brody has six
classroom hours to teach each week, and puts in three full days
of every seven days at the Davis campus in teaching, student
advisement, committee work, and preparation. Both are confident of their superior intelligence. Brody entered the scholarly life because he was a "smart kid." He excelled in school,
which helped him escape the mixed ghetto of Elizabeth, New
Jersey, for a scholarship at Harvard. Curiously, Ovsiew grew
up in Elizabeth, too, but as the son of a well-to-do builder.

Both are first-generation native-born Americans, the children of Polish immigrants who fled the constant threat of poverty and of the pogrom. "Brody" was the name of the port city from which many Poles emigrated. David doesn't know the original family name. Neither Brody nor Ovsiew claims to have encountered anti-Semitism in his career. Neither observes fealty to the religion of his parents.

Ovsiew and Brody are reluctant activists, and both have avoided union office.

They participate because they feel they must.

Brody resents any intrusion on his time, and says so. In the evening, out on the deck of his Berkeley home, the twinkling velvet carpet of the entire Bay area spread out behind him, he is edgy. He wants to get back to his study and his work. Brody has come to enjoy teaching over the years, he says, but his research and writing are what really matter. His wife brings out a tray of cookies and fragrant tea. There is, as with the wives of Brown and others, nothing of the servile housewife about her. Her gesture is simple courtesy. Brody accepts it accordingly. There is the sound of a television set and their three children from inside the house. He later concedes that he is not "skillful on social occasions" or at placing people at their ease. He is right. And he wants to get back to his study.

"One of the greatest difficulties about organizing professors," he is saying, "is that no one wants to do it. Who the hell wants to do it? Who wants to find out what goes on in Sacramento? They've got a tremendous apparatus of administrators, experts, so forth . . . huge! *And it's all they do!*"

The injustice of it rankles, and his voice is getting shrill. He understands the conflict for his colleagues all too well.

"And what they do affects us! The only way you can live in this system is to have people who are performing the same functions . . . on the other side. And professors don't want to do it. In other occupations, a union is an opportunity for upward mobility. If you go to work for a union, that's a step

upward for people in the blue-collar ranks. People strugg|
it. Professors don't want to do that. That would be a sacri|
It's a sacrifice of time to do *anything* for the union in\
continuing day-to-day way. So it's a tremendous problen,
finding people to do the work."

Moved to action in much the same way as Ovsiew, Brody
serves his chapter as self-described idealogue, as compared to
Ovsiew's "gray eminence." With his specialization in labor
history, he is equipped to prepare position papers and perform
similar writing tasks. His analysis of the need for unionism
echoes his opposite number at Temple.

"We're now going through what people in many other
areas of American society have gone through: a recognition of
the realities of power and organization. That's when you
discover that you're living under an illusion if you think that,
as an individual, you really can affect what happens to you.
The question then is how you proceed to respond to that
discovery."

It is customary faculty-unionist dogma that professors and
students are fighting the same battle. Brody, with a scholar's
objectivity, concedes that facts dilute that contention. The
issue of class size, especially at the megaversity where
economics dictate large classes to get maximum mileage from
professors' time, is not a burning one for most faculty. But it
certainly is for students. And if union demands for higher pay
succeed, the likely resultant tuition increase is the students'
burden, not the professors'.

"There is a whole series of issues that affect students rather
than us. In truth, we don't particularly care about class size,
except as it relates to teaching load. But on tuition . . . we
think it's a bad thing. What it does is make an elitist institution
more elitist."

Brody doesn't believe that tenure is of concern to students,
either, though many have protested that it keeps in office
uncreative old mossbacks who use twenty-year-old lecture

notes and who prevent younger professors from advancing. He doesn't dismiss that contention, but he claims it is not the view of organized students.

He thinks a moment, examining the inconsistencies. He has said that the union has tried to support the best interests of the students. Now he ruefully remembers a legislative hearing at the capitol.

"I was giving testimony. There were students there. I said something to the effect that professors had the interests of the students at heart. A state senator said that I 'sounded just as paternalistic toward the students as the administration sounds toward you, that you know best.' " Brody smiles briefly. "It wasn't what I meant, but it was exactly what I thought."

The compatibility of student and professorial interests, he believes, is their common need for an effective voice. He recognizes the dilemmas beyond that basic point. While he feels that faculty must share in decisions, he is not certain that all judgements must be shared with students.

"Do we claim that we know best? I don't know how that will come out."

For all their self-assurance, Brody and Ovsiew are refreshingly candid about episodes of violation of their own strong senses of integrity. Ovsiew remembers being courted at considerable length for a deanship at another college. At a point far into their negotiations, he decided he didn't want the job. But instead of saying so, he demanded what he regarded to be a ridiculously high salary demand, anticipating they would turn him down. They gulped . . . and agreed to the demand. Then he had to confess he really didn't want it. He wasn't very proud of himself. Nor was Brody, when he took a post at Ohio State with the stipulated inducement that his second year would be a sabbatical with full pay. Instead, he accepted the position at Davis after one year of work *and* the leave *and* the money at Ohio State.

Neither man pretends perfection. Both recognize their fallibility. And both remain firmly convinced of their rectitude, whatever the temporary setbacks.

Four weeks after the election which made the AAUP the collective bargaining agent of the Temple University faculty, Leon Ovsiew is subdued. An uncle had died the week before and the losing effort for the AFT was tiring.

"It was not only a minor disaster for Temple University, it's going to have a profound effect upon the other two state universities, Penn State and Pitt. That's because it's a very powerful argument that since the AAUP was successful here, the other two universities are going to go the same way."

He does see hope. "By a curious circumstance, that may help mitigate the situation. If the AAUP does win elections in all three, as I think they will now, it may give the AAUP some backbone. They may learn a little competency. For one thing, they may have enough money to hire some staff." He sighs gloomily. "It will still not do much about changing the basic orientation of the people at AAUP in Washington, which is a serious problem.

"What happened here is rather easy to reconstruct. Some strands of causality are clear enough. The basic mind-set of the professor at Temple is a helluva lot more conservative than we thought. The attitude of the faculty in general here—and I daresay at other universities—is what might be called a 'diffident militancy.' The other thing was that the AAUP very effectively got the vote out. Their slogan was 'AFT can't beat AAUP—Only apathy can.' They spent a lot of money and hammered that message home.

"Our campaign was more honest, but it was not more effective. The AAUP campaign was somewhat *dis*honest, but well within the limits people will tolerate in a campaign. They said things that weren't true about the contract they had signed at Rutgers, for example. That contract was a model of how *bad*

135

a contract can be. But we never got that message through. They got theirs through, and that's the way the game is played."

What will be the role of the AFT now at Temple? Ovsiew thinks it ought to be that of the loyal opposition. If and when the AAUP demonstrably fails, the AFT will demand another election. The record of AAUP at other places, he believes, is so bad that they *will* fail. Ovsiew won't attempt to undermine their efforts, but he will be waiting.

CHAPTER 8

The photograph on the flyleaf is of a clear-browed young scholar on the rise. In regulation Princetonian horn-rims and crewcut just long enough to part, there is just the trace of a smile on the finely etched lips. It is the face of a man who is without doubt. Even more, it radiates the most sublime confidence. With good reason. The man is Martin Duberman. The book is his biography of James Russell Lowell, and it was a finalist in the National Book Awards for 1966. It was preceded by his *Charles Francis Adams* in 1962. That one won the Bancroft Prize. In between, his documentary play, *In White America*, won the Vernon Rice Drama Desk Award. There have been five other books, other plays. He is reviewed, quoted, attacked, and published by the *New York Times*. Duberman was tenured by age thirty-five, a full professor by thirty-seven.

Now he is professor of history at Lehman College of the City University of New York. He makes $31,275 per academic year, plus a $5,000 bonus for his status as one of the fifty scholars and teachers designated by the giant institution as "Distinguished Service Professors."

At forty-three years of age, Martin Duberman is an aristocrat of the professoriate. If he is not exactly a household word, he is known to nearly all serious historians and to many laymen as well. Martin Duberman has made it.

He lives in a brick row house on Charles Street in New York's Greenwich Village. This is the *West* Village, the quiet residential part populated by upper-middle-class people in the arts and communications. Successful bohemians. It is a shimmering Sunday in May, when New York seems the very best place in the world to be. The streets are nearly empty. They will fill later, when several pounds of the Sunday *Times* have finally been read and the delis are about to close.

Duberman rents the top two floors. After several moments, he answers the doorbell. The contrast with the photograph is startling. He cannot be the man on the flyleaf. The hair is longer, tinged with gray, but that's not it. He doesn't wear glasses. Milky blue eyes. Contact lenses?

No, it's not those things, it's the set of his face. It's more pliant, vulnerable. That other man might have been a junior White House staff assistant with connections. This is a man less certain.

It is also a man hungover from a bad party the night before. His party. He invites his visitor upstairs. The invitation is courteous, if lacking in eager anticipation. The apartment fits the preconception. It is airy, tasteful, casually elegant; the home of someone who knows good design without the aid of a consultant and who didn't have to concentrate to put it together. The floor is scraped and polished. Oriental rugs glow, and outsize plants luxuriate at the shuttered windows. Abstract paintings and framed theater posters cover the white brick walls. A Sidney Greenstreet peacock chair and other rattan pieces stand around the edges of the room. The buttery leather sofa has artful straps pretending to hold squashy pillows in place. The floor-to-ceiling wine rack is half empty. A staircase continues up to the bedroom and workroom. The effect is bachelor dream pad, Manhattan division.

Dishes of peanuts and pistachio nuts are the only remnants of last night's party. He offers his visitor a drink, with a shudder. Or coffee, tea, orange juice? Declined, he drops into the leather Eames chair with a groan. He has a spare, hipless, small-boned body, and the physical bearing, even in his present state, to make the blue velour shirt and faded jeans seem a Bill Blass lounging outfit. The jeans have neatly pressed creases.

His visitor remarks upon both the conflicts and confirmations of his preconceptions and first impressions. When Duberman responds, he forms his words gingerly. He says something about "who *hasn't* changed in ten years." After a while, he mentions that he is working on a book he is calling *Halfway*. It is to be based, in part, upon journals he kept at earlier times in his life. About that other person, that flyleaf person, he says:

"I'm transcribing one journal now that I kept in the early Fifties. And I'm absolutely appalled. I haven't re-read it in God knows how many years, and appalled is the only word. . . . I can't believe this person was me. I'd like to believe it *wasn't* me. The smugness, all the clichéd formulas. I mean, I seem to have felt on top of the world. Unfortunately, I was in graduate school, twenty-five or twenty-six, when I was writing those damn things, so I can't ascribe the callowness to mere youth. The entries are so simplistic, whether about political matters or my love affairs. I just can't believe the formulations I came up with. But I have a certain yearning for the old time, and the book is turning into a dialogue between what I am now and that other person.

"I feel so torn in so many areas between an older kind of upbringing and training and a newer social model, or at least new alternatives as embodied in the counterculture. And I don't think the ambivalence is confined to me. It's a generational problem. A lot of people in their late thirties, early forties, feel this tension. They're having trouble making sense of their lives—professionally and personally. There's always been an in-between generation, but I don't think any that has

139

been faced with models on either side that directly oppose each other to the extent they do for us. People thirty years ago weren't faced with a conflict of quite this intensity.

"In every sense I was brought up middle class. Here I am living like a bourgeois. I have a lot of tensions just being in this apartment. This is too much space. And what am I doing here surrounded by all these creature comforts? Rhetorically, I say I admire the counterculture's rejection of materialism and accumulation of possessions. And yet I was brought up to define myself in terms of all those *things*."

And he's sitting in *the* Charles Eames chair.

"Exactly. Friends were here last night, a woman I was in graduate school with and her husband. We were talking about this, and it was a breast-beating session. They had just come yesterday from buying a ten-room house in New Jersey and she was saying, 'I can't live with myself, I can't stand it. The older I get, the more I find myself living out those middle-class values which another part of my head tells me are despicable. I can't put the two together, I'm terribly torn.' And her husband was saying, 'Oh, take it easy. What's so wrong with living in a nice home or having comfortable things around?' And she said, 'It is wrong. People are starving and dying and growing up ten in a room in Harlem, and these were all things we were taught to protest. Yet when it comes right down to it, we're living out the worst values of our culture.' "

Duberman quotes a Matthew Arnold line about "wandering between two worlds, one dead and the other powerless to be born." He considers that, then decides:

"That's really a cop-out. The one is *not* dead, and the other *not* powerless to be born. It's just that it's such a struggle, and I don't know what it is I'm struggling toward. Sometimes I feel it's just that I want to be twenty years old, and I'm not. The whole struggle is a function of never having had a sufficiently well-developed style of my own. The cross-identification comes from that. If I had truly been a product of my own generation, then I would feel less turmoil, less attracted to the new generation."

Yet everyone has an identity, and Duberman's, at least externally, seems more clear than most. Writer, teacher, scholar, historian, dramatist. . . . Or does all that just heighten the conflict?

"Well . . . I know I disapprove increasingly of this whole achievement orientation of which I am exemplar and victim. Work is all that defines my life. When I'm not working, I feel very guilty about not working. I don't know how to relax and enjoy myself, go away and spin out. I'm very bad at all that. And yet when I think back on my own family I can't remember their overtly inculcating all this in me. I remember the opposite, in fact. When I went to private school in New York, Horace Mann, I was worried that I wouldn't measure up. All those fancy kids with fancy backgrounds would be there. I remember my mother saying—with what I thought was genuine casualness—'Oh, look, stop worrying about it. You don't have to get straight A's. Forget it. Relax. Have fun!' So it's strange that though their words weren't the standard Jewish family words ('Get ahead, booby, and be a doctor'), somehow we all internalized it anyway. It was part of the subculture even though we weren't verbalizing it."

Nevertheless, he *has* achieved. He is of the elite of his profession, acknowledged a position of stature beyond the wildest hopes of all but perhaps two percent of the nation's professoriate. His salary is higher than that of most college presidents and most state governors. Before he was forty, his literary output and the honors accorded it surpassed the combined lifetime efforts of ten average professors. He is an undisputed star.

Yet even Duberman remains a notch below the summit. That is occupied in lonely splendor by perhaps a hundred men and a very few women. Most enjoy such renown as to assure their influence on their disciplines far beyond their deaths.

Some, given the popular exploitability of their interests, their flair for provocative comment, or their willingness to engage in politics or art or public service, are celebrated far beyond their campuses. Their associations with the mighty bestow that peculiar level of glamour which permits their ready identification merely by surname—Kissinger, Schlesinger, Galbraith, Moynihan. Slightly more informed members of the public are familiar with Chomsky, Ellison, Reisman, Kristol. Because their tools are words, subject to simplification for mass consumption, they are the best known of the academics. Those in the so-called data disciplines are less marketable, apart from an occasional Fermi or Oppenheimer, as they are more at home in laboratories than television studios. Molecular biology and mathematical physics simply don't have the pizzaz of political science and urban anthroplogy. Their practitioners win Nobel Prizes, but no one can remember their names unless they choose to speak out on social issues, as have George Wald or Linus Pauling. But if, say, C. N. Yang lacks celebrity, he belongs to the superstar caste nonetheless.

Yang won a Nobel Prize in physics. In 1973, he was one of five men holding an Albert Einstein professorship, a designation created by the New York legislature in 1966 to attract scholars to the universities of its state, perhaps the first open affirmation by a political body of the clout of academic superstars. The State University of New York, a scattered and ragged collection of unknown teachers' colleges a few years before, was an institution on the make. With the prodding of Nelson Rockefeller, new university centers on the Berkeley–UCLA model were planned and funded, some of them built from scratch. But buildings are merely settings. To achieve the recognized distinction of older state universities like Wisconsin and California, SUNY needed people. Not just professors, but giants. As already observed, name professors draw other name professors who in turn attract gifted disciples, all of whom bring good students and financial support and status—which draw more superstars.

The legislature simply formalized the process. With five Albert Schweitzer professorships to complement the Einstein chairs, they sprinkled presumed genius and undisputed glory over ten public and private universities throughout the state. To snare the superstars, they dangled annual stipends of $100,000. A portion of this, up to $50,000, was to be salary. The rest was to be used, under the professor's direct control, for laboratory equipment, office help, lecture fees to visiting scholars and intellectuals, books and periodicals, financial aid for students, and travel expenses. In short, the Schweitzer and Einstein professors were invited to become one-person mini-colleges, accountable to no department chairmen, no deans, and only the most gingerly supervision of their campus presidents.

There was, however, the often disapproving collective opinion of their new colleagues. Inevitable. The announced annual stipends were regarded by less honored faculty members as little more than bribes. Some chose to ignore explanations of the comprehensiveness of the $100,000 packages, preferring to regard them as salaries only. There were protests that the super professors would retire as millionaires in a field in which protestations of poverty ennoble the vocation of selfless pursuit and rendering of knowledge. Such materialistic excesses sullied the calling and its members, it was said. Individual choices for the posts were attacked, although they were not imposed by the legislature but determined by the individual institutions. Fordham invited Marshall McLuhan to its Schweitzer chair, insuring outrage on the part of professors infuriated by both his media cachet and his pronouncements, which many regarded as murky or fatuous. Feminists decried the relatively low salary ($29,500) of economist Barbara Ward, the only woman of the ten. The inaccessibility of the professors was proclaimed. Rumors circulated that certain of the Schweitzer professors would speak to groups of students on their own campuses only upon payment of their regular lecture fees, ranging upward from $1,000.

The several deadly sins had a field day. They do on any campus on which star professors are employed. It is to be expected that envy will result when a few professors are paid higher salaries not for what they do but in recognition of what they have done, especially when those accomplishments so honored are vulnerable to question, as they almost always are.

Some stars stoke the fire, furthermore, by the ways in which they project their personalities. In a profession in which practitioners believe themselves possessed of superior intelligence, arrogance is a trait so common as to be unworthy of mention. (In a persistent if not necessarily accurate anecdote, Arthur Schlesinger was once asked why he never bothered to obtain a Ph.D. The precocious historian is represented as responding: "Who would have given me the orals?") The implication assigned to the pronouncements of superstars is that their analyses and critiques should be accepted enthusiastically on the basis of the eminence of their spokesman. In the community of scholars, as in a republic, some are more equal than others. The others don't care for that one bit.

Martin Duberman's star status is undoubtedly one source of his past difficulties with colleagues. How does he cope with it?

"I have a lot of trouble with that. I don't know . . . and this is not a game of false modesty . . . I get very confusing messages. For example, at my classes at Lehman, once in a while a student is startled to discover that I've written a book. There seems to be a sense—and I like it—that I'm someone who teaches there and they don't know a thing about me. I enjoy that. Yet, since I *do* feel defined by my work, I'm a little concerned about it at the same time. How come they don't know I've written seven books? I'm very in the middle about all that, too. Nooo . . . I don't in any solidified sense see myself as an academic star. No."

But that is his reputation among his colleagues. The prizes, the honors, all those things confirm it. Does he reject the designation?

"Oh, God, it's hard to even think about. I don't know why. It doesn't *feel* like me. I know one of my mechanisms after eighty-seven years of therapy is that nothing that happened yesterday or earlier means anything to me. I'm incredibly present-oriented . . . without being able to enjoy much of the present. Yesterday is done for me. So the books that I've published don't seem to relate organically to who I am. It's like a whole separate presence. If, in fact, identity consists of memory, then I guess I've got an identity problem."

He insists that his fame has meant little to him professionally.

"When I decided to leave Princeton, I wrote to Richard Morris at Columbia and said I wanted to leave and was Columbia interested? I got back a letter saying no. And there were a couple of other attempts I made. I had a lot of trouble finding a job in New York. It took me three years to get out of Princeton after I made the decision that I wanted to leave. Since I moved to Lehman, I've had no offers, not a single one. So I've hardly been swamped. Part of that may be that it's pretty well known that I'm devoted to New York and certainly could never be moved from it. But I've never had any offers from *within* the city. That's why I'm confused about my 'star status.'

"I've always gotten these double messages about everything. At Princeton, there were people who were upset that I was writing plays. Countering that, there were people who thought of it as glamourous. The trouble with Princeton was that everything I heard was third-hand, which was one reason I got so pissed off. Friends of mine would be at parties and would come back and tell me what members of my own department were saying about me. I heard almost nothing to my face. Finally as these reports mounted in number, I got so angry that I said to the chairman of the department that I was tired of it and would like a meeting of the department called. If there were grievances against me, I'd like to hear them to my face, and if they couldn't be solved, then I would resign. If they could, fine, let's solve them. They were very reluctant to call a meeting, but I insisted.

"It was an unreal sweetness-and-light affair. You know, 'We don't know what you're talking about. We like you very much. We're delighted that you're living in New York and writing plays. You've been hearing malicious gossip made up by evil people.' Total unreality. So I said to myself, 'Okay, if that's the way you want to play it, fine. I'll just wait and see if I start hearing this stuff again.' And it all *did* break open again. An experimental course I proposed was vetoed by the dean of faculty. Both he and the president refused to even talk to me about the experiments, so I couldn't explain why I though they might be important as a pilot project. They refused out of hand even to talk to me.

"Then they started working the salary bit on me, so that as a full professor, when I left Princeton, my salary was something like $16,500, which was approximately $5,000 below the average in my department. It was the only way they could put the screws to me, and they did."

They just didn't give him raises? Did they cut him?

"No, I never heard of anybody being cut, but they didn't give me raises, even when they were being given across-the-board, and there were no merit increases. I had written as much as anyone in my department and was probably as well known. I finally got so angry at this that I told the chairman I wanted a raise, that I needed to live. He said no. So I told him I was going to the Committee of Three, which was one of those super-committees made up of three department chairmen.

After my first interview with them, they were appalled. After the head of the committee told me that he thought a merit increase was clearly in order, I got a letter saying the Committee had decided to give me a $250 annual raise. I was so angry when I got the letter that I sat down on the spot and wrote my letter of resignation. Then I thought, 'Don't be a damn fool, you've still got to make a living. Wait until you've got another job.' It took me three years to get another job, at which point I resigned."

What was it that was making them unhappy with him?

"I don't really know. The rumors still go on. I still have a few friends out there. The last thing one of them told me was that the current explanation at Princeton is that Duberman would constantly cut his classes in order to get into New York to see the theater, and this is why everybody got angry. And that's so outrageous! I can barely remember in my fifteen years of teaching ever cutting class. The theater is accessible on other nights, classes are during the day, and I've only been to five matinees in my life. I mean, the whole thing's bizarre! I've never been able to puzzle it out.

"Princeton was a terribly difficult community for me to live in. It was so smug and square and couple-oriented. I was in very bad shape. I was in therapy at the time and my therapist was actually worried about me. Finally I decided that I had to move to New York. I got a year off and moved to New York. I got back into all the excitement and wonder of New York, and I just knew I would never return to Princeton to live. (I only lived there for two years.) It was almost a matter of life and death for me. At that point, I was given a definite offer by NYU. I wasn't even looking for it at the time. I was 98 percent decided to accept it and I went to Princeton as a matter of courtesy to tell them. They begged me to stay—this was 1965, before I was doing a number of other things. I had already written *In White America*, but I had not written any essays of social criticism and so forth. I still seemed a traditional and productive scholar, with a good reputation as a teacher. So they said, 'Go live in New York with our blessings. We understand that you will be out here only two days a week to do your teaching, that you will not be available for all those extras—lunches for visiting firemen, administrative duties— but you will make it up with your teaching and writing. Nobody can do all three things at maximum capacity, and we're satisfied if you do two of the three.'

"But they weren't satisfied. The more years that went by, the more grievances developed over the arrangements they themselves had instigated and persuaded me to accept. It was mostly a few people at Princeton who were aggrieved, but they happened to be the people in power. As far as I know, they were the ones who wanted me out."

Because he wasn't a good citizen of the academic community?

"Yeah. And in a sense, they were right. My attendance record at faculty meetings, even department meetings, was worse than anyone else's. But I had made it clear at the time of the agreement that that had to be the case if I were going to live in New York. I couldn't be *schlepping* out there every day to attend this or that hour-long function and at the same time do any of my own writing. I tended to make department meetings only if they fell on days I was out there to teach or if a matter of unusual importance was coming up, like somebody's promotion being debated or a change in curriculum. But that was just an aspect of what some people took to be my rejection of them—the Princeton community, the academic lifestyle. Not being a team player was just one way I refused to join them. Living in New York was another way, writing plays was a third. Writing essays, raising questions about the utility of studying history was another way. Trying to change classroom procedures was a fifth."

Although no one at Princeton seems willing to give the accusation substance by specific rebuttal, Duberman was clearly the victim of what academics choose to label "campus politics." That he offended the conservative instincts of some of his colleagues can be assumed by his subsequent rejection by the history department at NYU, if only because the judgment that he was "too far out" was surely buttressed or even initiated by contacts with members of the Princeton faculty. (The faculty recruitment and selection process is an unbelievably protracted one, and inquiries on candidates at their previous institutions is the rule.) Conversely, Duberman surely provoked his Princeton colleagues by forcing a confrontation over pedagogical techniques he could foresee would be offensive to many of them. Self-appointed agents of educational change promote conflict knowingly, if not necessarily consciously, with the glee of all prescient martyrs. The resultant repression by these of the established order merely confirms the assumptions of the agitator-visionary and sharpens the virtuous scent of hemlock. The literature of innovative education is rife with associative parallels with Socrates.

Duberman confesses to courting contention and to prodding it when it is somnolent. Although his own paranoia probably gave unmerited conspiratorial dimension to what was more likely an informally allied opposition to his proposals, there is no question he was intentionally eased out. Rather, he was given no reason to stay, a common technique in the academy and the chief distinction between campus politics and those of the business world. In the corporate executive suite, people are kicked upstairs or simply discharged. With the institution of tenure, that was rarely possible in the university. Other means of retribution and separation had to be devised. Tenured professors who inspire the distaste of a sufficient number of their colleagues are denied salary increases or given insultingly low ones. Or it is made clear that they can never expect to reach full professor. Or they are given only freshmen or low-prestige courses to teach. Or their workloads are increased to the permissible maximum while those with less responsibility and equal or better compensation remain all too visible. Or, one by one, they are shorn of their perquisites or trappings of power.

The practice permeates colleges and universities now, and is employed as the customary technique of personnel management whether the person to be removed is tenured or not, a member of faculty or administration. There was, at one university, a professor who accepted the post of dean of university records, admissions, and student aid. When it was decided that the job was "too big for him to handle," the admissions function was separated from him and assigned to a newly created directorship. When he didn't take the hint, one of his assistants became the autonomous registrar. He persisted in ignoring the clear message, so three-quarters of his remaining function of financial aid was taken from him and distributed among the deans of the institution's several schools under the premise of more direct accountability. He was left dean of financial aid for the remaining athletic grants and the minority student aid fund, which no one wanted because they were the source of the greatest number of complaints and litigations. Still he persisted. They changed his title from the favored "dean" to "coordinator." Finally, he chose to take advantage of an early retirement plan created especially for him "in light of his years of distinguished service." He couldn't go back to teaching in his original field because, though he was tenured, the department regrettably had no openings on the staff . . . and didn't expect any.

Although admittedly amorphous and difficult to delineate in the cloud of justifications for their execution, these devices at least are susceptible to outline. Far more enervating to the victim are the assaults upon his character and/or competence which lead to these actions. Wallace Sayre of Columbia University is credited with the observation that "academic politics is the most vicious and bitter form of politics because the stakes are so low." Professorial maneuverings for advantage or revenge are difficult to sort because they are as often concerned with vindication of intellectual perspectives as for the accumulation of power and material benefits. A negative vote against a colleague's proposed and cherished new program, a debater's point scored in a faculty meeting, a simple disagreement over procedure or course content—all or any of these can inspire a campaign by one professor to impose punishment on another.

Frequently, the target is unaware of his vulnerability. Occasionally, the perpetrator sets forth with no intention other than exploiting opportunities to inflict injury upon his enemy. In that sense, the phenomenon is no more insidious than its counterpart in business or government. The methods, too, are similar: whispered accusations, rumormongering, veiled threats. But professors, trained in the subtleties of words and innuendo, are more skillful than most in the manipulation of the fears of others. Since the academy is largely an enclosed micro-universe without the complexity of personal motivation of the larger society, the seeker of vengeance shares the insecurities of those he would have as allies and can play upon them more skillfully. There are cliques to be rigidified, gaps to be widened, prejudices to be reinforced. Evaluations are tendered offhandedly, as: "His last book is merely a restatement of concepts discredited ten years ago." Gossip is recounted in passing, as: "I understand his proposal didn't make it past the first screening of the study section," or, "One of my students implied that he'd offered to jump her grade to an 'A' in return for her favors." Those adept at debate might attack frontally, exploiting every opportunity to humiliate the adversary before their colleagues. The exaltation of the put-down as a high professorial art makes this a tempting approach, but it's risky. Behind-the-back and out-of-earshot assaults are safer, for they can be denied or claimed to be out of context.

The escalating frustration experienced by the victim in

151

trying to force an open indictment to which he can respond is the most debilitating part of the experience. He suspects there is a folder somewhere listing his alleged crimes, and insists upon seeing it so he can enter his rebuttal. Such a docket sometimes exists, as when a student claims sexual overtures from a professor. More often, nothing is written. The professor knows what privileges and scraps of authority have been taken from him, but he cannot find out why. He flails about with increasingly hysterical counter-accusations, isolating himself still further. He claims his academic freedom has been violated, but he hasn't been fired, making that hard to prove. He cries of discrimination because of race, age, religion, politics, a preference for teaching over research, or for men instead of women. Despite those contrary cases reported in the newspapers, the odds are overwhelmingly against restitution. The professor has no proof. He leaves eventually to take another position, grumbling of injustice. Then he writes his book. It pretends to be visionary, but is a transparent defense against charges no one knows or cares to remember.

". . . and as someone who was a bachelor and gay," Duberman is saying, "it was killing me to be living in Princeton. I was in bad shape psychologically."

At his own casual reference to his homosexuality, Duberman shoots a glance at his visitor, perhaps to appraise any reaction. It is not a revelation, however. He has already "come out" in *Black Mountain*, his study of the famous experimental academic community published the preceding fall. And although the announcement was very much *en passant* in treatment, comprising no more than two or three oblique references, book reviewers subsequently treated the matter as if four hundred pages had been devoted to it. His visitor remarks that Princeton is a notably hairy-chested sort of place, and wonders if suspicions of Duberman's homosexuality might have been an underlying reason for his troubles there.

"I don't think it was. I doubt if it was even a matter for

speculation. I was still young enough so it didn't seem strange that I was unmarried. They never saw me, as far as I know, with either men *or* women. Certainly nothing ever happened between me and any students, because that was one of my rules."

What fail-safe mechanisms does he have to help observe that rule? Surely there must have been people at Princeton to whom he was attracted?

"Oh, yes," he laughs, "Princeton specializes in my fantasy life." Then he sobers. "Straight professors are much luckier in that the social sanctions against having anything to do with students or female colleagues are much less strong than the sanctions against homosexual contact. If it turns out that a male professor is sleeping with a female student—and we hear those stories all the time—or leaves his wife to marry a female graduate student, there's snickering and whatever, but it's rarely outrage that some taboo has been broken. I remember a case at Yale when I was teaching there. A man I knew very well made a pass at a male student at a drunken party. The way I heard it, the student had more or less invited it. I wasn't there, so I don't know what happened. In any case, the student not only rebuffed the pass, but ran distraught from the room and straight to the Master's house. They asked Mr. X to deny it so they wouldn't have to do anything. Foolishly or nobly, Mr. X refused to deny it. So they said they were very sorry, but he'd have to leave the faculty. He not only left the faculty, he left the academic world."

The incidence of sexual liaison between college faculty and students, whether homosexual or heterosexual, is difficult to assess. Given its status of taboo layered over taboo, professors are reluctant to estimate frequency, and some insist professorial-undergraduate fornication to be the rarest of aberrations. Perhaps this is merely an extension of the tendency to suppress news of the good thing professors have going. Conversely, to accept the picture suggested by some professors, one must

153

visualize a pen of rutting chimpanzees maddened by Spanish fly.

As hard facts are difficult to come by, only the merest dribs of data can be offered. As one example of journalistic enterprise, the student newspaper at San Francisco State sent questionnaires on the subject to 600 members of the faculty. Only 150 responded, 40 claiming to have had sexual relations with students, another 40 expressing receptivity should the opportunity arise, the rest outraged at the invasion of privacy.

Professor-novelist R. V. Cassill, in the course of wittily describing instances of coupling (his own and those of friends) between professors and coeds, takes time out to proclaim the rarity of the scoring scholar as compared to other professions. Professor Cassill muses more extensively on the psychological incest of relations between teacher-parent and student-child, on Abelard and Eloise, on Marlene Dietrich and Emil Jannings, on the potential for education of the *whole* person, and professorial responsibility thereto.

Lacking solid evidence, it can be fairly speculated that students of the present rarely require the extracurricular erotic tutelage of their professors; they have each other. Further, while it is clear that gay professors have more to fear from public disclosure than do their straight colleagues, it remains a matter of degree, as in other endeavors.

"I grew up with that kind of tale deeply imbedded. Earlier, there was a scandal at Smith College. There was a police investigation at Smith of dirty books going through the mail. It turned out that several homosexual professors were receiving pictures of nude men in the mail. They were arrested. One of the professors turned over his diary to the state police. It implicated still other gay professors, who at that moment were not known by the police. There were something like four or five firings. It was gruesome—the firings, the public accusations. Their lives were ruined, and that had not involved making a pass at a student, but simply looking at erotic materials in the privacy of one's home.

"So you know it's not hard to find fail-safe mechanisms when you grow up with these kinds of horror stories. I don't know what kind of pact I made with myself, but I was sufficiently traditional then and I told myself the pact made sense. Not only should I avoid at all costs any contact because I might get fired and indicted, but also the teacher-student relationship was sacrosanct. That relationship necessarily excluded any kind of erotic feelings.

"I have kept that relationship absolutely 'uncontaminated' by any outward erotic transactions. But transactions *are* going on in the classroom. They're people and they're in a room together, so all kinds of vibrations and physical sensations are getting set off. I don't mean we should act on it every time we feel it. That's crazy. The fact is, they do influence how we respond to each other. If you want to find out why you're holding the opinions you are in opposition to someone else, your *feelings* about that person have to be explored along with the opinions, since they're an essential part of the opinions. This is all very dangerous stuff. I myself have only just begun to move into it, not in terms of any acting out but by verbalizing my own feelings.

"I give a seminar at Lehman on the history of American radicalism. It lasts a full year and it's limited to roughly a dozen people. When my public announcement of homosexuality was due to come out, I felt sufficiently close to the people in this seminar that I felt it would be a betrayal of the closeness if they read about it in print instead of hearing it directly from me. So I steeled myself and told them. It was damned difficult to do. Terribly difficult. But it was an appropriate setting to tell them because as part of the history of American radicalism we were about to discuss Gay Liberation and revolution in thought about gender identification. I told them and they responded in a variety of ways. It convinced me more than ever that if these things are expressed they can make a valuable contribution to the traditional exchanges that we feel are our essential job in the classroom setting—the intellectual, analytical, rational exchanges."

Homosexual professors never dared make such pronouncements even ten years ago. It was all the evidence required of moral turpitude, even if the declaration of sexual orientation was unaccompanied by admission or proof of consummation of that inclination. It is widely believed, both on and off the campus, that disproportionately large numbers of college teachers are homosexual. Gay activists support the assumption. Peter Fisher, of the militant Gay Activist Alliance, makes the flat (and unsupported) statement that twice as many teachers are gay in relation to their occupational group as in the larger population. Bob Burdick of the Mattachine Society, the NAACP of the Gay Liberation movement, was himself a college and secondary school teacher. He guesses the proportion to be only 20 percent higher. In other words, anywhere between one out of three or one out of five college professors —male and female—are homosexual.

Neither Kinsey nor Masters and Johnson offered data or estimates on sexual preference by occupation. Perhaps someone should. In any event, the roughly 150,000 gay college professors in the country are regarded by Fisher as a particular blessing. Speaking of homosexual teachers on both the college and lower levels, he notes that it is often "the unmarried, childless teacher who is best able to relate to his students because he has no other conflicting demands upon his attention or interest." He also observes that many homosexuals "do not become involved in the gay world until they have finished high school or college, and they often end up spending nights studying rather than dating or searching for a marital partner. It is not surprising," he says, "that they are often drawn to academic life."

Duberman followed that pattern, but he was nearly forty before he made his public announcement of his homosexuality. How did he come to use *Black Mountain* as his vehicle?

"Well . . . let's see if I can put this in a reasonably lucid way. . . . I do feel that the model of objectivity through which most historians and social scientists work needs challenging. For a while, I was so discouraged with the enterprise of history—teaching it, researching it, writing it—that I thought as a matter of survival I might well have to give it up. I didn't know what I was going to do, but that's what I was feeling. When I started the *Black Mountain* book I wrote the first 40,000 words the way I wrote my other books. It was traditional academic scholarship, heavily footnoted, myself carefully distanced. I was so appalled by it that I stopped. That's the point where I felt I couldn't go on as an historian. I didn't know what I was doing anymore. There was a basic deception involved in all this and an encompassing anonymity that I distrusted. I felt it was self-destructive for me to continue in this role.

"I dropped the whole thing for a year and started to write plays again. What gradually emerged was that I could go back to the *Black Mountain* book, but only if I put *myself* in it. The subject matter required it, because Black Mountain was a subjective place. Every person I talked to had a different experience. If I talked to ten people about one event that took place there, I got ten very different versions of that event. Also, the book is so much about individuals and I had met so many of them that I felt as a matter of simple honesty I had to declare my feelings about the people I was describing. That way, the reader would be forewarned that those descriptions had been filtered through this particular person and this particular set of life experiences and attitudes.

"So I began to put myself more and more into the book. When I described a split at Black Mountain in 1944, for example, I said I'd talked to all the major principals involved and I disliked one of them intensely. A psychiatrist named Irwin Strauss. I knew that colored my view of the entire episode and I felt the reader should know this. So I actually included in the book my jottings in my motel room in Lexington, Kentucky, where I went to visit the Strausses for three days."

The jottings described Strauss as "super-aware, hawklike . . . as if waiting to catch you out. Brilliant, articulate, witty, seemingly very genial. But something I don't like or trust about him; the geniality isn't wholly believable. Traces of arrogance, archness; even a clever cruelty seems possible."

"The more I got into this mode of presentation, the more I felt that not only was it right for me, but it might serve as a possible alternative for other social scientists. And I mean it as an attitude to the historical enterprise rather than a conversion of that enterprise from one thing to another. In other words, I continue to feel that we should do our best to research in depth 'what actually happened,' but we must also recognize that all that research is being filtered through our persons and it is a matter of simple honesty to confess what those personalities are like and how the interaction between the individual historian and his data significantly affects the presentation of the data in the finished product. My argument is we can do traditional history better if we talk more about who we are.

"At one point in *Black Mountain*, the rector, as he was called, was discovered in a parked car with a marine and was arrested. He had to steal away in the middle of the night. Some arrangement was made with the judge so that he was released, but the agreement was that he would be gone by morning. The few people who really ran Black Mountain behind the scenes conspired with legal authorities, and this man was 'encouraged' to leave. Nobody stood up for him, nobody said, 'Who gives a shit that you're a homosexual? We like you and you're important to us and we're not going to let these redneck

158

state troopers drive you out of the community and the state.' Nobody said that.

"I was so outraged in writing about this that I knew my rage was coloring my description of the event. It seemed appropriate and a necessary point at which to say: 'It may well be that some of what I've written is a function of my own fear as a homosexual.' I also provided some excerpts from my diary about an experimental course, by way of comparing my experiences with the work that was being done at Black Mountain. One of the entries in my diary was whether or not to tell the class that I was a homosexual. At that point, it was five years ago, I decided not. I debated it with myself in my diary, and I included that those were the only two points where it felt not only appropriate but necessary to reveal this aspect of my personality."

Did therapy make him decide to "come out"?

"Quite the contrary. In my years of therapy, I was encouraged to believe that the only sign of adulthood and health was when I was sexually involved with a woman, preferably married to her and living monogamously with her. I was in both individual and group therapy, with several therapists. The group therapy went on for almost ten years, and the whole group had internalized the values of the therapist. Bizarrely enough, he saw himself in the forefront of psychoanalytical thought, one of the innovators; yet his model of human health was strictly traditional—and it wasn't only homosexuals. Women were defined as healthy when they had given up career ambitions and settled down to a life of domestic bliss and raising children. It was an extraordinary, tyrannizing situation."

A staff psychiatrist at a large urban university says there is, to his knowledge, no comprehensive study of the numbers of college professors who undertake psychoanalysis, nor is he aware of colleagues with practices specializing in faculty people. He comes as close as any, he thinks, if only because of his position. Loath to generalize, he nevertheless sees a correlation between the higher ranges of intelligence and emotional dysfunction. Because professors as a group are more intelligent, it is logical to believe that more of them *need* psychiatric help. As for whether they actually seek it, he observes that educated people are less likely than most to view emotional problems as weaknesses to be overcome by sheer will, leading to the conclusion that a larger proportion of professors will enter analysis than persons of other professions. On the other hand, city life exacerbates emotional problems and he works for a big city institution and many professors work in rural areas and . . .

"In the first few years," Duberman is saying, "I remember thinking that these definitions were arbitrary, that they didn't represent life experiences. Then, at one point, I was told outright that the group was no longer interested in hearing about the details of my life as a homosexual. They considered that life merely symptomatic of my character disorder, and to talk about it was to waste my time and theirs and served as an obstacle to my growth and health. And so I was literally forbidden to discuss my homosexual love affairs or any aspect of my homosexual life. There were people in that group who I loved—not including the therapist—especially one woman. And the group was so unified behind this view of normal human behavior that she would say to me in a truly loving way, 'Martin, give up the defiance, for God's sake. Get on your own side and become a healthy human being.' She would say this to me with tears in her eyes, and then there would be tears in my eyes. The result was that finally, after a few years of protest, I internalized the group's values and decided I was a desperately sick, defiant human being and I had to grow up and become a heterosexual."

He accepted his homosexuality as a disease?

"Oh, I completely accepted the sickness model of homosexuality. It's very hard not to when you're in a group and it is unified behind that theory and you care about most of the people in the group and love some of them—and they are all giving you the same message. As independent as I see myself, that kind of pressure is very difficult to resist. It has, as a result, made me very bitter about analysis, and particularly about the psychoanalytical model of sexuality. I don't condemn wholesale all therapists and all treatment. In fact, I went back into treatment this past winter with a different therapist for about two or three months. A love affair had broken up and I was very upset. Some questions arose in my own mind that I felt unable to deal with alone. I really needed some 'objective outside perception' and even my closest friends could not provide it. I feel I benefited from the insights of this therapist, who is a very fine and human man and open to a wide variety of human experiences.

"So I don't condemn the whole field. I just think it's very hard to find people, as in any field, who have not been trained according to a particular model. Just as it's very hard to find historians who aren't entirely wedded to the views of 'objectivity.' "

While noting that heterosexual life patterns are often troubled, Duberman is not blind to the problems that cause particular anxiety for homosexuals. He likes children, but has no particular drive to have his own. And some of his friendships have sustained over thirty years, but . . .

"The older I get, the more I find myself regretting a lack of continuity. Not having a mate can be damned lonely. Somebody has said that life's a choice between loneliness and boredom. If you have a mate, you get bored. If you don't, you get lonely. When I wrote about Black Mountain I decided that I could not have survived there because my hermit instincts are very profound. They alternate with highly developed social instincts. I *like* people, even crowds of people. I'm one of the few New Yorkers who enjoy the subways and large parties.

But I also need a lot of privacy and retreat. Last August, I thought I was going to be away doing a production of a play of mine in East Hampton for a whole month, so I gave my apartment to two friends. It turned out I came back a week ahead of time. I couldn't kick them out because I promised them the apartment and they were from Chicago and had no place to go. But they were sleeping in my bed! It meant I had to sleep on the couch in the study. It was going to be awful, but I had no choice.

"It turned out to be a wonderful week. I really enjoyed having people around all the time. The orderly routine of my life was constantly disrupted in ways that I found initially difficult, but finally very enjoyable. It broke the routine, and when they left I missed them like crazy. I went into a sizable depression. I looked around this big space and I thought that the way I thought of myself in the past, the need for privacy and isolation, was bullshit. I didn't need all those things. I *convinced* myself I needed them."

The patterns of the professorial lifestyle are necessarily dichotomous. Teaching requires the participation of other people; scholarly research demands solitude. The personality that cannot draw nourishment from both sorts of activity must accommodate or become maladjusted, at least in terms of job performance. Only a minority of professors succeed in achieving a semblance of balance, especially while maintaining a consistently high quality of achievement in both dimensions of the professorial experience. It takes the energy, humanity, brilliance, and consuming curiosity of a Martin Duberman to do it. In his case, however, and that of those relatively few who comprise the elite corps of academicians, even those twin accomplishments are not enough. To the communality of the classroom, he adds his work in the theater; to the solitude of meticulous research in library stacks and carrels, he adds the lonely production of social essay. In an era when most people are inhibited by responsibility and imposed specialization, he and his colleagues are among the last of the Renaissance men. And that professorial characteristic is fading. Duberman sees nothing wrong with obsession—whether "involvement with a poem or planting tulips or the French Revolution"—but feels that many of his fellows do themselves a disservice by living as incestuously as they do with their academic specializations. If their contacts and activities were broadened, he believes, their particular expertises would be enhanced. If pressed to define himself, Duberman says "writer," but feels that that is an umbrella for other things. Increasingly, one of those other things is commitment to the theater.

Years ago he was a seventeen-year-old actor in a semi-professional summer stock company touring Vermont, playing the lead of George in *Our Town*. Though he loved the experience, he was dissuaded from pursuing it as a career. A sense of drama is nevertheless a useful skill for a classroom teacher and his interest in the theater was deferred, not stifled. *In White America* resulted from the natural flow of his enhanced skills as a writer and his ability to instruct, his enchantment with American history, his concern with issues of social justice, and his desire to present his material in a more vital and less traditional manner. The resulting play documented the history of the black people of America and was described as a new theatrical form. Its success drew Duberman more deeply than ever to the potential of this new means of expression.

"I love productions . . . in both senses. I *am* theatrical. I like amplitude and crisis. A lot! I also like working with people on a common project. It's a wonderful contrast with sitting in the room alone, writing, especially if you live alone at the same time. I've worked a little in films, never successfully, but I love the unpredictability of the theater, and that may be why. In the theater, whether it's a rehearsal or a performance, you really don't know what's going to happen. I *love* it, the way everything is constantly changing. For somebody that leads a controlled life, as I do, the theater is a wonderful jolt, because you can work your ass off, and everybody else can work their asses off. . . . You think you got it right, then boom! Sally gets a sore throat. Or Jane starts screaming at Jimmy because Jane didn't sleep well last night or somebody coughs in the audience and the whole thing blows up. And if it happens when the critics are there . . ."

How far into a production does he remain involved?

"All the way."

He's not one of those playwrights who just hands his play over to the director or producer?

"Never, never, never. I once removed a play from Elaine May two nights before opening night. It was part of *Adaptation Next*, which ran Off-Broadway for a couple of years. Originally it was three one-act plays, written by Bruce J. Friedman, Terence McNally and me. Elaine May was directing the whole evening. It was by far the most traumatic of all my theatrical experiences, and they're always traumatic, happily." Duberman gives his odd snorting laugh at the reference to his penchant for crisis. He says that when there isn't a genuine crisis around, he elaborates some simple event into one. "But *this* one. . . . First they dropped Friedman's play in previews. The evening had been called *Three From Column A*. All the signs came down and it was called *Two From Column A*. Then Elaine kept getting further and further away from my script, and I was there every fucking day, and you ask about *involved!* I was tenaciously, naggingly involved.

"She loved my play, but, like all geniuses, she insisted that her stamp had to be made on it. It had to become a vehicle for her. That may be a definition of genius. She's an immensely talented woman. But the more recalcitrant the play became, the more hysterically she insisted that it yield. Which meant laying in Elaine May routines to the point of inventing dialogue and slapstick stage business. And this was a play

164

meant to be funny, but finally very serious. She gimmicked it up so that it became a kind of burlesque show.

"With increasing anxiety through the weeks, I asked the producer what happened to my play? He said, 'Be calm, this is the way Elaine works, she loves to improvise. She'll get back to the script.' In the meantime, we were getting closer and closer to opening night and she was getting further and further from the script. At the same time, the audiences were beginning to go with the burlesque. It was a terrible thing for me, because I had the feeling her version was going to be a success, but it wasn't the play I had written. I *liked* the play I had written, so it came down to my saying that changes had to be made. For example, she had the main figure arriving with a long yellow scarf trailing behind him to the floor. He was meant to be a man of mystery and presence and dignity, and she had this simpering fop arrive. It was wildly different from what I had written.

"I specified these few things that I wanted changed and then I would let the show open. Elaine categorically refused to change anything, saying that her whole conception would collapse. There were all kinds of screaming and hysteria and shouting in the lobby in front of audiences. I didn't recover for months. Finally I said okay, I wanted the play back. They wouldn't give it back. So I said I'd get up in front of the curtain or stand up in the audience or hand out leaflets to critics saying that this was a play by Elaine May based on a script by Martin Duberman and that I would not accept responsibility for what was on the stage. Under that kind of threat, they finally said, 'All right, here's your fucking play, get lost.' Then they cancelled opening night. Elaine put an adaptation of hers in place of mine. They went into rehearsal, moved to a theater on *my* street, and opened a month later. It was a *roaring* success, ran for two years. And every day I had to leave my apartment to see lines of happy theatergoers across the street trying to get tickets to this damn thing."

Duberman has laughed ruefully throughout this story. His visitor asks if it is gratifying to deal with people of Elaine May's caliber. He repeats that he likes crisis. His visitor asks if he has figured out why.

"I can give you at least twenty separate explanations, all of which are true and none of which is sufficient."

But isn't it exciting to work with people of that rank?

"Oh, sure. Not to the extent it once was, but I don't think it's only academics who are easily glamourized by meeting the rich and famous of the world. There's good reason for it, aside from an admiration for success. Often these people are interesting, unusual. There's fun and excitement in meeting them."

Has Duberman's own theatrical sense been useful to him in the classroom?

"Well, I'm very good at teaching. I know from past experience, from enrollment and feedback, that I'm good at it. I lectured entirely without notes. Because I'm theatrical, I turned in good performances. That's what they were. I finally realized it was bad for the students, but only belatedly that it was bad for me, because I was feeding a narcissism that needed no further encouragement. There I was on stage, with literal rounds of applause after a lecture."

Does he feel that the lecture method is ineffective?

"Generally, yeah. I've been turned on myself as a member of an audience by a particularly dazzling performance. But I think the dazzlement carries dangers, because theatricality can be at the expense of truth."

Are his current classes lectures?

"No, part of the agreement when I came to City University was that I would not lecture. Because I really don't think it's a good educational device. I had to give a course in which forty students were enrolled. I couldn't get anything going. Finally I broke it in half, scheduled entirely separate hours, and in essence converted it into two seminars."

Princeton and Lehman are very different institutions. Apart from distinctions by social class, endowment, or prestige, Princeton is one of the ten most selective universities in the country, while Lehman is a division of a megaversity of 126,636 full-time students with an open admission policy guaranteeing enrollment to every graduate of any high school in the city of New York. What difference does he find between students at the two institutions?

"One is that there's more emotional accessibility, at Lehman, at least with some of the students. There's more willingness to talk about their lives, to express their feelings. And that's startling. I mean, it's not middle-class emotional control. But what goes along with it is a much greater respect for authority than middle-class students have. A lot of students at Lehman come from lower-class socioeconomic backgrounds, and they're used to strong authority figures in the home— male, especially—and in church and the school. Often they're the first in their families to go to college. If you try to destructure and divest yourself of the traditional authoritarian roles, they get more upset than the students at Princeton did. Some of them get so upset they just turn off entirely. They physically leave the classroom or they sit there in a semi-catatonic state, dutifully bringing their bodies, but nothing else.

"There is also a strong feeling that I'm just getting in touch with, that there is a much greater sense of worthlessness which I find very hard to cope with. It sometimes ties in with my own feelings about myself, but I find it so touching and so difficult to deal with. All they have to do is hear the name 'Princeton' or 'Harvard.' They think of themselves as rejects and leftovers. They think of their fathers as failures. Their fathers are cab drivers, janitors. They feel they're destined for failure as society traditionally defines it, and it's very difficult to convince them that they have any kind of gift or ability in any human sense or the standard academic ways. This can

167

sometimes be overwhelming in a classroom. I've discovered only recently that sometimes a group is very quiet and inhibited not because they're bored, but because they distrust their own perceptions to such a degree they're terrified to verbalize them for fear somebody is going to say 'jerk.' "

Are there differences for him professionally?

"At Princeton, the chairman carried enormous, almost dictatorial weight. I think he was directly responsible for my salary being frozen. At Lehman, it is much more democratic. Most of the major decisions are made by two committees, the Ed Policy committee and the Personnel and Budget committee, and I don't think the chairman is a member of either. Most of their recommendations, not including tenure, I guess, are brought back to the whole department."

Is he more diligent about faculty meetings?

"I go to all the department meetings, none of the faculty meetings. I think I only missed one this year. It's funny, I like them. The people are so much nicer at Lehman than they were at Princeton, so much less self-important. And the meetings are fun, a lot of good humor and kidding and everybody seems to realize that the issues at stake are not world-shaking. We have a good time. Whereas at Princeton, every decision would change the bounds of the universe. I am a contributing member of the department. I've tried to steer clear of university-wide committees and meetings, and I do feel less guilty about all that than I used to. We all know there's just so much time and everybody's got to establish priorities. And I know what my priorities are. In terms of my own life, it's my friends and my writing."

He hasn't mentioned scholarship.

"Some of my writing is scholarly. Notice I sit up straight in my chair when I say that. We are not ready to be entirely read out of the scholarly community."

But is he drawing away from it all? Is he tending to use his professorship more as a base than a reason?

"Yes, and I worry about it. I tend to be hard on myself, and it's not just an excuse that I'm now about to present, although happily it serves as an excuse as well. The fact is, I know that, as a teacher, I am giving something of value. I'm also getting something for myself. That part of my professorial life doesn't worry me, only to the extent it worries almost everybody I know. Everybody is saying what the hell are universities for and why are we divided into these neat little departments and disciplines and how can you teach history without getting involved with anthropology and psychology and sociology. Everyone is raising these kinds of doubts about their professorial roles. I don't know if my doubts are more pervasive, but in some moods I do feel that the university is an outmoded institution and therefore all of us who hold jobs within it are doing something we should stop. That's one way to either bring these institutions down or convert them to something that might be more socially useful.

"The reason I don't feel I'm a fraud is that, in terms of my classroom experimenting, I'm doing as much as I can so that the experiences my students and I have are valuable ones. But along with that goes a lot of pessimism about whether the institutions *can* be converted and whether I know what I want to convert them into. Because of all that confusion, I often feel like a fraud. After a bad day of teaching in which nothing seems to get transacted at any level, I really don't think I'm earning my money—and I'm getting a fairly healthy salary. So what is this all about, I ask myself."

Nevertheless, he thinks of himself primarily as a writer. Where does he go from here?

"I'm not at this moment getting myself involved in long-term historical projects. In the last three or four years I've been increasingly trying to write plays. And I feel in my guts that my academic background and training have worked to stifle my inventive powers, because we historians have been taught that the cardinal sin is invention. In fact, in our subtle, manipulative way, we social scientists are constantly inventing because we are selecting the data. We invent a particular picture to present to the reader, but we won't recognize it as overtly as that. So it's very difficult to overtly allow yourself to be inventive. I've been having a very hard time writing myself out of the academic bag, yet that's where my drive is, and my prose trails along with it so much of this traditional baggage that it can be awfully *lumpen* at times. I admire carefulness and knowledge, but not when it interferes with the imaginative process."

What areas is he likely to explore in his future writing?

"I'm more sure of the new subject matter than the form. But I'm beginning to think sexuality may be my subject, as opposed to the coming of the Civil War. Oscar Handlin would never approve. But sexuality has always been very central to my life. It's just now that it's surfaced, I've become more conscious of how much my life is ruled by it. I want to find out more about it in terms of me plus the culture. Which is why I think I will be doing semi-autobiographical work or 'biohistory' or 'participant-observer history', as some people called the Black Mountain book.

"I think I'm going to try to take the year off, the year after next, stop teaching everything I have been teaching, and do more on the history of sex roles in this country. What it's meant, how the society has defined maleness and femaleness. . . . A lot of people are doing that, of course. . . . But also, a publisher has asked me to do a history of what it's meant to be gay in this country, about which there's almost nothing known. I'm tempted, and he said either a history or documentary anthology, whatever you want, but I'm pretty sure that would involve another of those five- or six-year research jobs which I don't feel I could do again. I don't feel I could bury myself in libraries across the country at this point in my life. It would be killing. . . ."

In an article on the Op-Ed page of the *Times*, Duberman

170

subsequently writes on "The Historian As Ghost." He says, in part:

The growing disinterest of this college generation in historical study has often been commented on. As is usually the case these days, the generation itself is held to blame—it will not accept the discipline needed to master detail; it will not curtail impulse and passion in the name of gaining critical distance. The reverse side of the coin strikes me with more force. I see this generation rejecting historical study to the degree that it seeks personal authenticity. The best of the generation rejects disguise; it wants to know who is responsible; it prefers the personal to the computerized response; it values the distinctive above the typical.

CHAPTER 9

The bloodied soil of many campuses during the last decade proved to be rich loam for the germination and growth of educational experiment. Every college attempting to appease or divert its rebels (or seeking to retard their development) clutched desperately at innovation. They were aided eagerly by visionaries. At traditional colleges and universities, the experiments were carefully segregated polyps dangling from the furthest extremities of institutional torsos. Some were surgically removed when the crises which fostered them had passed; others dropped away from their own weight. Some altered their structures but persevered.

Fordham University permitted the creation of Bensalem College in its bosom. Poet and professor Elizabeth Sewell was its first director. Her dream was to engage a few dozen students and faculty in a total living and learning environment, "to find out what education is, what we need in this day and age, how to learn, how to teach and what."

Bensalem (the name was that of an island utopia in Francis Bacon's *New Atlantis*) opened in 1967. It had no classrooms, no course credits, no term papers, no grades, no curriculum, no academic checkpoints whatsoever. It *did* have six directors in seven years. During its lifetime it granted only 79 degrees, even though students needed only to hand in signed statements testifying they had been enrolled at least three years in order to qualify for the B.A. John Coyne and Tom Hebert, advocates of alternate education and authors of a guide to same (*This Way Out*), called Bensalem "the sump of experimental colleges." On their visit what they mostly found was hostility: of students for faculty, faculty for students, of both for Fordham and the world beyond. One of the six directors later wrote: "Bensalem endors[ed] the utopian vision that there is a common ground between people and that rationality and goodwill are sufficient to find that common ground. Little in Bensalem's experience indicates this is the case." Bensalem died in 1974, a lingering corpse, dispatched by the Fordham board of trustees in 1971, but permitted to discharge its last admittees.

Bensalem was quickly conceived, soon abandoned. Hampshire College enjoyed a longer gestation period. An excessive one, some have said. A gleam in the eye of neighboring Amherst, Smith, Mount Holyoke, and the University of Massachusetts since 1958, it did not register its first students until 1970. With such auspicious parentage, it is not surprising that Hampshire was given to such pronouncements as: "Hampshire's impact on education will be felt for two centuries," and describing itself as "A Model for Innovation in American Colleges and Universities." In sustaining its chosen image as the Harvard of educational innovation, Hampshire sternly enjoined prospective students not to assume that the absence of grades, set curriculum and credits meant four years of watching sunsets over the Berkshires. There were to be periodic comprehensive exams, faculty supervision, a respect for what was past. Within two years, the hordes of students beating at its gates had thinned, and the original seed monies tendered by its sponsors had been depleted. Hampshire will survive, but only because of its upper-class clientele (50 percent of the students were from families making $50,000 a year or more), prestigious overseers, and essential conventionality, not its imagination. Nothing it proposed or accomplished was unique or even particularly advanced. No new answers have been discovered, and Hampshire's goals are now more modest. It was inordinately pleased to receive provisional accreditation from the New England Association of Schools and Colleges, a designation often shunned by more venturesome colleges. But, it will survive.

Change is the key. Innovative colleges and programs that are ready to alter themselves cling most tenaciously to life. Once upon a time, Bard College (near Poughkeepsie, New York) informed other colleges and graduate schools to which their students applied that it was Bard's policy not to give grades. They offered written teacher evaluations instead. Their students had difficulty gaining admission to more conventional institutions, so the college compromised with graphs of student performance along with the evaluations, sustaining an illusion of integrity. Finally they did assign grades, protesting in their transcripts that *they* didn't use grades, but if someone else chose to measure students that way . . . well . . . here they were.

Old Westbury changed. Initiated by fiat of the State University of New York, first president Harris Wofford (very soon of Bryn Mawr) gathered a gaggle of ex-Peace Corps people, Great Books devotees, and avowedly hip student planners to set about making themselves a college. In an age of revolt-for-the-revolution's-sake, Wofford found himself in the middle of what he described as a "free firing zone." Being president, he was, of course, the primary target. College presidents, no matter how warmly accepting in nature, stand in for Daddy, Establishment, Repression, Authority. Wofford sharpened his utility as symbol by his openly expressed determination that he would not be reduced to technician and servant of the majority, that decisions would not be made in a structure in which students outnumbered the faculty and administration. Faculty were to bring their experience, students their imagination. These would be blended, with students as partners, not tyrants.

But Old Westbury attracted primarily upper middle-class utopians, not the mix of blue-collar whites, inner-city blacks and Puerto Ricans, suburbanites, scholars, and achievers they had hoped. They lusted for relevance, ignored history, resisted recognition of external realities, retreated from books, assaulted authority whatever its source, rejoiced in the anarchy of a thousand students doing their thousand very own things. All in all, they were the typical student body of the typical experimental college. In a series of spasms of conventional sit-ins and confrontations, though, Old Westbury changed. The focus moved from the affluent and alienated to the disadvantaged and disaffected. These latter wanted in, not out. Relevance was the gathering of marketable skills and the building of self-esteem, not getting in touch with one's karma. Old Westbury became known as the "Poor People's College." Years later, when SUNY's revised master plan insisted that more local community college students be permitted entry at Old Westbury, the faculty decided to hire a lawyer. They sought to sue to block the master plan, which they believed would dilute the college's commitment to the "educationally by-passed" of the cities.

The moment faded almost before it had really begun. By 1971, students were staying away from colleges—traditional *and* progressive—in droves. When they began to return, in a time of inflation and recession, it was to gather credentials and training in exchange for which employers paid money. Graduates with courses in Polymorphous Reality, French madrigals, and Guerrilla Warfare in the Videosphere simply aren't in a position to compete for jobs with physical therapists and taxation lawyers and the anointed of the Harvard Business School. Conventional colleges closed at an accelerating rate, and experimental institutions were twice as vulnerable. It is difficult at any time to attract significant financial support to avante-garde educational programs. The people who have accumulated that kind of money are not inclined to favor places called Friends' World College or Fairhaven, not when Yale will name buildings for them. Innovation and experiment thrive in economically flush times, but wither when money is tight. Progressive colleges lacking the backing and protection of a public university or the solid sponsorship of established universities most often simply expire.

The evidence of decline and retrenchment is everywhere. As one instance, Brown University startled the educational establishment in 1969 when it completely revamped its curriculum, made grades optional, eliminated most required courses, and promised a freedom and flexibility not seen at a prestigious university since Robert Maynard Hutchins' grand scheme at the University of Chicago almost forty years before. Within four years, reevaluation saw students opting for grades and the return of traditional programs and professors teaching courses as they always had. Central to the 1969 concept was a core group of "modes of thought" seminars intended to elevate methods of inquiry over the inculcation of mere facts. A *New York Times* reporter found that the number of these seminars had been halved, from eighty-four in 1971 to forty-three in 1974. He further discovered that enrollment in no-grade courses had dipped from 63 percent to 36 percent over the same period, and that only 10 percent of the student body chose to undertake independent study projects.

Brown's students, as those at other colleges with such offerings, still want to go to graduate, medical, and law schools. The lack of conventional grades puts them at a serious disadvantage in competition with other applicants. The periodical *Educational Record* published a survey in the Fall of 1973 which showed that only 17 percent of graduate schools of art and science, 14 percent of law schools, and 6 percent of medical schools looked upon credit–no credit grading systems as acceptable. The message was clear.

Nothing can be said about experimental education by antagonistic outsiders that the participants do not level against themselves, or, more likely, about colleagues who fail to recognize the proper path to enlightenment. Lifted from context, the same charges could be those directed against conventional education. Again, it is a question of degree: The system encourages intellectual arrogance; it also reinforces self-doubt. It provides no meaningful measure of achievement; but the standards it does impose are oppressive. It fails to provide purposeful direction; it is also restrictive. It fosters ignorance of reality; but it suppresses imagination.

Whatever their internicine battles, however, advocates of innovative learning rush to one another when threatened. That is to say, most of the time. *They* haven't produced the educated men who sent boys to kill and be killed in foreign wars. *They* haven't produced corporate price-fixers, political thugs, the violators of the ecology and of dignity. But then, there is no consensus among them as to what kinds of people they *have* produced.

Under these circumstances, any thoughtful but uncommitted educator is immobilized when attempting to assess the effectiveness of non-traditional colleges in producing better citizens/students/human beings. Persuasive definitions are lacking. Backed against the battlements, reluctant analysts surrender observations rather than conclusions, then withdraw from the field in disarray: (1) people of any age need standards against which to measure themselves; (2) some can function under self-imposed sanctions, but most cannot; (3) it is higher education's function to explore approaches to knowledge of self, not to dictate answers; (4) diversity must be cherished, fealty to temporary truths denied; (5) institutions and people must be given the opportunity to fail and to try again; (6)

whatever the structure of the environment of that opportunity, its inhabitants must be able to accept responsibility for their own failures.

Much of human endeavor is foolish and mean-spirited. Higher education, in all its permutations, reflects humanity. Its virtue is that it is neither required nor proscribed by law.

Partly under those assumptions, a number of alternative colleges persist. If not precisely flourishing, they continue, usually with no visible means of support beyond student tuition. Goddard College is one of these.

The history of experimental education did not begin with the discovery of love and trees by 300,000 city kids at Woodstock. Goddard was founded in 1938, and the other "respectable" non-traditional colleges still in existence include Antioch (1953), Reed (1911), Bennington (1932), and Sarah Lawrence (1926). Purists dismiss most of these as the maiden aunts of alternative education, once promiscuous, now haughty and girdled. But not Goddard. It remains true to its birthright. Continual free-flowing experimentation is what Goddard is. Beyond that, it defies classification.

For eight months of the year, northern Vermont is not a particularly hospitable place for people who favor dry socks and warm ears. The other four are glorious. This first week in April is permitting an unusually warm glimpse of June. Patches of snow remain only on the northern slopes of the worn green hills around Plainfield and in the shadows of trees and woodpiles. The foundations of farmhouses are banked with dirt or wrapped in plastic sheeting to ward off cold drafts and prevent frozen pipes. Christmas wreaths still hang on the doors of many houses, and the Vermonter's habit of drying clothes on the front porch prevails.

Plainfield, where Goddard is located, is not picture-book New England. Life is rawly fundamental here. But vistas of rolling hills and tumbling streams and weathered barns and deer in pastures are soothing to the visiting city person

179

diligently shun-piking from the Burlington airport. The multi-centered college peels back along a road above the town. The Greatwood campus is first. Most of the dormitories are here, and the cupolaed barn of the old Barker estate serves as a community center. The Northwood campus is a mile beyond. In between is the Eliot D. Pratt Library. Parking his car in the muddy lot near the road, the visitor walks along a path heavy with the smell and feel of melting snow and pine. As he reaches the entrance of the incongruously modernistic brick and concrete library building, an emerging student smiles a greeting and says he likes the stranger's coat. The visitor is both warmed and startled.

Tony Pearce, he is told, can be found at the NRT office, which turns out to be an alcove just large enough to hold a desk and two chairs. Pearce rises, apologizing for the size of his niche. In a softly drawling British accent he explains that they are frightfully short of space all over the campus. He offers a chair and a cup of tea, the ingredients and equipment for which he has some difficulty assembling.

Though under six feet, Pearce gives an impression of greater size. His head is large, his face big-featured. The thick nose is sunburned, and there is the outline of a white mask around his liquid blue eyes, for he is an avid cross-country skier. He is uncaring about his clothes, wearing rumpled denim shirt, sea-green chinos, and thicksoled work boots. When he was teaching international politics at NYU, he was noted nearly as much for what came to be known as the "Pearce Strip" as for being one of the most demanding and capable teachers in the field. Although he felt obligated to enter his classroom in coat and tie, the coat was shed by the time he reached his desk. As he started to get into his lecture, the tie was loosened, then pulled off, as if a hindrance to the clarity of his presentation. Soon, the shirt was unbuttoned and the sleeves rolled up past the elbows. His students smiled at each other knowingly, for with the discarding or loosening of each article of clothing, they knew that a major point was about to be offered and dissected. At a teach-in on the Vietnam War, he had remained fully clothed well into his segment of the program. Then a cheer went up as he ripped off his jacket and threw it at a chair. The standing-room audience knew he was taking the gloves off, too.

That was when he was Professor Anthony Pearce, associate professor of international relations, B.Sc. (econ.) of the London School of Economics, Ph.D. (theories of imperialism) from the University of California at Berkeley. That was when he presented his classes with lists of forty required books to read by the end of the semester. That was when he snapped at a student clicking his ball-point pen and at another popping his chewing gum. That was when not a few students cowered before the ferocity of his intellect and his impatience with ragged analysis. That was before he was "Tony" to his students, as he is now, when one of his advisees arrives—late— for consultation on her project for her three-year plan.

Pam wears a flannel shirt and jeans, button earrings, and a red bandana tied artlessly around her hair. She is about to leave on her non-resident trimester and she wants to talk about her proposed project. In theory, Goddard students are in on-campus residence for two four-month trimesters, away for a non-resident learning trimester, followed by a vacation. The non-resident term is given to independent study projects of limitless variety. The only readily identifiable academic requirement for graduation is completion of the senior study. Pam intends to start hers next term, when she will take a job with her father, who runs a farm in California.

Pam and Tony go outside to take advantage of the unfamiliar sunshine. Sitting on a damp hillock, they can see out across the Onion River valley, black with pine and flowing cloud shadows. Pam sits yoga-fashion, elbows on knees, chewing a bit of straw. She asks what Tony thought of her proposal.

"I did not like it very much at all." His tone is gentle, but direct.

Pam slumps back on her hands, her open face tightening. Her voice takes on an edge that wasn't there before.

"Then why? Maybe you could suggest and help me write another one."

"Well, to start with, this is a large part of your third-year plan, the forward-looking part. That's important, your statement about where you are and where you want to go." He points to a page in her written proposal, then continues, absently flipping the pages. "The critical things are these questions you want to get into. Why are friendships so difficult to develop? Why are people afraid of living with each other on more open terms? I respect these questions, which are profound . . . and general. But I think that, as something closer to the heart of your work, I'd like to suggest that you develop a set of more specific questions, too. Remember that what you're aiming at is an understanding of a total agricultural commercial operation in California. You want to understand the people who are working in the fields, the people who are overseeing that work, the management, and even the people who have financially backed the whole operation. Work by yourself in the way we talked about before, putting down the things you're really curious about, until you leave here with a preliminary set of things you want to find out."

Pam's difficulty, she says, is separating her total objectives for her third-year plan from the issues motivating her to undertake this specific project.

"I really don't know how to write the damn thing," she says, her tone still hurt. "Not only do I have to plan for this summer, but it has to tie in with what I want to do in my seventh and eighth trimester. I know from experience that that's almost impossible to calculate. It's like previsualization without any type of data, except for my basic personality."

She shakes her head in futility and starts pulling grass with her fingers. A mongrel dog trots by, pausing to sniff at each of them. From among the pines behind the library comes the muffled buzz of a chain saw. Tony is carefully restating his suggestions, pulling her forward, rebuilding her momentum. It starts to take hold. She talks it out, sorts through what he has said, adds some observations, plays with it.

"There are two different ways of looking at this," she says. "I have my own basic needs and curiosities about living and what I want to do with photography and writing and studying different cultures, and that goes into putting together this project." She pauses, brightens. "Maybe I just answered my own question!"

It is a good moment, if a small one. The outsider cannot fully understand the conversation, or its bits of unspoken self-knowledge, or the relationship between these two people. The episode seems simple, and unnecessarily drawn out, but it reflects some of the frustrations and joys of both teacher and student in a non-traditional learning situation. Tony walks a thin line between direction and support of his student, trying to help her discover her needs. Like therapy, the procedure takes time and involves repeated travel over trampled terrain. True to form, this conversation goes on another half hour. Pam is laughing before it is over, promising to send photographs of herself among the workers in the fields. She is eager once more to begin.

"I'm going to tell my Mom and Dad to get on my ass out there and not let me screw off. It's all going to be a very supportive thing." She is talking very fast, her words tumbling over each other. "Dad has this great communication . . . he's in an incredible position where he's really good friends with Cesar Chavez and with the Teamsters and . . . I mean he's in the middle and I guess that's why things haven't really blown up. He's working closely with me, even writing a paper on what he visualizes I may do. I've got a hard ass, but you'll see a changed person, I guarantee. I'll send you pictures, Tony, O.K.?"

Later, Tony drives his visitor back down the road to eat lunch at the student center. There are many more people here. Some dormitories run their own dining rooms, including soul food in the Third World dorm and the inevitable organic food service in another. Goddard has about one thousand students altogether—no one seems to know the exact figure—about six hundred of them on campus at any one time. The atmosphere is decidedly Summer Camp, with screen doors and thick white coffee mugs. In appearance, the student style is Whole Earth hip. That's not surprising, of course, nor particularly illuminating of how they think. Certainly, "straight" people are nowhere in evidence—not a tie or a suit in sight. But there is contention here. Carloads of it.

The communal flavor of the college is not shared or approved by all. There are pragmatic, private people here who are contemptuous of those who embrace Eastern mysticism and assume that all will go well because they wish it so. There is substantial hostility to the motives and actions of others—layers upon layers. Feminist radicals are at loggerheads with male chauvinist radicals, blacks with everyone else, dog-lovers confront dog-haters, meditators annoy doers, communalists oppose loners, couples drift from groups, heads sneer at Jesus freaks, and everyone is against the President. None of this is unique to Goddard. The same observations can be made about most colleges. But it is all so much more intense here. These students and teachers are looking hard for a way to live their lives, and the magnitude of potential choices presented by Goddard can be paralyzing. It is the nature of experimentation that much of it must fail, if only in the sense of its inherent fragility. Predictably, Goddard people proclaim the *value* of failure, and seem to mean it, in contrast to the similar lip service of traditional educators. But it all takes its toll. Goddard attracts the disaffected, the disenchanted, and the alienated. Seeking firm answers and not finding them, most of them leave. Only about 20 percent of those who enroll eventually graduate from the college.

Settling down at a long table in the rustic dining hall, Tony observes that the meal before him cost less than $1.

"And the food is consistently good here. They have limited choices, but excellent food, I think. Different dorms take over all the work in the dining room, preparing the vegetables, washing the dishes, mopping the floors. . . ." (The floors, it must be said, are dirt-streaked from the most recent mopping and the food is, at best, noninstitutional.) "This is in addition to Work Day. That student cutting trees at the parking lot is a poet. Part of the contract of Goddard students is that they must contribute one day a week of work to the place. It's absolutely essential to the running of the College, but it also provides an important change of pace for the students."

Student work days save about $150,000 a year in operating costs. On an annual operating budget the financial office will describe only as "around five million dollars," the work obviously is vital to the solvency of the College. Goddard has no endowment. Its operating funds come almost exclusively from student payments, supplemented by federal "work-study" and opportunity grants which are distributed to the students. Since 40–45 percent of the students receive financial aid of some kind, Goddard's undergraduates are financing others of their classmates as well as themselves. With only 750 undergraduates, Goddard's expenditures are high. Antioch College, with a bigger physical plant and nearly two thousand students, had a budget of $5.5 million the same year (albeit with a deficit of $1.27 million hanging over its head). Various guesses place the Goddard deficit—a fact of life in higher education—at anywhere from zero to over $1 million.

If students are away from campus four months of every twelve and they work to defray costs, why does Goddard charge $4,350 a year per student?

"The short answer is that Goddard depends entirely on tuition. There's no endowment worth talking about. All this work is essential to avoid the costs going up even higher than they are already. Most students accept it, and most rather enjoy their jobs, I think. The question is still very open, nevertheless."

Tony excuses himself to get dessert. He pauses to speak with a hot-eyed, intense young Puerto Rican who is one of two elected student trustees. There is a heated exchange about a plan to reduce administrative services. The heat is largely on the part of the student. When Tony leaves the table, it is clear that the student is still dissatisfied.

"That's Joe Perez. Very interesting guy. Older, sharp. He was someone who did not get a chance to go to college earlier. He's here now because Goddard is paying his way, and he's being crazy. No one seems to like him. I kind of do."

Tony is silent, thoughtful. A dog ambles by, sniffs the tail of a German Shepherd lying under a table. Dogs are a matter of fierce debate on campus. Many feel that the packs of dogs that roam the campus freely are responsible for this spring's dearth of deer and rabbits and chipmunks. Others note the possibility of fox-carried rabies. The local police have threatened to shoot on sight any dog not properly licensed. Still, they are everywhere, for there are no locked doors at Goddard.

"Joe is the leader of the dissident group here. They've gotten together and published what they call an ultimatum to the President of the College. Basically it involves reducing administrative services very drastically indeed. They put a lot of work into it and came up with a very detailed budget. They put a lot of hard research into the actual costs of the college. Now they feel this hasn't had an adequate hearing. Without asking him to buy the President's reorganization plan—which

186

is a very controversial document here—I felt the students should cooperate on a certain level without compromising their total position. This is a classical revolutionary dilemma."

He turns this over in his mind, then decides he must make another point about the Goddard experience.

"A college like this attempts, in many ways, to be run along collective lines. This does not mean that everyone is forced to join in every aspect of work, but if a large number of people don't join in, the system won't work. It's easier to run a communal system in a small school like Friends World College than a place even the size of Goddard.

"Unfortunately, families pay for Goddard, and parents are often reluctant to support students going to a school like this. It has a very free lifestyle, and when middle-class parents from Queens find out that they've paid $4,600 for their daughter to live in a hippie-type dorm, where drugs are sold openly and where there's a great deal of sexual acting-out, all in order to learn to play the Javanese gamelan, do glass blowing, and take a course in Celtic literature . . ."

He leaves the thought uncompleted. It is time for a community council meeting. In this case, "community" refers to the Goddard community, not the town of Plainfield. The people of Goddard seem to hold themselves aloof from the people of Plainfield, but few town–gown strains are apparent. This is unusual, for in almost any community dominated by even a small college or university, suspicion and long-nourished animosities are the rule. Although chambers of commerce characteristically tout the presence of a college as an asset, townspeople as frequently mutter about long-haired Commie dope fiends despoiling the landscape and their children. The eminence of the institution exacerbates this friction, if anything, for the odor of privilege and sanctuary is still more pervasive. Both Yale and Harvard, for example, have been pressured by their host communities to make substantial contributions to municipal coffers in lieu of taxes on their exempt properties. A New Haven politico sandbagged a $16 million Yale construction project in 1973 in a transparent effort to force the university into making larger contributions to the city. His quoted remarks at the time highlighted the antagonisms present in every proletarian community with an aristocratic academic haven in its midst:

"They were flabbergasted. They thought they owned us. They are going to have to realize that we are not peasants and they are not the manor on the hill. They are going to have to come down off their high horse and change their relationship with us."

On the way to the meeting, Tony encounters other faculty members and students. With one, he talks about his two daughters, both of whom have undertaken study at experimental colleges such as Friends World. With a harried administrator, he discusses room assignments. He comes upon Joe Perez again, and, after a few words, the clenched set of Joe's jaw softens just a bit. The council meeting, held in a small cabin nearby that serves as an art studio, is attended by five young men. All of them could be students, but two are professors. As most of the other Goddardites seen during the day, they share an earnest solemnity. Apart from Tony Pearce, there is much of the true believer in those committed to non-traditional education, with a not always kindly tolerance for those who have yet to see the light. Pearce shares their conviction of the efficacy of experimental education, but not the defensive zealotry found among many of his colleagues. The meeting, which covers a variety of topics with no discernible solution, breaks up when one professor announces he must go tell someone how good her third-year proposal is, despite the fact he hasn't read it yet.

Afterwards, Tony talks about his evolution from traditionalist to innovator.

"The London School of Economics was a series of disconnected lecture courses, sometimes given by brilliant lecturers,

188

sometimes by big names who couldn't lecture. In my last year there, I started naïvely asking questions: Where did the social sciences come from? What are they trying to do and what connection do they have with each other? What were their moral objectives and wherein lay their unity? By and large, I was patted on the head for being a bright boy to ask such questions. In many ways, my graduate work was an attempt to find out for myself—by reading in the history of the social science disciplines. I concluded that there was an absurd sort of *inefficiency* at the London School. I'm enormously interested in trying to get highly condensed sorts of dynamic pictures of a world in change. For all the work I did at the London School, I had not been successful in creating in my mind any kind of useful working model of world trade, of commodity flow. Now after years of graduate study I find myself working toward that. When I look back at the earlier work, I find it hard to see that there was anything of permanent value except the questions I took away from there.

"When I followed those questions in graduate school, I was supposed to be in another program which demanded highly abstract answers and exercises. But I went ahead and followed my own concerns. In consequence, when I came up to take my Ph.D. exams, three of the committee were in favor of flunking me and the other three wanted to give me an 'A.' No one had received an 'A' in political philosophy for the last seven years. So they sent me back for a year, saying it would be good for my soul. I continued my search largely as before. When I came back, it was the same result—three to three. The third time, they unanimously voted to give me an 'A.' But you see, what's educational efficiency, really? What's efficient about presenting bodies of abstract knowledge which are not connected to recognizable human concerns? And I don't even necessarily mean urgent concerns for social change, but just plain old human curiosity. All the work I did in economics never once gave me an introduction to cooperative principles, and my work in sociology never drew me to the whole notion of a planned intentional community. Yet now this is the crux of my concern."

What is a planned intentional community?

"It's the classical name for what we often call a commune—as opposed to a community which grows organically through the individual choice of many people. A 'planned intentional community' is where people come together voluntarily and purposefully to build toward definite ends and goals and usually sharing some or all their property."

Is Goddard a planned intentional community?

"To an extent. And I'm convinced that the kind of efficiency of education I was talking about is greater with this type of environment."

Having come to that conclusion in graduate school fifteen years ago, why did he go through ten years of teaching in such traditional places as Mount Holyoke and New York University?

"It was a very, very gradual thing for me. I had been a member of the Society of Friends—the Quakers—for many years. After I moved to New York, I became more and more involved in Quaker operations, so I was not held so much within the confines of a secular job and a culturally isolated suburban home. I was in touch with the Society of Friends and involved in action projects. When I taught at Berkeley and NYU, I was teaching about peace-and-war issues and was also involved in the peace movement. But I treated the things as separate. I recognized the basic personal connection, but when I taught I would try to very objectively do justice to the times. I would have been appalled if anyone had felt I was proselytizing for the peace movement. I took a general position in favor of peace and against war, but apart from that, I felt I had to be rather detached.

"Then at that teach-in at NYU, I offered my analysis of

how the United States had become involved in Vietnam. I read a lecture to them, something that I put together very, very carefully. At two in the morning, the hall was jampacked with people, and they all got up and applauded. Afterwards, groups of students collared me and said, 'Well, what do we do now? How do we get out of this?' I was startled and they pushed me on that point. My interest in Quaker activities began to focus on the peace effort."

At about the same time, an effort was begun to create a new college, based on Quaker principles. Its campus was to be the world, its students working at centers in Mexico, Kenya, England, India, Japan, Los Angeles, and Long Island. Its educational perspective was to be utterly new, its method, of course, experimental. Tony worked with the founder of the college at the Long Island center as a member of the summer faculty in 1963. They had twenty-six students from twenty-six countries. Tony felt he had found the vehicle to meld his convictions and his professional skills. He worked hard for the establishment of Friends World, first as a part-time teacher; then in 1967, he left NYU to become a full-time faculty member. The loss of academic rank, tenure, and title seemed— and still does—unimportant. His evolving belief in the efficiency of learning in an experimental situation took on a more concrete form.

Tony is fond of pointing with pride to students he has known at Friends World and Goddard. He describes Sanno Keeler as one of his most gifted. She and one other student found positions at the Gombi Stream Reservation in Africa, where Jane Goodall was studying animal behavior under natural conditions. At first, the two students typed notes and made tea. They read the research drafts as they typed, relating these to their own experiences with chimps and other animals around the compound. Their interest stimulated, they moved into other related literature, then actual field work. Standard zoological texts were available to them, but, within six weeks, they were doing field observations six days a week, twelve hours a day.

"I can imagine no better way of education," Tony insists, "than to start right off working with people doing the things in which you're interested. The Smithsonian Institution regarded the preparation of the Friends World students as so superior that they gave employment to a number of them in India. Their senior theses were published as articles in the proceedings of the Smithsonian Institution. Now, at the very least—*at the absolute rock-bottom minimum*—these Friends World students were doing work which was superior to almost all master's degrees being done in ethnology."

When Sanno Keeler was ready, Pearce sought an appropriate person to conduct her senior year external exam. He wanted a "humanist scholar concerned with integrated learning" to determine if Sanno was, by that person's standards, "a well-educated human being." He asked Dr. Carl Rogers of the California Center for Studies of the Person to speak with Sanno, assessing her sensitivity to others, her imagination, her analytical skills, and her preparation in comparison with that of graduates of other kinds of colleges. Tony was very pleased with Dr. Rogers' reply:

My examination was based on a quite extensive reading of different portions of Sanno's journal and a one and one-half hour oral examination. I found it genuinely incredible to think that a girl of Sanno's age could have had the breadth and depth of intercultural experiences that she has had. She has faced solitude in a foreign culture, hard living conditions, faced very difficult personal and group problems . . . and is unquestionably the best-educated world citizen I have ever seen at her age. . . . I found her an open, growing person with an awareness of the strength she has developed during her four years and also quite capable of a realistic assessment of her own educational weaknesses as well as [those] of the curriculum of the Friends World College. There is no doubt, for example, that she has slighted or been unable to have the resources for such subjects as mathematics and science. This, however, is more than compensated for by the richness of her experience in other directions. It is also obvious that one of the beauties of this kind of self-directed learning is that the person never feels that she is fully educated but is sharply aware of the learnings which are still ahead of her.

Walking back across the Greatwood campus to his car, Tony stops to speak with other students. Most of them smile, unbidden, at the stranger with Tony. Others cock their heads in mild curiosity. Once inside Tony's battered Volvo, he says he will take the long route—"Pearce's Pretty Places Package Tour."

What does working at Goddard as a faculty member mean to him in concrete terms, personally and professionally?

"I think of myself not so much as a member of the faculty but as a member of the college community. A very privileged member, indeed. I only work eight months of the year, closer to seven months, in fact. And while my pay is modest over the whole year, when I work I get paid more than $2,000 a month, which is not starvation pay."

But it's certainly less than he would get at a conventional college, isn't it?

"Oh, yeah. But Goddard has an incredible number of attractions. It's the mystique of experimental education. So many professors themselves feel trapped in the classroom instruction and want to get the hell out of it."

Tony points to an unusual old round barn. His passenger observes that, in the main, this country seems an economically poor area.

"Oh, definitely. This is one of the real problems around here—the genuine problem of rural poverty. It's really very difficult. . . . Anna and I happen to be rather wealthy, and this is one issue about living here. In the bad old days I used to drive a Ferrari . . . but I just don't do things like that now. When we came up here, we did not want to live a wealthy New York lifestyle. We came up here to live relatively simply and we don't have particularly extravagant tastes. We have a 140-year-old farmhouse which we thought about furnishing with antiques. . . . Now it's odds and ends of stuff . . . but then there'd be that anxiety about being ripped off."

He wants to change the subject, so he waves at the view beyond the windows as the Volvo begins to strain up into the hills. The car churns up roads that turn from ragged macadam to firm gravel to rutted mud, past increasingly large farms with two and three hundred acres of now fallow land, ungrazed and unplowed. Most of them are for sale, he says, resignedly, and inevitably they will be snapped by developers. From high broad rolling fields, the road suddenly plunges into woods. Tony notes that his land starts here. Still the car goes up, and in a few minutes stops at an unprepossessing structure hugging the road. On the other side, a white Samoyed named Tushka leaps about at the end of a long tether, ecstatic at the sight of his master. Tony goes to free him.

The air is markedly crisper here. It was a difficult winter, foot after foot of snow. Tony is looking forward to clearing some land this summer, after they return from England, and his wife Anna plans to break in a new horse. She is also taking off the fall trimester from her own teaching job at Goddard, because Tony says she has had a rough year. After he had ended his first marriage and met Anna, they decided they wanted to live in the country. As it happened, there were jobs for both of them at Goddard. Tony glows as he says that Anna beat out several other candidates for the job.

"I was incredibly proud of her. But then she had an incredible amount of work pressed on her. This last term, she had to carry all the load in the elementary teaching course."

The front door opens into a warm room that used to be the summer kitchen. Tony calls for Anna, then goes to another part of the house to speak with her about the events of the day. They return to sit at a large table by the window which looks out on a spectacular panorama of the Wooster Mountains.

When the tea is ready and Anna has located the brownies, the conversation turns to experiences at other experimental colleges and about Tony's pleasure at dealing with the students at Goddard.

"They're really charming. One of the things I love about life is the strangeness of individuals, how remarkable and strange people are. A place like Goddard permits this to come out. That kind of strangeness flourishes around here, as in a tropical jungle. It grows rank and runs riot and all sorts of strange forms emerge. It's fun. Fascinating."

Tony, despite his willing receptivity to people, has a very personal, private dimension, a part of him he won't bare to others. Anna presents the same quality. Don't they have any difficulty with their lives being so involved with the College? No, they say. They strike a fair balance between the College and their lives here.

"We're only pursued by our own thoughts," Anna says.

Tony nods. "That's something else again."

"Every once in a while Tony will look at me and say, 'Let's leave Goddard behind.' "

"Teaching at an experimental college," he says, "is a very exciting, anxiety-producing process. Inevitably you get teachers, especially older ones, who are asking students to do things they haven't done themselves. There are real questions about the legitimacy of this, about the validity of what they are doing for students fifteen or twenty years younger than they. In time, these experimental colleges will be increasingly staffed by people who are themselves graduates of this kind of college. Many of the teachers here have to go through a process of re-education which can be very hard and very painful."

"The other thing I find," says Anna, "is that it is all very fragmented. Students go off on non-resident term or on vacation, and it's very hard to keep some sort of continuity. When Goddard works best is when a counselor really sees a student and can do some guiding and talking on a regular basis. It's very hard when you're trying to get self-motivated students to know what kinds of requirements or contracts you can make in a course . . . and then try to stick to it."

Doesn't it take a special breed of student for this form of education to work?

"It depends," Anna says. "I don't really see a good cross-section, because I'm teaching in teacher ed, and most of our students are more together and motivated than most others."

Because of their professional goal?

"Yes, because they have a sense of direction. Also, we're always working with kids in the field, so they have real experiences to judge themselves against.

"Talking about anxiety . . . I was speaking with one of the teachers who's been here about five years. His feeling is that faculty people come to Goddard as their counterculture. I mean it's not just a job. It's something they personally invest in as a lifestyle, something they want to see succeed. At this point, with Goddard in the shape it's in, that's where the anxieties come in."

In the shape it is financially?

"Yes. And the faculty not very together, pressure from the external degree programs—they're getting bigger and the resident program isn't—all that's part of it."

External degree programs?

"Yes, the Adult Education Program is really one of the very exciting programs around. Each student comes here to Goddard for two two-week cycles and does independent study, corresponding with faculty for the six months in between. It's very much a program for people who are really doing something in the outside world. Another program Tony and I are excited about is called the Goddard Experimental Program for Further Education. It's for lower-income people, sort of like AEP, but with weekend work and more frequent contact along with the independent study."

Are there moments when she'd like a more conventional authoritarian structure?

"I do wish the faculty would get itself together to develop a really strong academic philosophy where the checkpoints were a little more consistent. I don't think there should be any radical changes, just that we could do better in terms of evaluation and careful planning. But I don't just see my students in class, I have regular conferences with them, I really get to know them. That's the great part about the place."

Then why the feelings of discouragement Tony expressed?

"I feel very overloaded, too many students to do well with, very fragmented. You can be just constantly thinking about Goddard's issues and Goddard's problems. I mean, it's never-ending. The responsibilities aren't clear, either. You can teach two, or you can teach four courses in a term, with ten or twenty students, fewer counselees or more. The loads are very unevenly distributed."

During lunch, Tony had spoken of the need for students leaving the classroom to find people who are "future-oriented." With the pummeling of values, Tony had said, the impact of scientific discovery on those values, and the changing perceptions that had been caused, young people were being forced to develop new standards and new ideals. He said he had felt that a shift from Aristotelian logic to a more pragmatic approach for higher education was critical, that it must be oriented toward changes taking place in the world right now. Given those futurist beliefs, how did he reconcile this with an institution exemplifying the alternate lifestyle, the back-to-the-earth

197

withdrawal from society? Most of the people of the civilized world live in cities. How was it going to help students to learn how to be blacksmiths or how to make water wheels?

"I am convinced," he replies, "that it is wise to assume that the future of the world—if it is to be a decent future—is going to be tied in with a new attitude toward the rural areas. The problems of the cities have their roots in the countryside. This was a dairy farm. It's no longer operating because the Hood dairy company bought many of the local creameries and began closing them down and shipping the milk to Boston. Except in a town called Cabot. They held on to their creamery and turned it into a cooperative. Now that is a town of flourishing dairy farms, with a lot more vitality than most of the other communities around here. I am interested more and more in towns like Cabot, which may have a small industry or two and which gradually *could* include a blacksmithing job. It could be someone settling there to do very practical welding jobs, along with an old forge for doing ornamental iron work. I hope that the future is going to be in that direction. Not only here, but throughout the entire world. The revival of rural life and culture is the thing most needed."

Along with the decentralization it would bring?

"Along with decentralization."

And dispersal of concentrated populations?

"Right. And with that decentralization, the reduction of the power of nation–states." He pauses a moment, marshalling arguments. "I read David Lilienthal's book published in the mid-Thirties called *TVA: Democracy on the March.* Right in the preface, Lilienthal said the basic reason he supported TVA was the question of how to reduce the power of the nation–state. He said we're going to do it by breaking the nation into functional regions. He suggested working around river basins as a natural kind of unit and transfer power from the central to the regional area. Along with the dams of the TVA system, you had to re-educate farmers and their agricultural style or the dams would have been useless. They would have silted up in twenty-five or thirty years. That meant contour plowing, reforestation. TVA planted twenty million trees in the first two years. That whole area was denuded of trees and is now getting to have fine forests again. Farming, which was absolutely appalling, has now become prosperous there. With local control for soil conservation districts, you see, you begin to reduce the power of nation–states. I could have come to this point of view by staying in the library and doing some intelligent reading. Except no one I knew (back in the city) was talking this way. Everyone was locked into basic assumptions about the profession of political science—the principle of hierarchy, taking the nation–state for granted. I had to get out of there and find people who were not prepared to take it for granted, to begin to even dream about alternatives."

How does he describe himself now to other people? What is his identity?

"I look at them in a glazed sort of way when they ask what I do at Goddard. I say I do quite a few things, which is accurate. Then they try to pin me down: Well, what do you teach? I say: I don't teach. So they say: Oh, what *are* you doing? Then I say: Come to think of it, I do teach some. I've become very evasive. No doubt about that, is there, dear?"

He reaches across the table to squeeze Anna's hand, laughing.

"What *do* you do, To?" she teases.

Anna leaves to brew more tea, then to dress for the evening. They're meeting friends for dinner down in Hanover. There is a quiet moment, watching the sun sliding in a low arc to the mountains across the valley.

His identity? the visitor prompts.

"Certain Quaker beliefs have become more and more a part of me. I hold to a few beliefs which are very simple and very strong. There is something divine within each human being,

199

therefore each human being is deserving of respect. Each human being is unique in the particular ways in which he can express his own being. The Quaker discipline is not a set of dogmas, but a set of questions, and this has come to influence me a great deal. Both intellectually and in terms of spiritual belief this guiding oneself by questions becomes more important to me. It's a humanist belief for one who no longer believes conventional religious dogma, but who has retained the ethics of that religion."

He excludes then, the possibility of a superior being?

"Definitely. The idea of a superior being is a human construct. I find myself smiling with the Chinese Confucian sages who met the Dominican monks who came to them through the deserts in the Middle Ages. The Chinese sages were tremendously interested in the ways in which these Westerners could make calendars and clocks, but when they heard the story of our Western teaching of God as a king in heaven, they looked back among their ancient records and found that, yes, there was a time somewhere back in an ancient dynasty where the Chinese felt that, too. But they had now dispensed with the notion.

"I do find myself heir to the ethics of this faith, and in Quakerism I feel profound respect and gratitude for those who created these simple, strong beliefs. Yet I do not have the sense of a ruling, judging God to sustain me, or, for that matter, to regulate me. Instead, my theology owes a great deal to my studies of science, particularly astrophysics and biochemistry. These show me a world of almost unbelievable beauty and wonder whose conception I do not attempt to analyze in mere human terms. The particular scientific work which fascinates me is that on the probability of forms of intelligent life on other planets. We will build new myths of immortality from contemplation of the origins and probable future of the organic atoms of which we are organized.

"I was at a conference a couple of years ago at MIT and

200

heard Carl Oglesby, one of the founders of SDS. He said that at the heart of the revolutionary change of our time is a renewed search for the sacred. I was very moved by that, and I think it is true. The search proceeds by quietness, understatement, and a great sense of uncertainty, lack of assurance and direction."

A great many professors concede, with prodding, that one of their greatest satisfactions is getting up before a class and spinning off some well-developed intellectual concepts. Tony's ego-needs seem less strong.

"On the contrary. I certainly enjoy just exactly that kind of thing, very much indeed. One of the things Anna must put up with in our marriage every now and then is when I get together with someone who has been, or is, a professor and reads a lot, who is full of information and opinions about everything under the sun. When that happens, I start talking an enormous amount. I have a weird mixture of information but very strong opinions. And Anna often has to listen while I go into this performance."

Anna, who has returned to the room, nods vigorously.

"But my ego-needs right now are to find educational ideas and get them realized in programs. I think this comes largely from my astonishment about where I've been in life. I have rarely set an ambition for myself. I've gone much more at the intuitive level. Reflection on my own experiments in life has made me open to young people who are searching. People are moved by what I call their "hidden agenda"—the things they will and might do in life if they are in touch with themselves. It's a marvelous thing to find someone who's confused about where they want to go, and suddenly, from intuition, put them in touch with their hidden agenda . . ."

"Another way of putting it," Anna interjects, "is that we try to help students *give themselves permission* to do things they've been educated not to do."

How did Tony Pearce come to this point? What personal

201

"agenda" led him here? He was born in the duchy of Cornwall, in a border town between Cornwall and the rest of England. Not far away, on a freehold farm of sixty acres, his fertile grandparents had produced four sons and two daughters. One of the daughters married a local miller, a son became a carpenter in St. Ives. Tony's father left school to join the army. The family was solidly of the yeoman class (the British peasantry, in the honored sense of the word). Tony's father returned, educated himself, became a journalist for a local paper. As such, he showed ability which was recognized by the local member of parliament and was subsequently rewarded with the post of constituency agent for the Liberal Party of North Cornwall. It was an organizational job, not only for elections, but for interceding with the bureaucracy, arranging social functions, hearing grievances. So successful was he that he never lost an election, and continued in the post for the rest of his life.

When Tony entered grammar (secondary) school at the age of twelve, he became a successful layabout and hookey-player. By the time he was fourteen he was twenty-first in a class of twenty-two, and by fifteen he was thrown out of school. His father was away in the army at the time—it was 1943—but his mother leaned hard on him, and he managed to do well enough on the Oxford matriculation examination. He didn't do well enough to win a scholarship, though, and was then drafted himself. He became an army officer after a nine-month training period he remembers as both physically tough and intellectually vigorous. It was the first time in his life he had worked in such a challenging program. He was asked to accept a regular commission and seriously considered it. But peace came, and Tony became bored. He started playing hookey again, and thinking once more about college. Then he resigned his commission as a conscientious objector.

He discovered with horror that Oxford and Cambridge required Latin. Hearing that a place called the London School of Economics *didn't* demand Latin, he decided to take their entrance exam. Economics sounded vaguely interesting, and he thought a degree in the subject might help him support himself. Of over 700 applicants, 200 were admitted. Tony was one. After a pleasant summer traveling around Europe, he showed up at the London School two weeks late for registration. He filled out a brief form, and they told him to come back in three years and take fifteen three-hour exams. The registrar gave him a library card, a list of lectures he might attend if he wished, and a tutor he could see if he wanted.

Living in tiny rooms around Russell Square, he again became absorbed. He read every book on every reading list handed out. Wrapping himself in a blanket so he wouldn't have to put coins in the gas fire, he began reading every morning. at seven o'clock. The electric light was free. He sustained the regimen five days a week, never doing a stroke of work on weekends or in the summers, when he hitchhiked around the Mediterranean. He graduated with a first class honors degree—one of eight in the class—and an American wife who had studied in London on a Fulbright. He accepted a fellowship at the University of California and they moved to Berkeley. American social science was, he felt, years ahead of England and Europe, where the field was then still regarded with some suspicion.

Increasingly, he became interested in the problems of peace and war between nation–states, of imperialism. In his doctoral dissertation, he dwelt upon the ways in which the governments of nation–states induced their citizens to engage in war. As he worked on the thesis, he focused even more upon why people risk their lives to kill others. At the end of that very abstract and theoretical study, he realized that all this had come very directly from his own experience. He was the son of a man who had fought all through World War I and had been seriously wounded. Tony himself had been a commissioned officer and had resigned. All these deep, personal things were

203

expressing themselves in his work. It was then that he felt he could ask his father what his service in the First World War had meant to him.

Now, in the summer kitchen of the old farmhouse in East Calais, Vermont, Tony hands his father's letter to his visitor. Then he leaves to dress for dinner. The letter was written May 2nd, 1960. Tony's father died shortly thereafter.

"Dear Tony,

How pleased I was to get your letter, if only to feel that you could still write to the "old firm" and ask for my opinion. It was a nice thought on your part and I hope I shall not disappoint you.

When I first went to war I put Patriotism very high in my outlook. To me, it meant that I was offering myself and my service to maintain and put forward a series of ideals which were incorporated in England of the time. I remember telling my Dad, the morning I left home, quite young, for active service, that I felt just like the Crusaders must have felt when they too went on active service many years before.

This feeling persisted and I am certain that it helped many of us to bear privations and hunger, to withstand pain and suffering, and to comfort those who passed on.

And yet Tony life has since taught me that whilst I was perhaps right to think that way then, war can never in itself be the means of men understanding each other—or only after the bitterness and hatreds of war have been softened and blotted out by mutual understanding and cooperation after war is over.

The real patriotism is the feeling and desire to look upon ourselves and our neighbors, whatever their country or colour of their skin, their race or religion, as being equals. Not perhaps in the wealth of this world, not perhaps in their education, not perhaps in their outlook, but in the sight of God.

It is not often I think of war and all its memories. It

was the after period that meant most. We suffered, like Christ, but in a greatly lesser way, for the future and for mankind to live as men and not to be caged and to lose the right to be free men. In the first War, I believe we nearly all felt that unless we (our side) prevailed, the world would sink back into a jungle life in which decent free men and women would be hunted and exterminated unless they accepted a life that was slavery to them.

Men with little education would often discuss this with others of deeper knowledge and education, and the second would often learn from the former on fundamental things, of "losing the little to retain the greater" when freedom was being discussed, of those who would come after and what we owed to them. That was what patriotism meant to those men. To be able to save and pass on those things which they cherished. Decency, freedom of expression, of religion, of the vote, of democracy.

Perhaps my clearest memory of suffering was to be shot down whilst carrying a fellow Warrant Officer, himself mortally wounded, and to see my life ebbing fast. I do not remember feeling sorry in any way that I had exposed myself to danger. But a stretcher-bearer braved a perfect hail of bullets and got to me and stopped the flow and I was dragged back to safety. He did not count the possible cost. To him it was a duty, and that was his vision of patriotism.

Four of my men carried me over two miles on a stretcher and risked being shot for being behind the lines . . . they knew I would have done the same for them. That was how they viewed patriotism. . . . Duty, love of men for men . . . submerged any thought of danger or holding back.

That journey had more hours of pain and danger, of being lashed to an ammunition carrier until the back of my head was almost a pulp, of nearly being captured by the Germans, of having a tourniquet on for thirty-six hours and retaining my arm even though the doctors told me that life would be lost. . . . In life, from time to time, there must be conflict. Without it there would be no real addition to knowledge or any real advance. I mean by conflict the pitting of one's thoughts and memories against each other in a striving to find the best, to live and to give in life.

Patriotism is not enough but it is the kernel of many good things in those we love, esteem, admire. . . . For those things we have the same feelings that the patriot has for his country and his freedoms. *But life is the goal.* It is now 11:30. Mum is alone as Jill went to a post in Warwickshire today. It is time I went home. My love to you all. As ever,

Dad

Tony returns to the summer kitchen, his hair now combed back over his ears, dressed in clean shirt and trousers and wondering whether he must wear a tie. Noting that the letter has been read, he scans the visitor's face, decides to say nothing. The sun is a red ball touching the rim of hills across the valley.

CHAPTER 10

The only abiding thing is change, but the past should control it, or at least its pace. How else are we to know anything? What is the use of empty "rationalists," such as were discovered at many a university some years ago, who, being confronted with various demands for instant change, found that they believed nothing and could not judge any change as better or worse than another? They drove the very seekers after change up the wall in frustration. Nobody wants everybody not to believe in anything. . . .

In our time of dogma to the left and dogma to the right . . . when "rival follies" mutually wage an unrelenting war, a time when change is widely counted a self-evident virtue, an age of futurism and millennarianism, there is much to learn from Burke. . . . "Men thirst after power," he wrote, and whether they want it "vested in the many or the few" depends chiefly on their estimate of their own chance to exercise it.

The words are Alexander Bickel's, writing about Edmund Burke. The *Times* describes Bickel as a "leading [C]onstitutional expert and specialist in the First Amendment." The dean of another law school calls him a "mossback." Bickel says he's a Whig.

After graduating from Harvard Law School, Bickel was

Supreme Court Justice Felix Frankfurter's law clerk, and campaigned for the Kennedys. He successfully defended *The New York Times* in the Pentagon Papers case, was AFTRA's lawyer in its suit against William F. Buckley (who didn't want to join the union), and has been a contributing editor to the liberal organ the *New Republic* since 1957. He is also a professor of law at Yale University.

Bickel's views and ideology defy facile classification, a distressing circumstance for those insistent upon their own unchallenged freedom of choice while demanding that everyone else stand in place for pigeon-holing. Alexander Bickel is a moving target. In addition to working for conventionally liberal men and publications, he is against capital punishment and believed the White House should have released the Watergate tapes long before they did. On the other hand, he is a close friend of minor liberal demon Robert Bork (who fired Archibald Cox), agrees with the 1972 Supreme Court anti-obscenity rulings, and remains uncertain about the morality of abortion. Although he exudes a well-bred Brahmin-style competence, he emigrated from Rumania in 1939 at the age of fourteen.

He concedes no inconsistency in either his views or his activities and does not invoke Emerson's "hobgoblin of little minds" rejoinder. That would suggest defensiveness and hauteur. Bickel is not defensive.

What he thinks and how he acts is important to any assessment of the professoriate, for he exemplifies a segment of his profession which wields considerable influence beyond the campus. To his possession of a body of knowledge of immediate applicability in the larger society, Bickel adds a solid forum in which to circulate his views *and* a powerful and prestigious home base that lends his pronouncements impact beyond measure. (Consider the attention likely to be afforded an equally gifted man employed by, say, South Dakota State University. The Eastern Establishment lives.) Yet Bickel is, first and foremost, a college professor, not a lawyer or diplomat who happens to teach. His views are more worthy of examination than those of most professors because people in positions of influence solicit them.

Here in his office at the law school, he has accepted a telephone call from a United States senator. During the course of this muggy June morning, he receives calls from his editor at the *New Republic*, from a Connecticut assemblyman, from a colleague at Harvard Law, and again from the senator. The room is Campobello-summer-cottage in style. It is also very hot, but there is no air conditioning, probably because the machines would spoil the external lines of the Gothic building. Anyway, one suspects that Bickel doesn't sweat.

He does weary of explaining the personal principles that shape his evaluations of events and issues, however. When pressed, as now, he sighs with genteel impatience.

"I'm a very particular kind of liberal. I'm a conservative in my judicial functions and in my judicial philosophy. I supported Robert Kennedy in 1968 because he was my kind of liberal. To my mind, many of the things he was saying were echoes of Brandeis. I worked with McGovern, though I was distressed with his campaign. I vote Democratic almost always. But in academic politics and attitudes toward the counter-culture and the 'greening'—or browning—of America, I've been staunchly conservative. I thought Charlie Reich's book was an infantile production." (Reich was a law professor.) "I've done many other things that would be classified as 'liberal,' but I've done them in my own way, for my own reasons.

"I have no objection to people using these 'location' terms, so to speak, but I know what I am. I fall on my own nose."

The particular key to his philosophies as seen in his writings appears to be a carefully tuned and scholarly balance: His disinclination to accept mass judgments is counterweighted by an insistence upon mass consent, his conditional pragmatism by skeptical idealism, his appreciation of what has been by a gingerly recognition of what must yet be done. In others, all this might result in perpetual indecisiveness and ethical waffling. In the student upheavals of the last decade, as Bickel pointed out in the article quoted above, that's exactly what happened. Faculty people caved in before the onslaught of the first discouraging words, because they didn't really know where they stood.

Bickel, on the other hand, knows where he is on virtually every issue, and if what he says or does today fits liberal dogma, and tomorrow, conservative cant, he knows how he got there.

The Watergate hearings are underway at this moment. National ennui has not yet set in. The proceedings are perversely gratifying to liberals—most of them eager that the conspirators continue to be publicly skewered. The same liberals were appalled at the investigations conducted by Joe McCarthy and demanded an end to them. As Bickel has said he favors the Ervin hearings, his visitor wonders aloud whether he falls into the same inconsistency.

"I happen to be in the fortunate position of having said the same thing then. I didn't like McCarthy. There are *ways* to conduct investigations. I also said the same thing about Robert Kennedy, for whom I later campaigned. There are ways of conducting investigations that are an invasion of civil liberties, and they were doing it the wrong way. But I said then that the power of Congress to investigate is essential, founded in the Constitution. You can't just say you'd rather do this by grand jury, make them stop, any more than you can say the grand jury must stop.

"That's what separation of powers is about. Separation of powers is not our problem, it's part of the *solution* of the problem. What happened with Watergate is that separation of powers is not working. These fellows locked themselves in the

White House and ran a Gaullist presidency. In the long run, that can't work. That's what we're now seeing."

But isn't the form of Congressional investigation more subject to abuse? Witnesses are pretty helpless before the innuendo and brow-beating and political harangues of the Congressman on the committee, who are themselves immune from legal retaliation. Aren't those serious deficiencies?

"Both are subject to abuse. I thought Judge Sirica abused his powers by using threats of enormous sentences to make these guys talk and by intervening in the trial. It's an abuse of power liberals regard indulgently because it worked out nicely. But suppose the defendants had been the Chicago Seven, rather than the Watergate Six or Eight or whatever it was? Liberals would have been up in arms!

"Congressional investigation is subject to considerable control by the Congress as a whole, and ultimately by the courts. I don't think the possibility of abuse is necessarily greater in one place than in the other. Maybe there are some differences in degree, but it doesn't matter that much. These hearings seem to me to have shown no abuse at all. They're not vigorous enough for my taste. They don't go after these guys. They're too bland. They don't push enough.

"One of the ways Bobby Kennedy abused power in some of those labor hearings in the late Fifties was that he'd get a guy he'd *know* was going to plead the Fifth Amendment. His lawyer *told* Bobby, but he put him on the stand anyway. He sat him there for an hour and asked him a hundred questions . . . to each of which the answer was the Fifth Amendment. And then Bobby'd end up saying, 'Ah ha! So you think all those questions would incriminate you. You must be guilty of something!' Now *that's* a form of imposing sentence on someone. McCarthy did it all the time."

Still, a man is called before the committee. There is an imposing panel of senators and high-powered lawyers. Aides scurry about. Television lights blaze down. And there is the witness—virtually alone. It seems a terribly super-heated situation, with all the odds against the witness.

"So it is in a grand jury," says Bickel. "You walk into a grand jury room and you don't even have your lawyer with you. You're *all* alone. There are twenty-five people shuttling in and out. If you don't answer a question, they take you right across the corridor before a judge. Now you can have your lawyer with you, but there's a judge on the bench. There's the eagle with the arrows in his claw. And any time you don't answer, you go to jail for contempt.

"That's worse than a Congressional committee. Before them, you have your lawyer with you. It's public. The press is there. If the committee is overbearing or abusive, they're doing it out in the open. If you don't answer, the committee has to go back and vote a citation of contempt against you. Then that has to go to the floor of the Senate or the House, and it has to be voted by a majority. And *then* it goes over to the U.S. attorney. He has to empanel a grand jury, they have to indict you. And then you get tried. That all might or might not happen two years later. It's much less intimidating and disturbing than to be called directly into a grand jury. In that room you are in an infinitely more frightening and overbearing situation than before a Congressional committee. There's no press, no public. Nobody to protect you, just you and them. You don't even know if you're the accused, or what they're investigating, or what they're after."

In light of his deep interest in Constitutional law and his salability as an attorney, why did Bickel choose to be a professor?

"A teaching career is a universal joint, whereas practice is a stationary thing. In practice you're tied to a very structured job—at least until quite late in life when you get some independence—whereas in a teaching career you can face any way you want.

"And don't overestimate the extent of my practice. It's not unusual, by any means. There are any number of law professors whose practice is more extensive than mine. What may be less usual is that I have a professorial career that includes both practice and fairly extensive scholarly and other written production.

"The great thing about an academic position is the independence. I am my own master. During term, a third of my time is given to being a citizen of this academic community—teaching and preparation, committee assignments, talking to students, making appearances at their groups."

That comes to about twenty hours a week during the academic year, none during the summer. It leaves ample time for the cases he chooses to undertake and for his writing, which has included five books in the last fifteen years. Given his success in the courtroom, he must be tempted from time to time to leave the campus. But he insists the options aren't always open, twenty-five years ago or now.

"In my thirties, I was at a low point of 'salability' as a lawyer. I was too senior to be taken in at the apprenticeship stage of practice, and not sufficiently experienced and established on my own to be worth the money to a law firm at a senior level appropriate to my age. Then in the next decade, when I got to be reasonably well known, established as a figure in a branch of the law, then I was again salable. Even that is not that clear.

"There are other attractions about law practice, but your imagination is pretty well captivated by the money factor. At the beginning, young people face starting at the bottom. It is not . . . um . . . *interesting* at the bottom. You begin as a law clerk in somebody's basement. It's another apprenticeship, after three years of law school and sixteen years of other schooling. It's not the most exciting thing. You have to have a high capacity for postponing gratification and let your imagination range pretty far into the future about the kind of career you'll have.

"The only thing you can tell for sure is that if you're any good you'll make a lot of money and live well. . . . But that's the only thing you can tell for sure."

Barring incompetence or a poorly located practice, a lawyer of any experience can charge an hourly fee of at least $60. Some charge as much as $120 an hour, but even that's not the ceiling. Even a green, middling graduate of a decent law school can anticipate a starting salary of $13,000 to $15,000, with the really good ones drawing $20,000 before the ink is dry on their diplomas. A powerhouse the likes of Clark Clifford reputedly accumulates as much as one million dollars a year.

"If I wanted to go into full-time practice, I could probably make an arrangement that was suitable, but it would take a while to do. Or I could take a chance and set up practice for myself. That's almost impossible to do any longer. If you get a batch of people together as the Fortas firm was formed twenty years ago, you can do it. But it's an investment, a risk.

"The much easier thing to do is to latch on to a going concern. But for that firm to keep you in the manner to which you've become accustomed means at least five figures to them. That money comes out of the pockets of the partners until you begin to displace the appropriate amount of water. The risk is transferred to them. It's their gamble—that you work out and earn your keep."

Nevertheless, it is a skill marketable outside the university. And many professors have the same choice. The stereotype of a classics teacher in a muffler and slipping eyeglasses is not extinct, but it's feeling poorly. Physicists and systems men and agronomists and labor economists (and doctors, dentists, and lawyers) who draw their paychecks from colleges can double and triple their incomes "on the outside." For many firms, the cachet that professorial consultants bring to their annual reports and sales meetings is almost as valuable as their services.

And the professor retains his freedom of choice because the college is a secure base. Bickel isn't going to throw in that hand.

"At my time of life, you don't have free choices. There's inertia, there's all kinds of things that come to bear on you so that you don't want to start fresh. You don't ask yourself at age forty-eight, 'Let's see, what would I rather do?' My life is arranged and it takes a fairly cataclysmic event to eject me out of that life. How many people change vocations? It's very rare in mid-career. It's got to be advantageous by several orders of magnitude.

"Whereas in a teaching career, the gratifications begin immediately."

And there is Yale, with its tradition, its highly regarded faculty, and remarkable students. It's one of the best, but it's not *the* best. Harvard is. That's really why The Game is so important every November. Yalies care if they win, Harvard men don't. Not really. Yale has the second largest university library in the United States. Harvard has the largest. Harvard pays its professors better. Harvard has a larger endowment. Harvard gets more applications for admission. Harvard is given more money by the government, alumni, and foundations. Harvard is in Cambridge, a city of some charm and much vitality. Yale is in New Haven, a city notable primarily for its knack for attracting urban renewal grants. The American Council on Education ranks Harvard's graduate liberal arts departments higher than Yale's. Harvard produces more baccalaureates, more M.D.'s, more Ph.D.'s.

But there is redemption. Outside of their respective alumni, it is virtually impossible to find a knowledgeable person prepared to commit himself on the relative quality or status or prestige of Harvard Law and Yale Law. It's a dead heat, and it's better than second.

All professors can reel off lists of the ten top departments in their fields, supplemented by comers and dark horses. Ask about law schools, and you hear something along these lines: "Well . . . Harvard and Yale, of course. Columbia, Stanford, Michigan, Pennsylvania. And Chicago. Duke, these days, maybe Northwestern, NYU. Some might include Virginia, or Cornell. But Harvard and Yale at the top. Of course."

That's what Bickel is talking about now—what makes a great law school. (There are 107 in the country.)

"They draw nationally," he is saying. "They're highly selective, they've traditionally been so. Their faculties are substantial men and women who write and are leading figures in their branches of law. They're active in other ways than their scholarship. They're at the top of the profession. That's what draws students, that's what draws more faculty of that sort. That's how these places maintain themselves. If you look at the student bodies of Yale and Harvard, on any quantifiable basis, they outrank everybody else. And the alumni . . . they are a group of men of marked achievement.

"There are cycles of change even in that. Some schools decay and others build themselves up."

But not Yale, not Harvard. In the sixty years since law schools came into their own, Yale Law and Harvard Law have always been at the top. And the rich get richer. That's one reason why Alexander Bickel remains, although he could undoubtedly make a comparable living as a full-time attorney. He has the best of both his worlds. He teaches law, and when he chooses, practices it. He seems to need that flexibility. There was the *Times*–Pentagon Papers case, for example.

"This was a great big interesting case and there were obviously two sides of it. I wouldn't have had any grave difficulty arguing the other side of it . . . any *moral* difficulty, although I felt quite comfortable on the side I was on. But I haven't taken cases, in the past, for a variety of reasons. If I don't particularly like my clients, for example. Or if I don't want to impair my position in a public forum. I never allowed myself to be retained to argue a school desegregation case precisely because I have testified on the subject before Congressional committees a dozen times, and I've been active in trying to draft legislation and influence the course of public policy. The minute I took one of these cases and became an employee of some party, my independence and my public expression of views on the issue would be impaired.

"I'm not in regular practice, I'm in academic life. I am what I am and who I am. If someone retains me, they don't just retain my technical skills, they retain my name. I have to keep an eye out for that.

"I have to feel free to like or dislike my client. If I dislike him I don't feel I'm obliged to take him on, at least not if he has adequate access to legal counsel. There were lawyers in the Fifties who wouldn't take one of the loyalty and security cases, who wouldn't accept a Communist for a client, or someone accused of Communist connections because it might've hurt the Continental Can account. They were doing the *wrong* thing. They were being derelict in the exercise of the responsibility the bar has.

"But if you're dealing with clients who have full access to the bar, they're not hurting. And if you're not in the general practice of law, as I'm not, then at least you're entitled to just plain not like your client. I haven't, many times. So even though I could comfortably argue their cases, even agree with them, I didn't take them on."

When he chooses, Bickel contributes his services. He helped Yale's activist chaplain, William Sloane Coffin, Jr., on a *pro bono publico* basis. Unpaid, that is. He testified against the Vietnam War before the Senate Foreign Relations Committee. He worked with George McGovern on the reform commission of the Democratic Party.

"I don't get anything for that sort of thing. It's a form of practicing public law, and everyone worth his soul does that. You do it because you want to, because you believe in it. It's gratifying, too, not a hateful chore. But it *is* unpaid."

As if to punctuate the remarks, the phone rings. It is the senator. Bickel's voice changes just a touch in tone. The conversation appears to relate to a point of law in the Watergate investigations. When Bickel hangs up, he is asked his opinion of the willing criminal fealty of Nixon's Pretorian Guard compared to the moralistic disloyalty of Daniel Ellsberg.

"First of all," Bickel responds, "I don't approve of what Ellsberg did. It was wrong. Whether it was a crime or not is another matter. That depends on statutes. It happens that our statutory body of law applicable to this kind of situation is very porous. Probably he committed no crime. That's not because what he did was right but because the laws aren't very good. And Ellsberg wasn't acquitted. He was *not* held innocent. His trial was frustrated by procedural difficulties. If there was any doubt about Ellsberg's guilt, it was because the laws weren't good enough to support a criminal prosecution.

"That may hold for some of Nixon's people, too. There are any number of things that may be charged to them that the criminal law doesn't necessarily cover. It covers breaking and entering quite nicely, and obstruction of justice. It happens that the Espionage Act of 1917 under which Ellsberg was tried is a statute full of holes. If one is persuaded—as I'm not—that Ellsberg was engaged in an act of civil disobedience which was legally wrong but morally justified, then we rejoice when he gets acquitted. Any healthy, decent system makes some allowance for acts of conscience which are considered morally right even though they may be technically wrong.

"If you hold that view—and I do not—you then have to ask yourself, can't that be said of Ehrlichman and Haldemann and Mitchell and the rest of those fellows? But they aren't citizens performing acts of civil disobedience. They were the guardians of the law, violating it. I don't have any hesitation in saying that there are no circumstances in which abuse of power can be equated with civil disobedience.

"The whole notion of civil disobedience is that the private conscience is entitled to resist the legal order. But corrupting and debasing the legal order on the part of those in whose charge it is . . . that's not tolerable. It never is. There's no tradition behind it. Civil disobedience goes back to Socrates. But this other thing goes back only to men viewing themselves as above all. That's never tolerable."

The calls are increasing, people are coming to the office. Bickel must excuse himself, with a promise to meet in the future.

That turns out to be three months later, at his home on a quiet, tree-shaded street in an expensive New Haven neighborhood. The Bickels economize with just one station wagon. He can walk to his office in fifteen minutes. His study is on the second floor, up the stairs from a living room in which the Los Angeles Rams could run pass patterns.

A few weeks back, Bickel had been quoted again in the *Times*. The Supreme Court's anti-obscenity rulings had just been released: "Prof. Alexander Bickel, who welcomed the Court's attempt to cut down on hardcore smut, suggested that the Court was hoping to draw the line between what is permissible, and what is not, 'somewhere between *Deep Throat* and *Last Tango in Paris.*'"

A few days later, he was invited to appear on the Dick Cavett Show as a member of a panel discussing the ruling. Arrayed in opposition to him were Truman Capote, Anthony Perkins, an Episcopalian clergyman, Bishop Moore, another lawyer, and Cavett himself, who felt no compulsion toward neutrality.

Perkins spent most of the time looking aghast, Capote was bored with the rampant ignorance around him, and the bishop was uncomfortably dogged. Bickel and the other lawyer dominated the discussion with courtly thrusts and parries. The audience groaned a lot, usually when Bickel patiently restated the reasons for his approval of the rulings.

"All we were talking about on that show, after all," he says now, "was that these court decisions enabled state and local legislatures to call some kind of halt to the really hard core stuff. And that's highly qualified. I don't think it's really a conservative view that society can take only a limited amount of total public license. I believe that. Yes, I do. No civilized society has ever existed in which that position did not prevail."

Bickel has seen neither *Deep Throat* nor *Last Tango*, he concedes. But that's not the point. It has been alleged that the Court decision will give local authorities the chance to suppress a film or book which does not satisfy their personal moralities. That's not the point, either, insists Bickel.

"There's nothing the Supreme Court can do to regulate every police department in every city in the country. No matter how libertarian the Supreme Court decisions, there's nothing that can be done about some cop taking interpretation of the First Amendment into his own hands. There's nothing that can be done about the timidity of film producers . . . or changes in taste. Those things aren't within the control of the authorities in Washington or anywhere else."

But isn't there a real potential for a chilling effect upon the efforts of creative artists? Publishers and producers are in business. Mightn't they play to the lowest common denominator?

"The most libertarian interpretation of the First Amendment has to be based upon a judgment of the good sense of people. That is, when they see sadism performed on the stage or screen, they don't go out and do likewise. We should let them see and hear anything and everything. Truth and morality reside in the wisdom of the people. That is the basic First Amendment, we say, and if that's the faith, no authoritarian restrictions should be imposed on what comes to people's ears and lives.

"But! You have to ask yourself how far you're willing to let personal autonomy go, not just in the way of pornography, but in all aspects of personal conduct. Let's say I want to put up an ugly billboard on my lawn or a statue that represents copulation or stand out there and masturbate. . . . There are thousands of things that an organized society doesn't let me do, thousands of ways it infringes on my personal autonomy. Why is it, then, that so many restraints are imposed on me, but not this one about pornography? The burden of justification is on people like that poor confused bishop on the Cavett show. He has to draw the distinctions.

" 'Well,' he said, 'this doesn't hurt anybody else.' But he doesn't *know* that! That's a value judgment he makes and attempts to impose on me and the majority of his fellow citizens. He kept reminding me of an incident involving Disraeli during the Darwinian debate. The high Church and the Conservatives took the position that man was descended from the angels, not the apes. Disraeli held that position and once found himself in an argument about it with an Anglican dean. The good dean was arguing the liberal position. 'We mustn't be bound by dogma,' he said, 'we must let the human mind roll.' Finally Disraeli said to him, 'No dogma, no dean, Mr. Dean.'

"Curious for an Anglican bishop to be taking that position. I can understand Truman Capote . . ." Bickel's voice curdles, "but what the hell do we need bishops for if that's the position they take?"

There seems, in all this, a strain of patrician paternalism. Would Bickel regard that as an an unfair interpretation? He would, of course. His face darkens as he struggles to mask his irritation at the suggestion.

"The standard liberal rhetoric is internally inconsistent. The fascists and populists are consistent—cynically so. They think they can maneuver masses of people into taking the position they want, and there's no problem about any restraints on the reach of the people's power, because it can be managed. I believe in democracy, but I'm limited in my faith. Yes, I want to test out notions with the majority of the people I live with. Of course I do. *Only,* however, when it's carefully structured and the pace controlled so that no power is ever based solely on plebiscite. I think that was the view of the founders of the Republic. It's a Whig outlook, a Burkian position. It includes, it's true, a clear mistrust of the people as well as a need for their support and an acceptance of the belief that government depends upon their consent."

That's a rather fine balance easily subject to abuse, isn't it?

"But it's not paternalistic. I view it as realistic, hard-nosed. Liberal dogma suffers from profound internal contradiction, because nothing is more sacred than *The People.* Everything is for *The People, The People* are always right. Every election ought to be as uncontrolled as possible, with the clearest kind of access. Yet, on the other hand, there are all kinds of liberal insistence on a whole catechism of principles and highly moral standards. It results in that internal contradiction which is falsely resolved by saying that every time you put it to the people they'll vote the Bill of Rights.

"That's bullshit. Every time you put it to the people, they'll vote the Bill of Rights *down,* given half a chance. Now I think there's infinitely more decency in human beings than there is evil. If I take any given individual off the street and sit him down here an hour or two, he and I will agree on every one of the first eight articles of the Bill of Rights.

"But that's not *The People.* That man votes as part of a mass of 75 million, and that's a different article altogether.

"Nothing is more elitist than liberal dogma. It is a profound geological fault in the work of the Warren Court, for example. The work of that Court divides into two main streams, at least as it relates to political philosophy. On the one hand, populism: enlargement of the franchise, one man, one vote, removal of residency restrictions, everybody vote, twice, if possible. The other stream is the exceedingly dogmatic imposition of absolute Constitutional principles, of which Brown vs. Board of Education is only the faint beginning. The contradiction is never resolved. 'We're not afraid of the people. We can control them by imposing the most rigid kind of Constitutional restraints on what they may do. Let everyone vote because that doesn't really matter. It's only unimportant things they vote about. The important things, we decide. When we do that, it isn't anti-democratic, we're speaking for the people, we're doing what they want. It's in the Constitution. It's in their behalf that we're saying this.' Nothing is more elitist or patronizing than this attitude."

Bickel obviously believes he avoids that fault. On the other hand, he expends no energy denying his membership in the aristocracy of his profession, and that undoubtedly makes it difficult for him to deal with those less favored or less gifted. This is understandable for one whose colleagues, clients, and disciples share or surpass his own brilliance. After all, he overcame the drag of a useless childhood language in an alien country to become, in barely ten years, top graduate of one of America's finest institutions of higher education, garnished with the rare honor of a year as clerk to one of the most distinguished of its jurists. The nature of that honor cannot be overstated, although Bickel soft-pedals the achievement while relishing the experience.

"Oh, certainly, it was a tremendous plum, a great boost, but that was some time ago."

How did it happen?

"Well, Frankfurter had two requirements. One was that you had clerked before. I had clerked at the U.S. Court of Appeals in Boston. Two was that you had to be selected by Henry Hart. Hart was a great man, a member of the Harvard Law School faculty, and an old student, protégé, and dear friend of Frankfurter. Hart selected Frankfurter's law clerks. That meant you had to be a Harvard Law graduate because how else would Henry Hart get to know you? So I got a cable in Paris saying, 'You're it, if you want it.' I wanted it."

223

Bickel swivels to look out the window. He is not seeing the trees.

"Felix was a tremendous formative influence for me, even next to my own parents. And intellectually, he was the most powerful personal presence of my life. From early on, we stayed very close. I saw a great deal of him in the years after. There was a huge correspondence between us, he was incredibly active in keeping up with people. He was heroic to me."

So many attorneys enter public service or politics or its fringes. Did Bickel's associations ever inspire such an ambition in him?

"Politics is not an ambition a sane man entertains. Felix gave me some splendid advice early in life: 'Never set your heart on a particular job. Have aspirations, career lines, general goals, but never set your heart on a particular job that is in the power of somebody else to confer. Along that road lies heartbreak and bitterness time and time again.' So I do not entertain ambitions for things other people can give me. Felix also said never take any job because you think it'll lead to another one, one you wouldn't take on its own merits. You'll do it badly and it *won't* lead to something else."

Frankfurter, Bobby Kennedy, Dean Acheson, McGovern, senators, judges, congressmen, university presidents, publishers, scholars. Bickel has known them all as friends and colleagues. He spent his non-classroom hours at international conferences in Venice, at think-tanks in California, in courtrooms and hearing rooms in New York and Washington.

He requires little diversion. When he does, he likes tennis and cocktail parties. He says good parties are those in which he can, as Justice Holmes said, "compose the mind" through observing attractive women. His eyes crinkle again.

"As for tennis, I resist calling what I do 'playing.' I go out there and do *some*thing, but only on a back court where no one will see me." A friend says it's the only activity in which

Bickel faults. "I'd give a cookie to be able to play tennis the way others I know. But I've just got to resign myself and find my satisfaction in the ultimate proportions of final justice."

Crinkle.

CHAPTER 11

"The *current* legal system obviously doesn't work," says Howard Zinn. His use of a temporal modifier is not frivolous. He intends that the American legal system will be changed. He's helping to push.

"It maintains economic privilege, on the one hand. But, in its corrective or punitive aspects, it doesn't do *anything* it's supposed to do. And the laws against crime cannot possibly work in maintaining harmony because the other laws, the civil laws on contracts, property, torts, corporations, all act in such a way as to distribute property and wealth in such a manner as to stimulate crime."

Zinn has become something of a professional witness for the defense at the series of trials of activists beginning with Philip Berrigan in 1967. He has found it a heartening progression. Berrigan got six years. But in 1973, every last one of the Camden Seventeen was acquitted.

"The two parts of law are working against each other, so that forking people into jail does about as much good as slapping mosquitoes in a swamp. To my mind, a system of law will have to evolve, *de*-volve, to one in which law does not play as important a part as an accepted, traditional act of norms of human behavior, of amicable behavior of people toward one another, of cooperative sharing of resources."

He calls himself an independent radical, and is more,

perhaps, a gentle variety of anarchist. He's cautious about accepting the latter label, but doesn't reject it, either. He went to North Vietnam with Daniel Berrigan to bring back the first three POWs, and testified at the Ellsberg trial. Zinn has found gratification and friends in The Movement, of which he is a charter member. He's a writer and teacher, and he likes that, too.

"Obviously, I am talking in long range terms. Our purpose has to be to create a society which needs fewer laws. Right now we have one which requires more and more."

Zinn's office is in an antique building on a cul-de-sac between Commonwealth Avenue and the Charles River in Boston's Back Bay. There are punters on the Charles under a threatening slate sky. Inside, it is dim and cool. The open-cage elevator might have been transplanted from a no-star Montparnasse hotel. It wheezes and creaks to the third floor, where the corridor circles the staircase and people turn sideways to pass each other. The anteroom for a suite of faculty offices is as narrow, the illumination murky. There is no one at the receptionist's desk, and apparently the offices are empty. Zinn's visitor settles on a wooden bench, the only available seating.

After ten minutes, a very large man with hair and beard matching his tennis costume strides through the anteroom, swinging a racket. He plunges into one of the offices. Through the open door, he can be seen stripping off his sweat-soaked shirt, kicking off his shoes, whisking a beer can out of a refrigerator, popping the top, sitting down at his typewriter. He begins typing immediately. The whole tableau is a smooth flow, without contemplative pauses. He must have started thinking what he was going to write during the last set.

After ten minutes more, the clattering of his machine stops. A stereo swoops into a Bach concerto. He sticks his head out the door to inquire if the visitor is waiting for him. He had to get that first paragraph written while he had it fixed in his head. But he is not Howard Zinn, and he returns to his work, grateful that there will be no interruption for a while. Professor Levin is a flamboyant fixture of the department, one of its most popular lecturers. He's a bachelor, so rumors burble constantly about him, a fact he relishes. He's given to initiating rumors about himself, such as his nonexistent playing years with the Green Bay Packers.

All this is offered by Howard Zinn, who soon appears from what had seemed to be an unoccupied office. Squeezing down another corridor, the visitor passes a tiny rumpled seminar room. On the blackboard, a few scrawled words include something in Russian, an elaborate mathematical equation, and a free-form shopping list including "brownies, Zonkers, and chalk." The people who occupy these rooms are of a whimsical turn of mind.

Certainly Zinn does not convey the evangelical fervor that his reputation suggests. Rather, his manner is diffident, tentative. He is tall, almost gaunt, with widely spaced large eyes and prominent nose and cheekbones. His hair is thick and black and unfashionably cut. He might be a marginal Off-Broadway character actor who finds himself in his first interview after the opening of an unexpected hit.

The crowded office is filled with memorabilia of The Movement. Every flat surface is piled with books and underground newspapers of the non-sexual, radical persuasion. Posters announce past demonstrations against war and racism. There are photos of Daniel Berrigan with a police number and of an army deserter being dragged from sanctuary by federal marshals. Zinn had been at the church, locking arms with other professors around the soldier. They and about a thousand students had been there for days. It made all the papers.

"It was a horrifying scene, the power of the government reaching into this very peaceful scene. Who was bothering

229

anybody? He wasn't bothering anybody. He just didn't want to go to Vietnam. That was a reasonable notion, one that became legitimate years later."

Zinn contributed to that legitimization. "I'm a teacher," he says. "I teach the things I believe in. I try to involve students in those things, not to force them, but to invite them to know ideas, people. The Berrigans come and talk to my classes, Elizabeth McAllister comes, Dan Ellsberg. I talk to them about the war, about the law, and justice and police, about government, socialism, anarchism, poverty. Teaching is very important to me, but it's not enough.

"I don't believe people learn most of what they know from books. They learn from action. So I'm a participant in action. Not an organizer, not a leader. A participant. I participated in the demonstrations in the South. I was teaching there between 1956 and 1963. Before the sit-ins even, I and my students declared as a project that we wanted to integrate the Atlanta Public Library." (He was at Spelman College in Atlanta at the time.) "We sent people, black people, down to the library again and again to ask for books. Always, we conjured up titles designed to make the librarians feel just a touch of remorse. That was their concern, right? Human understanding?

"I had said to this group of social science students, 'Let's study the process of social change, let's take a problem—the desegregation of the Atlanta Public Library—let's do it and study it at the same time.' We'd see what kinds of tactics and pressures worked, what lawsuits were effective. Eventually there were negotiations with the head of the library. He was very flustered by all this. Librarians take pledges like doctors take pledges. They can't turn away anybody who's in emergency need of a book! We went through all the things—sit-ins, the threat of lawsuits—and then we got a phone call one day. There was a hurry-up meeting of the city council, and they decided to desegregate the library.

"It was a great moment for the four of us, two black, two

white, when we walked down to the library, went in, and got the first books that were issued to blacks in the Atlanta Public Library. And there were other things, sit-ins at the department store, for example. I don't want to blow up my life as an activist. But I've always been a demonstrator, I believe in demonstrations."

Atlanta was not a new experience for Zinn. When he was eighteen and working in the Brooklyn Navy Yard, he helped organize a union of apprentice shipwrights and fitters. Three years later, at twenty-one, he went into the air force. With his discharge, he joined the American Veterans Committee (not to be confused with the American Legion, he says with a laugh). After a short spell back at the shipyard, he went on to jobs in a brewery, digging ditches, the garment center, the Housing Authority. The first time he was arrested was when he was chairman of the militant local AVC chapter. He had set up a table on the street to collect names for a petition against the removal of price controls. A policeman ordered him to move. Zinn refused, and he was arrested. He didn't spend any time in jail, since he had witnesses that the officer was drunk. The charge was dropped.

"I suppose I've been arrested about seven times since. Once, I wasn't put in jail. The other times, it was just for a day or two. That's not counting borderline things. Like when I was on the executive committee of SNCC in Atlanta. We went up to integrate the state legislature. They ordered our arrest, but just to evict us. Then I was arrested at peace demonstrations—twice in Washington, three times in Boston. I'm not the most active person, really. Most of the time, I'm teaching and talking about the war, testifying at trials, failing sometimes. I've done a lot of speaking on the Boston Common, from the very first anti-war rally in 1965. There were a few hundred people then. Four years later, during the Moratorium, there were 100,000 people. I spoke then, too." His eyes move away for an instant. That had been a good moment.

231

The mist outside has turned into a downpour. The faded kite hanging in the window bobs in the freshening breeze. Zinn swivels back to his visitor.

"If someone were to ask me my most memorable teaching experience this year, I'd have to say it was when I went to Los Angeles to testify in the Ellsberg trial. Well, maybe when I went to Camden. I was actually lecturing to the jury on the war, on the Pentagon Papers, on civil disobedience . . . and I never felt so good in my life. You feel good when you're before a class, talking about things that matter to you and that you hope will matter to your students. You feel really good about that, but who knows, it's a gamble, what will they do with it? What effect will it have?

"But this is so direct and immediate. Here's a jury, and here are people whose freedom is at stake. You have the possibility of helping win their freedom instead of letting them go to jail. I don't want to over-dramatize the part one witness plays, but you feel that that's what the teaching and reading are all about. That's what it's for.

"I'm interested in teaching as a social act. By the time I was a freshman at NYU, I was twenty-seven. I'd done a lot of things before I entered the academic world. I was *involved* in the world . . . and in depressions, because I'd grown up in one. My family was immersed in it. And I was interested in war . . . enlisted as a bombardier in the war . . . [World War II] in the labor movement because I got involved in that. I'd done a lot of reading in politics and history. So by the time I was a freshman, I knew that I wanted to do something which would have an effect on the world. That's a grandiose aim, of course. Since then I cut it down slightly."

His quick laugh is self-deprecatory. Unnecessarily so, for Zinn doesn't radiate the unshakeable certainty of, say, Alexander Bickel, or the intellectual *hubris* of the true believer. While convinced of the correctness of his stances, he recognizes the existence of other views and is willing to concede the possibility of at least partial validity of those contrary to his. Perhaps that is why he became a teacher. He's not entirely sure himself.

"I . . . hmm . . . I thought history was a good place to start. It seemed reasonable and logical. If you want to do something which would have some effect on the world, you've got to know a lot of history. So I started studying it. But I've always felt some distance from the professional historian, the super-professional. I never wanted to live a life devoted to producing articles for the American Historical Society, or to be what is called a scholar. To some of my friends in the profession, that's the worst thing about me. But that doesn't bother me, because I make a distinction between scholarship and intelligence. If scholarship only feeds the world scholarship, then I don't want it."

Zinn put it another way in his collection of essays, *The Politics of History*:

Is it not time that we scholars began to earn our keep in this world? Thanks to a gullible public, we have been honored, flattered, even paid, for producing the largest number of inconsequential studies in the history of civilization. . . . Like politicians, we have thrived on public innocence. Occasionally, we emerge from the library stacks to sign a petition or deliver a speech, then return to produce even more of inconsequence. We are accustomed to keeping our social commitment extracurricular and our scholarly work safely neutral. We were quick to understand that awe and honor greet those who have flown off into space while people suffer on earth. . . . Read the titles of doctoral dissertations published in the past twenty years, and the pages of the leading scholarly journals for the same period, alongside the lists of war dead, the figures on per capita income in Latin America, the autobiography of Malcolm X. We publish while others perish.

"So I don't really care," he is saying now, "if I'm classified as an historian or a political scientist. I guess it's that I don't want people to think I'm a cop-out, that I'm idle, that I don't care about what's happening. So it didn't matter what my 'specialty' was . . . I sort of roamed all over the place . . . I didn't have the trepidation that scholars have when you ask them to go teach something in another field. I'm not saying that I was *qualified* to teach all these things. It's just that I don't think that you had to pile up enormous credentials in a field in order to convey something of it to someone else.

"When I was teaching speech and spelling in Atlanta, as a result, I was willing to teach a course in Russian literature. Which was, of course, horrifying to anybody who has what we call 'standards' in the academic world. Me! Teaching a course in Russian literature! But I had studied a few years of the language and read Tolstoy and Dostoevsky and Chekhov, and I thought I knew enough to get my students interested and talk about it with them. So though I'm in the political science department, I get half my mail addressed to the history department. Friends look at me askance, as if I'm a traitor to the discipline, but I'm happy."

But isn't that the nature of the social sciences? Mustn't an economist know something of history and mathematics and psychology and politics and sociology, and each of them, the others?

"I guess so. We have, to an extent, discarded that sense of discipline—you know, this is ours, that is theirs. People talk about interdisciplinary work, but they talk about it as they do of interracial marriage. 'It's ohhkaaayyyy,' but it's not as if we were just talking about two human beings who got together. We're very stern in describing an interracial marriage, as we are this interdisciplinary thing. But I'm still struggling with how to make teaching useful, to make it relate to the world.

"I'm very happy that yesterday a lawyer called me and said he'd like me to do some research on double jeopardy. His clients were in the Attica uprising and were going on trial in Buffalo. He was asking me to help. Well, I'll drop everything! For scholars to use our abilities to read and put things together and do research for people who are resisting the system and trying to change things . . . well, that's the greatest thing we could do.

"At Camden, they were all acquitted. Every last one! Totally acquitted on all counts! It was the first political trial of draft board raiders in which this happened. All the defendants were caught redhanded. I mean, there was no question about the facts. They were caught by one hundred FBI men who were waiting for them to enter the building. They had been tipped off by one of the Camden people. The facts were clear, there was no question about it. And they were all totally acquitted!"

On what grounds?

"Well, the nice thing about an acquittal by a jury is that the jury never has to say why. If a defendant can get his message across, it will help a lot. For a long time in political trials, defendants have been trying to get across to juries the doctrine of jury nullification. That doctrine goes back to the middle of the eighteenth century. It was used in the trial of John Peter Zenger." (Zenger was a newspaper printer who was jailed by the governor of New York in 1735 for libel against a Crown official. His attorney argued that Zenger's statements had been true, and therefore not libelous. The jury agreed.) "But the doctrine hasn't been used much since. It's operative, but not dominant. In a political trial, though, you're desperate. You'll pull out anything, especially if you think it's right.

"The doctrine of jury nullification says that no matter what the judge's instructions are, the jury can judge the facts. It doesn't *have* to abide by the judge's instructions. The jury can judge the law, the higher law, even conscience. It can decide that morally these people are right, even though legally they are wrong. You can acquit and no one will ever be able to ask

235

you a question after that, for there is no appeal from an acquittal.

"At Camden, those people defended themselves. That was very important. They presented themselves to the jury as human beings. Parenthetically, that ties in with my view that we have to break down the whole idea of specialization, or 'professionalism.' It gets in the way of human encounter. The specialty of a lawyer creates an obstacle between jury and defendant. If defendants can plead their own case, overcome the idea of specialization, then it seems to me we'll get closer to justice. It's just the same with the notion of teaching as a profession, that only certain people can do it, that you have to have these degrees, that kind of training, this kind of background. That an ordinary intelligent person cannot read ninety-two books and write history. This, even though the opposite has been proven many times to the shame of historians who have worked so hard and produced so little.

"Anyway, the Camden people defended themselves. And over a period of weeks they got into the jury's mind that this was a petty violation of law they were accused of, compared to the gross violations of law of the government in conducting the war. These were acts of conscience. This is a point I tried to make to the jury. That is, even in other than political cases, defendants can give reasons which exculpate them from their deeds. Even in something as gross as murder, if you murdered in self-defense or in defense of others, it's okay. There is legal precedent for not prosecuting people for technical violations providing there's some overriding urgency. Going through a red light to take someone to the hospital, breaking a window to get to a fire alarm. There's been a double standard, though. This allowance in ordinary crime has never been permitted in political trials. The Camden people succeeded in getting the jury to accept this."

All this was most gratifying to Zinn and those who share his views. A cause which was condemned in 1965 as at the very

236

least unpatriotic, at most traitorous, had been embraced by millions of Americans a bare few years later. The government, determined to prosecute dissidents, had failed with Ellsberg, failed with the Seattle Seven, the Kansas City Four, the Evanston Four, Spock and Coffin, the New York Panthers, the antiwar veterans called the Gainesville Eight, even Angela Davis. But whatever the abuses of either side, there remains, for many, an uneasiness that sanctioned disregard for law can benefit zealots of other persuasions. Watergate was an obvious example. But one thinks of those who burn buses and bomb churches to deny integration. Can they not make a similar plea?

"Well, yes. I think so. That is . . . I think that defense can be made, but I think . . . it's perfectly proper for somebody to have the right to make that defense, but . . . but the fact that there's that right doesn't mean that the verdict should be the same in all of these cases."

It's all right for "us," but not for "them"?

"I'm arguing the principle that violations of the law may possibly be right under certain circumstances, not that they're *always* right under *all* circumstances. I'm willing to trust more to reasonable judgments about what is *right* than rigid judgments about what is *legal.* Notions about what is legal are in any case tinged with prejudices. It's not true that we maintain a line between the legal and the moral. We don't always rule according to the law. We *don't!* There are all sorts of biases. Well, let's let the biases out in the open, let's judge acts on their moral rightness and wrongness. If you say this is open to abuse . . . of course it is. But so is the other system, the present one. I would rather have a system based on some reasonable weighing of right and wrong in human terms rather than in rigid adherence to a law which is administered by biased people."

Zinn's interest in law is not recent. In 1961 and 1962, he went to Albany, Georgia, to do a report for the Southern

Regional Council. Things were happening to blacks in Albany which seemed to Zinn to be violations of federal law, but the federal government wasn't doing much about it. He researched civil rights legislation enacted immediately after the War Between the States, and moved from that into the much broader field of Constitutional law itself. Given his perspectives, it is not surprising that he finds a sizable gap between the presumed protection of the law and the reality of enforcement.

In his course on law and justice—Zinn's writing and teaching and life are all of a piece—he tells his students that the law clearly protects a citizen's right to distribute leaflets on the street. But if that citizen stands on the corner giving out his leaflets and a policeman tells him to move on, all citations of Constitutional protection will fail before the reality of power as the officer chooses to impose it. He teaches a course in political theory, in which he introduces questions of morality, ends and means, the nature of democracy, the secrecy of representative government. There is also a seminar in Marxist theory, another in anarchism. And another on the philosophy of history, in which he talks about the subjectivity of history.

The presumed objectivity of the historian is a matter of considerable concern to its practitioners. Zinn and Martin Duberman know each other, have for over ten years. They share a disbelief that objectivity is even possible. But where Duberman focuses on how the recounting of events must be screened through the personal biases and life experiences of the observer, Zinn contemplates the unlikelihood of neutrality on the part of historians serving class and dogma. He talks about it in *The Politics of History*:

> The myth of "objectivity" in teaching and scholarship is based on a common confusion. If to be objective is to be scrupulously careful about reporting accurately what one sees then of course this is laudable. But accuracy is only a prerequisite. . . . Too many scholars abjure a starting set of values because they fail to make the proper distinction

between an ultimate set of values and the instruments needed to obtain them. . . . Our values should determine the *questions* we ask in scholarly inquiry, but not the answers. . . . There is no question of a disinterested community of scholars, only a question about what kinds of interests the scholars will serve. There are fundamental humanistic interests—above any particular class, party, nation, ideology—which I believe we should consciously serve. I assume this is what we mean when we speak of fostering certain "values" in education.

Certainly Zinn maintains no pretense of objectivity in his courses. There is no distance from his subject, and he does not feel that he deceives his potential students.

"It starts right out with my selection of topics," he says. "Anyone can tell that I'm not keeping separate my subject and the things I believe in. I teach an 'Introduction to Political Theory' course. Last semester, it had the Vietnam War as the running example for all the problems in political theory. When I dealt with 'means and ends,' I discussed Machiavelli and Kissinger, Sir Thomas More and Daniel Ellsberg. When I dealt with human nature, I talked about My Lai. When representative government was the subject, I talked about the role of Congress in the war. And when I talk about the uses of history, I had to use the Pentagon Papers.

"I had them read the *Apology* of Plato and I placed Daniel Berrigan against Socrates. And Socrates saying, 'No, I won't escape, I'm going to take my punishment like a man.' And Berrigan saying, 'No, they'll have to find me.'

"No, I don't place distance. If there's validity in the notion of objectivity, it lies in this, which I try to honor: You don't lie, you don't pretend there isn't another side. You make it very clear that what you are telling the people is subjective, that your point of view is one of a number of points of view. But also, you don't feel honor bound to give all those points of view equal credit and attention. I go on the assumption that mine is the minority view, that it hasn't been adequately represented in the literature, and that therefore I should give it as much attention as I can. They get others all the time."

Zinn usually teaches undergraduates, normally in one large lecture and one seminar each semester. He's a popular professor. Although he placed a limit of 200 students on his lecture course this last semester, 350 registered. Although flattered by the interest, he was distressed by the number. It meant he had to use a microphone, which made him unhappy. He has seven T.A.'s, so the class can be broken down to smaller discussion groups. But that's still 50 per group.

It's a great burden, he says. "These kids are signing up for two one-and-a-half hour lectures a week. It's costing them a lot of money." (The tuition at Boston University this year is $2,950.) More important—Zinn gets irritated when people talk about money—they're expending a lot of time and energy, and they're all gathered there as if he had something very special to offer them.

"It's quite a responsibility. As a result, during the school year, I'm even more gaunt than I am now. I work very hard at those lectures. The night before, I'm up very, very late working on them. It's not just the subject matter, the content. It has to be *alive*. People have to be involved, awake, alert, and that is hard."

Zinn's weekly routine differs little from that of other senior professors. There are his three hours of lecture, three more in seminar, nine to twelve in individual consultation with students from his classes and those engaged in independent study projects. He must spend more time in preparation than most professors, since his wide-ranging interests involve him in different courses each year. He cannot rely on ten-year-old lecture notes. Not that he is likely to conduct the carefully ordered presentation of a Eugene Santomasso.

"I work with a few basic ideas and a lot of raw material. I have it before me in rather disorganized form . . . notes, clippings, books. I have found, over the years, that my most organized lectures are my least successful ones. I don't mean that an unorganized lecture is therefore the best. But when I come in with a general idea that I feel strongly about, with maybe two or three sub-ideas I know about, that's when it works. When you come in with a very detailed lecture, you feel you have to use all of it. I prefer to give myself looseness, plenty of leeway. There's a combination of centrality and spontaneity which is essential for there to be substance."

He avoids committees and involvement in departmental matters. He goes to the campus Tuesdays, Wednesdays, and Thursdays. He stays home Mondays to work on his lectures. Fridays, he turns to other things. He teaches in a community school for working-class people involved in tenants' unions and peace groups. He travels, lectures, writes.

Considering his late entrance into the professoriate, Zinn has been a remarkably prolific writer and thinker. He didn't get his doctorate from Columbia until 1958, when he was thirty-six. His first book was published soon after. Since then, he's written seven more, and he doesn't remember how many articles. That means he's averaged about one book every two years of his professional life. It didn't hurt his career or his achievement of tenure. On the other hand, his activism probably didn't help.

"Let me tell you about that. I've sat in a lot of committees granting tenure. What happens is they weigh a person's publications and his teaching and then . . . everything else about him. They claim they don't, but they do. 'Do we really like him? What are his politics? How much of a troublemaker is he?'

"Well, when it came time to decide if I would get tenure at BU, there was no doubt I had produced enough—more—than anybody in the department. No problem there. The reports on my teaching from the students were such that the committee simply could not say I was a bad teacher. But still, it wasn't

241

impossible to deny me tenure. No, political things are such that it is still possible, if the feeling against me was strong enough. In fact, it was very close.

"But when they hired me they didn't know me as a radical activist. It was in '64, just before the Vietnam War. They knew me only as someone who had been active in civil rights in the South. It was a time when a civil rights person was very respectable, almost desirable. When they offered me a job, they said I would get tenure in a year. They *promised!* Next year, when I thought I would get it, I didn't ask any questions. I was sure it would be automatic. Then I got my contract and it didn't call for tenure. I asked them why and they said, 'Oh, we forgot. Was this the year you were supposed to get tenure? Well you know how things are, we forgot . . . next year.' Next year, no tenure. They said, 'Clerical error, something went wrong.'

"By that time it was '67, the war, my action on it, my articles, a book. And in early '68 I went to Hanoi with Berrigan. I spoke on the Common, I was known as anti-war. This was before a lot of professors had gotten around to seeing that the war was bad. The chairman of the department was not an anti-war person and so the senior members of the department were not. There was one member of the department who was ferociously anti-Communist and a terrific supporter of American foreign policy. He had welcomed me when I had first come in as a civil rights person. Now he was wondering if I was a monster. He and the chairman were the driving force. With a few others, my tenure was a tie vote. I had a secret informant in the meeting. Then they held another meeting and somebody changed, so I was voted in.

"But that wasn't the end of it. It had to be okayed by the dean and the president and finally the board of trustees. The dean and the president went along. There was some question how the board of trustees would go.

"This was the Spring of '68. The trustees were having a

dinner on Founders' Day at the Sheraton Plaza. And Rusk was the honored guest! It was the height of the anti-war movement on campus. Teach-ins, demonstrations. It was infuriating! Some people came to me and said they were going to have a picket line and a meeting outside the hotel. They'd set up a microphone and they wanted me to speak! And . . . well . . . it was one of those moments!" His laugh is infectious. "The board of trustees was about to decide on my tenure, but I couldn't say no. I couldn't say that I wouldn't speak for that reason. Anyway, they told me there would be six other speakers and that I'd be the seventh. I'd be there, walk the picket line, speak, and that would be it. When I got there I found out I was the only speaker. The others hadn't shown up. So I had to hold forth on the mike for what seemed a very long time. It seemed longer still because all the guests in their tuxedos were filing in at the same time. They were all stopping a moment, looking at the demonstrators, looking at me. At least it seemed to me they were looking at me. Every member of the board of trustees!

"Two days later I got a letter from the president's office. I was sure I knew what was in it. But I had been given tenure by a vote of the board—the afternoon of the evening dinner."

Zinn usually was involved in Movement activities outside the university. But when students occupied a dean's office in protest of the ROTC presence on campus, he joined them. That led to a committee to investigate Zinn, and what seemed to him the first steps in depriving him of his tenure. It was dropped, however. BU was relatively quiet for a while . . . until John Silber became president. Silber, it is safe to venture, is controversial. As dean of the liberal arts college at the University of Texas, he tangled publicly with the head of the Board of Regents. He left to become president of Boston University. Judging from private comments of a number of faculty and administrators, Silber's personality cannot be described as soothing. Zinn is less guarded in his observations.

243

"Two things. One, he doesn't waste any time calling the police. The first time, the police used their clubs indiscriminately. It was a very bloody scene. It was a peaceful although an obstructive demonstration. People sitting on the steps. They could have been arrested quietly. Sixty of us were. I was.

"There's no doubt about it. A cooler, shrewder, more moderate character could obviate a lot of these demonstrations. The University of Massachusetts has banned ROTC and military recruiting and *their* president isn't rushing to put them back. He's playing it cool. Silber isn't. Silber is a man of high principle, in the sense that once he decides he is right about something, anything goes to defend it. Once he decides that he is right to have military recruiters on campus, we must have them on campus. He'll call the police, he'll arrest people, he'll put people in prison, he'll have them clubbed. He'll do anything to hold that principle inviolate.

"But I suppose what's most irritating is that he doesn't seem to care what students think. He gives off an aura of believing in democracy, but when the students voted overwhelmingly against having military recruiters on campus, he went ahead and brought them back.

President Silber is not fond of Zinn, either. In a speech to the American Association for the Advancement of Science, he accused Zinn of abusing academic freedom by falsifying evidence and distorting the truth. According to Silber, Zinn "shamelessly" distorted and degraded the ethical positions of Martin Luther King concerning the extent to which one should show respect for the law. Zinn rejoins.

"He hired this outfit, Price Watergate . . ."

Price Waterhouse?

"Did I say Price Watergate? Ha! Anyway, he hired them to conduct a mail ballot of the faculty, accompanied by a strong letter from him saying that BU is foundering, is desperate, money is at stake, and we won't get this money unless we bring back ROTC. He got an overwhelmingly favorable vote.

He intimidates the faculty and gets the Senate Council to obsequiously pass a resolution giving him the power to draw up a code of conduct. It reads like something out of 1984. It permits a campus security officer to order any student or faculty member off the campus, if in the opinion of the officer it would be better for the mental or emotional well-being of that person to be off the campus."

That seems farfetched. Boston University is an urban institution, vulnerable to street crimes and loiterers. Some of its students have been raped and murdered, as have those at many other universities. The code requires only that a person challenged by the campus police produce an ID card. If such protections, however porous, were not available, protests would inevitably ensue condemning the administration for failing to provide protection. Of course, the potential for abuse by individual officers persists. That's inevitably true. Zinn sees a darker dimension.

"I'm not exaggerating. It's weird—a system of ID cards where every student and faculty member must present the card upon demand to any officer of the university. If they don't, they can be ordered off the campus. If they refuse to leave, they can be suspended. This is the part of the rules that aroused such tremendous opposition. It was even too much for the usually timid faculty. My department was unanimously outraged. The department of sociology said the same thing.

"Anyway, it's this sort of thing that has aroused so much opposition to Silber."

Given his sincerely held views it might be thought that Zinn experiences some distress that he is paid by an institution representative of much that is oppressive in our society—big government, big business, big education. His position offers a comfortable salary, a home in the suburbs, leisure, prestige. It brings lecture fees in the hundreds of dollars, annual book royalties in the thousands. One might expect qualms.

"But I really like my job! Those things don't bother me. My

notion of social change requires people to be in the machinery of the society at every point. The only way we're going to get change in this country is if we are where people are. If you're working for a big outfit, what's important is the kind of job you're doing, not that you work there. But if you're in that big outfit and you're trying to undermine it, well then. . . . Oh, we may be fooling ourselves. They're taking a risk that they can absorb and digest a number of troublemakers. So big, our society, so powerful, they can let us putter around and yell and demonstrate. 'It's not going to get them very far,' they think, 'and we will contain them.'

"Obviously there's a strong element of truth in that, because they've done it for a long time. But the only way we're going to get some change in this country is if we are where people are, if we're in the schools where ordinary people go, if we're in places where people work. We use this opportunity to try to make them lose their gamble."

Then it doesn't trouble him that part of his salary may come from Union Carbide or Dow Chemical?

"Oh, no, I think it probably distresses alumni in Union Carbide that part of their salary goes to pay me. In fact, our alumni association gets letters from alumni saying they resent the fact that Boston University is paying a salary to Howard Zinn."

A janitor comes in to empty the wastebaskets. He smiles and exchanges dutiful comments with Zinn. After he leaves, Zinn says:

"That guy works four hours in a factory every morning, and eight hours here. Now that's a terrible deprivation of a man's freedom, engaged in activities which are not the most rewarding. But by putting two jobs together he can make $10,000 a year. And I make a lot more for doing . . . this. There's terrible disproportions in the way people get paid in this society.

"It's troubling, but some time ago I came to grips with, and

246

half-defeated, the guilt feelings associated with not being a twenty-four hour revolutionary. I have a nice place to live, vacations, a little car. We go down to Cape Cod for a month in the summer. I could torment myself over this, but this is what I've chosen as my life. I know that the conditions of my life are always going to predispose me to be softer, or not as energetic on certain matters. Yes, I'm going to devote some time working on changing prisons, but not as much as if I were an ex-prisoner. And I'm not devoting as much time as when I was working in a shipyard and closer to the heart of what I was struggling against. The conditions of my life are such as to make it necessary to constantly remind myself of how bad things are for other people. I mustn't get complacent."

But what of The Movement? Certainly it is quiet, and college kids seem to be returning to apathy and beer parties. Is it just a breathing spell?

"Nooo . . . that would imply that we are again on the verge of something big, another era of dramatic campus protest. That would be too big a claim. But we aren't back in 1953, either, even though student action is not very visible and a lot of them are thinking along traditional lines again. This whole anti-war movement has had an effect on today's college generation. They're thinking differently. I can see it in my classes. They're way ahead in their thinking.

"The one good sign I see in what seems to be the silence of The Movement is that a lot of people have been affected by it. A lot of them . . . no, I don't want to exaggerate . . . *some* of them are involved in small organizing projects, very local, in different parts of the country. These are very modest and obscure, unnoticed, not the kind of thing that attracts attention, like a march or demonstration, but which involves long-range plodding, organizing . . ."

That's "plodding," with two d's?

"Yes, yes," he grins. "But it's work which is, in the long run, more important to the transformation of American society than a series of demonstrations. They're going back to their own block, organizing tenant groups or where they work or go to school. This is a kind of anarchist belief—revolutionary change is not going to come about through seizure of power at the center, taking the Winter Palace or San Clemente. Those kinds of revolutions have been disappointing in many ways.

"I see revolution coming through a huge number of local actions, which will be sporadic and uneven. They will be snuffed out here and there, but they will grow and grow and grow. Eventually there will be enough to transform their immediate environments, and, yes, change the society. Not in a day, not a coup, but it's going to happen."

The sky opens up on the way to the bus stop. There aren't any buses, anyway. A cab finally stops. Before his passenger has leaned back, the driver begins a whining litany on his disgust with the prices these days of Rolls Royces and Peugeots. Give him a Toronado anytime, he says.

CHAPTER 12

At the height of the art boom ten years ago, *New York Times* critic John Canaday estimated that there were 250,000 artists in the United States. Serious, practicing painters and sculptors, professional in every sense of the word, except for their bank balances. He guessed that maybe 5,000 had ever had, or could ever expect to have an exhibition of their works in a New York gallery. And there were, perhaps, 300 who might be said to make a living from their art alone. The rest had to look elsewhere—they night-clerked in hotels, apprenticed themselves as carpenters, or painted billboards. Or they taught.

Canaday believed that fully half of that quarter million lived in the metropolitan area of New York City. It was, and still is, the Big Apple, the center of the art universe, despite mild challenges from Los Angeles and Chicago. The influential museums, the powerful art dealers, the important critics, and the moneymen of the arts were in New York. And they still are. Admittedly, American art has lost much of its puissance in the last decade. Painting pictures has seemed a hopelessly irrelevant act in the face of My Lai and Watergate. Film, gratifying in its immediacy and communality, has contributed to the attrition. So has the fourth generation of Abstract Expressionists, gumming the cud of a form none too substantial in 1955. And so did the uncaring affluent, who sheltered their excess profits with Nebraskan cattle herds, oil shale holdings, and Jackson Pollacks.

Withal, hope remains. Halve Canady's estimate, and there are still over 60,000 artists in and around New York. And they still have to find other work to survive. It means that New York art schools can find high-level faculty easily, and often dirt cheap. Even artists of prominence beg for jobs. "If I could only tell you the names of the really fine artists who have applied for teaching jobs here," says one department chairman, "and who I had to turn down because they didn't have a doctorate." Artists don't, as a rule, bother about Ph.D.'s. They weren't expecting to need them when they started out. They were going to be the exceptions. They were going to be among the 300. But university deans fail to see why art teachers should not have the credentials of everyone else on their faculties.

The penthouse of the Education Building was converted to studios eight years ago. It almost doubled the space available to the art department, but it still isn't enough. Art departments characteristically get the short end of the budgetary stick at universities. It's hard for administrators and trustees to take art seriously, for they are practical men.

This particular studio is large enough for the sixteen students taking Advanced Painting this term. They huddle around the edges, like children who want their beds in contact with a wall. The center of the room is empty, for live models, when they have them, and for Robert Kaupelis, when he has announcements or observations to make. Kaupelis teaches this class. Rather, he guides it. It is not a lecture course. At start of term, the students propose a "contract" with Kaupelis, set a project they want to pursue, a goal they hope to reach. After discussion and agreement, the students proceed. Kaupelis spends the rest of the course helping them with work in progress. This means touring the studio two or three times a day, working for a time with each individual student. His "rounds," he calls it.

At this moment, he is speaking with a student, a nun who teaches art at a parochial school. She has arrayed the five small paintings she has done this semester around her easel. They are portrait heads and tentative abstractions. Given her professional position and the formal training required to hold it, the paintings are remarkably inept. Bob Kaupelis is attempting to mask his incredulity with something less than complete success. The nun smiles gamely, as if concurring with his unspoken appraisal and soliciting his tolerance. From time to time, they both shrug, their mutual charade crumbling.

He motions at the painting on the easel, a portrait of a crowned Christ. "You like it now?" he asks her.

She glances at the painting, then at him, then back at the painting. "I think I'm at the point where I'm satisfied," she ventures. "Maybe the crown needs work?"

"A crown has to be gold," he says. "Yours is brown." His eyes fix on hers, but she looks away. She knows that, but she doesn't know how to change it. "How can you have a crown not gold?"

"Eventually," she offers, "I plan to build it up with a heavy impasto . . ."

"Ah, good. Gold paint, jewels, in a heavy paste. Terrific!" He is trying very hard to work up some enthusiasm, in her, at least. She must *try!* "Look here. This cloth." He scoops up a scrap of blue velvet and holds it to the Christ's robe. "See the color relationship? You're suggesting jewels. You need *real* jewels in there, and *real* cloth. And *real* buttons. It needs substance."

The nun nods. He's right, but she still doesn't know how to do it. Among artists, words have meaning beyond conventional definition. The uninitiated listening to a conversation between artists can never know the shadings of intent in a discussion of a brush stroke or a splotch of red. American painter Albert

251

Ryder, once asked to comment about a ghostly seascape on which he had worked intently for six months, reportedly responded that "the sky was beginning to look right." With first-year painting students, a teacher might demonstrate ways that a figure can be given fullness, or the flesh transparency, or a room depth. But with the more experienced artists, he will simply say "more red" or "less yellow" or "feel the form," and he will be understood.

These are supposed to be experienced artists, many of them graduate students, several of them teachers. But Kaupelis isn't getting across to the nun. He decides he must revert to specifics of technique. He tells her that the ground (the base layer of pigment upon which the painting is constructed) doesn't work, because it is too intense and seems to come forward visually, rather than recede. The colors of the figures are muddy, he says, a condition that comes about from over-mixing of paints and working them into a gray, soupy tone. He explains that when a dark line is traced around the edge of a figure, it tends to flatten the roundness of an arm or head. If that's what she *wants* to do, fine. But the nun is trying to create a realistic representation of Christ, so she shouldn't outline the figure in black. He talks about hue and value and intensity and volume, all first-year stuff, because nothing else has worked. Now, the term is nearly over and this isn't working either. The nun is smiling and nodding. And shrugging.

She pulls out another piece of canvas, unrolls it on a chair for Kaupelis' comment. He considers it.

"Sister," he says finally, "is this a placemat?"

Shrug. "What you said yesterday inspired me to do this." He had said that one didn't have to stretch a canvas over a wooden frame, necessarily. You could just tack it to a wall or lay it out on the floor "like a placemat."

"But I just meant . . ." He gives up, says resignedly, "Okay."

They laugh, together, both recognizing the futility of the situation. He moves to the next easel.

Kaupelis tries to alter visual and auditory stimuli in the studio, to change spatial perceptions. Periodically, he makes them change the position of their easels or move to another part of the room. Today, he has strung yards of purple ribbon about the room. They must duck it, or step over it, or push it out of the way, or untangle it from their feet. They must become aware of it, its texture and color, the way it redefines space. All of this, of course, is unspoken. Most of the students in the room don't have to be told why the ribbon is there.

But he does make his students think—hard—about what they are doing in responding to those stimuli. In his figure drawing classes, he uses conventional techniques. He has the model change poses every few seconds, forcing the students to make very rapid gesture sketches with broad, quick strokes. It helps to break them of the laborious, fuzzy, tight little scratchings nearly all beginners produce, to build their confidence and make them worry less over details of eyes and toes and eyelashes in favor of capturing the essence of the total movement and articulation of the whole figure. And he has his students draw the contours of a figure without taking their eyes from the model, an exercise in mind-eye-hand coordination.

These are common enough devices in the teaching of art. Kaupelis has his own variations. In one instance, the students are made to blindfold themselves and draw an object or scene they visualize like a photograph in their heads. In another, Kaupelis tells a story of a street incident. While he does, the class must illustrate each element of the story, from imagination. He gives them perhaps ten seconds to execute each sketch. A simple story, five minutes in the telling, may produce forty drawings from each person in the class. The sketch paper and charcoal fly. It helps get all those yellow pencils with erasers out of the room. Art teachers hate those yellow pencils.

Kaupelis' students are expected to be able to verbalize what they are doing. It's not easy, as anyone who has ever tried to define "esthetic" can confirm. After a blindfolded drawing session, one of his students wrote about the experience:

"About seeing: We do very little, actually. Ask anyone in the room to close his eyes and describe what someone else is wearing, or ask me to close my eyes and without hands describe what I am wearing—and I won't know! *But,* ask me to close my eyes and imagine I am unclothed, and to dress myself, and I will know vividly what I am 'wearing,' because I will call into play all useful knowledge and experience and will reject all useless information. I will construct and select and design fabric, color, fit, feel, texture, shape, size . . . the works!"

Finishing with another student, Kaupelis pauses to change the LP on the turntable. *Tommy,* by The Who. Painting is a multi-leveled endeavor. It requires neither the solitude nor the quiet of scholarly activities. The artist's mind learns both to blot out unwanted stimuli and to bring them back on cue. At one moment, rendering the curve of a nude model's hip and thigh is an exercise in defining form, at another, it stirs longing. Both are needed, they support each other. The technical and the emotional become the whole. Non-artists never believe that painters can set aside the sensual reality of the live, fleshy nakedness of the model before them. And artists who succeed in reducing the experience to mechanics are doing only half a job.

Kaupelis adjusts the volume and moves to the next student, whose paintings, much larger and more inventive than the nun's, are pinned up over a whole corner of the room. The young man who produced them is quite a different person as well: short, curlyheaded, voluble, with a rushing, jabbing conversational style. Mesh shirt, jeans, sandals. Aggressively self-assured, he is a prototype New York neurotic, positive division. He treats Kaupelis as a colleague, rather than teacher. It is likely that he would deal with the president of General Motors or the Guru Maharah Ji the same way. He is obviously bright, graduated the top fifth of his class at competitive Bronx High School of Science, and talented. Whether his particular gifts are best applied to painting is an open question, one he might ask himself in a rare moment of introspection.

Kaupelis looks at the paintings a while. The student almost pants with anticipation. *Confident* anticipation. The pictures are largely abstract, swirls of oranges and greens.

"I'm glad you're finding out a little bit about green," Kaupelis observes. In the paintings completed earlier in the term, the greens are raw and harsh, clashing violently with the warm colors. They are smoother in the later pictures.

"That's why I got to limiting my colors."

"These *are* the early things?" asks Kaupelis.

"Right. And they were going nowhere. That's why I moved this way. I mean, I could have gone on forever, just turned them out, without any particular significance here or there."

"Why does that," Kaupelis points to the latest painting, "have any more significance than the first one?"

"Well, I thought there was more discipline in the limiting of the colors over several canvases. I don't know . . . I seemed to develop a closer relationship with them. Something seemed to happen. As I got to know them, things seemed to happen, they became more expressive."

"You're saying that discipline is critical to production of a better kind of art?"

"Right. First of all, in *my* production, limits are very important. And since we artists don't have limits anymore— like making it look like an apple—where do we put them? So we move out and experiment. But being able to handle that, no limits, is an incredible debt to pay for freedom. You really have to attack that freedom after a great deal of time and study. That's a distant goal for me. This one," he dismisses one of his paintings with a wave, "just didn't work."

"But this is one of your latest ones, isn't it?"

"No. It may look like it, but it's really superficial. I mean, it's very easy to like. I put it up on a stark white wall at home and it really looked good. It's . . . it's snappy . . . but it might make a better silkscreen than a painting. These others I like more and more. I wasn't sure how I felt about them, so I stopped for a while. They really grew on me, the more I looked at them."

"I'm glad you brought these in for me to see." Kaupelis is pointing at the earlier pictures. "And glad I didn't see them before. These later ones are such a radical departure. These first are such pretty, pretty things." It is not a compliment for an artist to describe his work as "pretty." He turns to three Van Goghish self-portraits. He isn't thrilled by them either, except by the improvement in execution he sees. "You *like* these?" he asks with some skepticism.

"Yeah. At least, I like the middle one." He glances hopefully at Kaupelis, who is making a face. "But I don't care for that one."

"Maybe the middle one has a *few* values if we dug deep enough."

"Well, I'm partial," says the student, trying to be light. "They're of me."

"I just don't like super-realistic art," says Kaupelis, making a small joke in return. The student misses it.

"Super-realistic?"

"They're a perfect likeness," Kaupelis says, embroidering. The portraits are tortured, seamed, contorted. They have no resemblance to the artist.

"They're different moods. Ha, ha." The student gets the jest, lamely rejoins.

"But, you see, the color doesn't make any sense," says

256

Kaupelis, serious again. "Here, it doesn't. Over here, it does. This other is disciplined. That's what you're talking about."

"But part of that is because it's background. I didn't feel like putting a background, but I didn't want to leave it white. An anti-way of making a ground is to use a color which is a major part of the subject itself. In which case, you play with transparencies to reflect the foreground, to support it visually." The student is lecturing again, his confidence only slightly shaken.

Kaupelis shares with him a technique for building transparency with pigment and thinner. They chat more. Kaupelis would be happier if the student weren't quite so certain in his judgments. He pokes a few holes, but the student seems only to draw strength from challenge. The student has a quick mind and glib patter. He might even be a serviceable artist someday, but. . . . Finally, Kaupelis strolls to the neighboring easel.

Over near the middle of the room, a man in his middle twenties is gluing pieces of painted canvas to a gessoed board. (Gesso is the white paint-like substance with which most artists prepare a surface. It dries hard so it isn't picked up in the later coats of pigment, and the brushstrokes of gesso leave a "tooth" to which paint can adhere.) His name is Don Porter. His long blond hair is tied back with a scrap of the purple ribbon strung about the room. He is wearing only chopped off jeans. He has a handsome face, with gentle eyes. A flower child, the kind parents worry about, but who makes mothers soft inside because he's such a good boy at heart. Don has tried most things—dope, yoga, meditation—and he's still looking. He's a cab driver now. Half the artists and actors in New York drive taxis. Don has been an actor, too, and writes poetry.

The inescapable conclusion is that Don is a dabbler, with painting just his latest enthusiasm. When this is suggested to him, he insists that he regards himself now as an artist, and that this is to be his life work. For the moment.

The collage of reapplied pieces of the original painting looks

257

nearly continuous, with only the seams showing. About a third of the board underneath is still visible. Don is coloring the resultant negative space. He talks about his last course with Kaupelis. It was figure drawing, and much more structured than this class. Kaupelis had said that it was one of the best he'd had, conceding that he's always saying that.

"In his figure drawing class, we were given assignments every day. It was a much tighter group. Here we're left pretty much on our own. In that one, we had critiques every morning. And really, it was a very, very inspiring class. Right now, I'm still running on the energy I picked up there. Kaupelis is an inspiring man. Incredibly energetic. The first day, we came in and he said to do a figure composition, then we put them up on the board for a critique. That was our schedule for the whole time we were in class. Every day we would tack up on the wall the assignment we had the last time. And he pushed to get out a lot of honesty. People were often hesitant to say bad things, but he pushed it, and we became able to say those things. He was able to do it in a way that didn't intimidate us, and would allow us to say things to other people in the class. Really extremely important to us."

Kaupelis strives for candor in working with his students and in making them interact with one another. The niceties of social relationships must be broken down, he believes, before any meaningful work can be accomplished. He uses a variety of devices toward that end. Usually, only a few people in each class know each other. At first, Kaupelis gave each of them a card and asked for name, address, telephone so he might get in touch with them if necessary. He began making notes on the cards about them—"great-looking blonde," "big nose"—so he could learn their names. Then he decided to ask them to make notes about themselves on their cards—their outstanding physical or emotional or psychological characteristics. He spun it out further: Name your greatest prejudice, your favorite artist, your personal painting inclination. Or, ten things you

258

love, ten words describing yourself, your most profound experience, your most embarrassing moment.

All these give Kaupelis some insights into each student. Because the cards must be filled out rapidly, the students have less chance to throw up defenses. They are telling things to a stranger—Kaupelis—and making themselves vulnerable. That helps Kaupelis. But he wants his students to give to one another as well. He doesn't want them to end the class as strangers. He has each student whisper one deep secret to another, then listen to someone else's revelation. After that, he arbitrarily pairs off students and instructs them to visit a gallery or museum exhibition together. They must talk about the art they're seeing, maybe have lunch. Some continuing relationships are formed, which is nice, but that isn't what Kaupelis is looking for. He wants them to begin to be honest with one another, to let down the barriers. By the second week of class, they are talking about the drawings or paintings of people they know, not the strangers with whom they were thrown together through the vagaries of class schedules and registration cards. They are learning from one another as much as from Kaupelis.

Not that everyone in a class connects with everyone else. The art department at NYU is not comparable to the more comprehensive and single-minded schools like Pratt Institute or the Rhode Island School of Design which are concerned exclusively with training professional artists. NYU attracts and permits the presence of dilettantes, the blending of serious creative artists with those who plan to teach merely as a pleasant way to make a living. There are advanced students mixed with beginners, graduates with undergraduates, college art teachers with elementary school art teachers, visiting students taking just one course to transfer back to Wisconsin, French majors who need a few credits to graduate, foreigners groping for a specialization. Don Porter finds himself making judgments about the relative ability and intent of his classmates, and he interacts well only with those he regards his equals or superiors. But no one leaves a Kaupelis class untouched.

Partly, it's because he is a person of awesome energy. His schedule of up to twenty classroom hours a week would make most English and physics professors blanch, and he is active in school and departmental activities as well. In addition, he spends forty or fifty hours a week on his own painting. But more important to his success as a teacher is his ability to step outside his personal artistic preferences and work from the student's personal vision instead of his own. In classes of such variable intent and talent, it's a critical skill. It's why Kaupelis is the consensus choice as the most effective teacher in the department.

"I've been in classes where the instructor pushes everyone all in the same direction." This is Ellen Pitt, one of the most capable students in this class. (Also the messiest. Her hands and arms are stained with paint almost to the shoulders.) "My first year in college, I had a drawing instructor. When I looked around at the end of the course, I saw that everyone who took this guy painted and drew the same way. He put his stamp on everyone's psyche. Kaupelis isn't like that at all.

"He encourages you to move in your own direction. He's just great. First of all, he creates an atmosphere in class that I've never had before. People are very willing to share ideas. When they look at your work, they want to know what you're thinking. He sets up an aura where there is communication among everybody. And he has a very good eye in perceiving where you're going."

Ellen rubs her cheek, successfully smearing a brilliant green smudge down to her jaw. She glances at her painting as she talks. It is cool and Rothkoesque in its treatment of open fields of color. She is concerned about an edge between two aqua squares. Upon reflection, she decides she is pleased with it.

Asked about the contrast between students here and at

Cooper Union, which she attended as an undergraduate, she says that she finds communication among students better here. True, they were more committed *there,* and the level of talent was generally higher. But it was more competitive, too. The students weren't as willing to share creative information; they were afraid of offering advantage to classmates. At this stage in her development, she thinks she needs the freedom she can get here.

Activity in the room is beginning to slow. Some of the students are walking along the overhead balcony, surveying what their classmates have done today. Others are cleaning brushes and palettes, stacking their work in lockers, packing away paints. The chatter increases as they tell one another of the day's discoveries. Kaupelis reminds them that the next session is the last, and that he will want to see everything they've done this term. Then he removes his apron—which bears the words "I got my job through the New York Times"—and puts away his record albums.

The stunning redhead who had spent the class languidly toying with a vivid painting of hard-edge squiggles smiles at him as she leaves. She is immaculate, not a smudge on her or her trim boutique jeans and striped T-shirt. Kaupelis shakes his head when she has gone, partly because she is a delectable woman, partly because he discovered early in the course that she was not at all serious. Although he felt she had some talent, her work was just "little designer exercises, no sparkle, no warmth."

That is a problem for all teachers of art. Students can be carried along only to the point where talent or commitment desert them. The last decade has seen a surge of interest on campuses in the visual arts, a logical extension of the push toward individualism and self-expression. At first, dabblers dominated. They resisted learning basic techniques as intrusions on their identities. As in their zeal for social change, they had no intention of being confused by facts. To a large degree, they have been replaced by students genuinely concerned with developing what talents they might have. Ceramics, weaving, sculpture, and the graphic arts are seen as antidotes to the artifacts of a dehumanized, mass-produced industrial society. This does not guarantee that increases in art class enrollments will usher in a new era of vitality in American art. Much of the student interest is of a very personal sort, turned inward, without external ambition. As such, individual breakthroughs beyond elementary technique and into true creativity are no more likely than before. Burgeoning enrollments tease art teachers into believing in the revivification of the arts by a generation thought lost to moving pictures. Students like Kaupelis' redhead deflate the hope. She has learned technique, but will go no further. Painting is a diversion for her, not a need.

Each of us is issued a creative instinct. However it manifests itself—in turning ash on a wood lathe or arranging flowers or embroidering antimacassars—it is there. It cannot be taught, only exploited, honed, focused. There is not even agreement on what creativity *is*. The American Heritage and Shorter Oxford English dictionaries don't list the word. Webster's Seventh Collegiate chooses to illuminate with the definition that creativity is "the ability to create." Even Freud was thwarted. He wrote that psychoanalysis could "do nothing toward elucidating the nature of the artistic gift, nor can it explain the means by which the artist works." Jung asserted that "the creative act . . . will forever elude the human understanding. It can only be described in its manifestations; it can be obscurely sensed, but never wholly grasped."

Given that circumstance, teachers of art can only hope to lead their students by example and through progressively more complex creative acts to the threshold of comprehension, not beyond. Thus the compulsion of the academy to codify the sensory elements essential to the construction of works of art. Perspective and color theory and anatomy are reduced to rules, on the premise that to break them successfully (i.e., creatively) first requires knowledge of their existence and skill in their manipulation. Instruction in the mixing of paints and welding of scraps of metal is necessary, but is primarily a device to help the student discover relationships between the components of space, texture, line, color, and form without which no creative work can be constructed. Since talent and creativity are not susceptible to delineation, the student can only be helped to discover his personal vision on his own.

In this, the college art teacher is severely restricted by the conventions and economics of the larger institutions of which they are part. Ideally, art instruction is conducted in an informal, non-directive workshop atmosphere, as was true from the Greeks right through to this century. Apprentices observed their masters at work, drawing and sculpting and painting alongside them. They worked, ate, swept floors and ground pigment in the workshop every waking hour of every day. Their masters did not sap their own creative energies in designed instruction. The disciplines guiding the apprentices were only those of the studio. With the institutionalization of higher education imposed by training in those traditional professions in which credentials *were* desirable, the creative arts were boxed into compartments labeled as courses, credits, distributions, degrees, class sessions, and the whole man or woman. A student engrossed in an esthetic problem had to clean up and close his locker simply because a ringing bell signified it was time to hear of Charlemagne or the Counter-Reformation.

All that could be made tolerable by devoting entire mornings, at least, to studio work, and afternoons to economics and Latin. The mind could make that adjustment, even if it could not accept a physics professor's notion of what a painter need learn. More critical is space. Artists need light and airiness and very much space. An aircraft hangar or railroad station would do nicely. But construction of such a facility is expensive, not just because of its dimensions, but because of its resistance to ready conversion. A sculpture studio simply cannot be transformed to a classroom during a ten-minute break. Lithograph presses, pottery kilns, easels, and pottery wheels must stay in place. And, of course, they too are costly.

Finance officers, accomplished in "useful" skills, are not sympathetic to these needs. They are not the progeny of John Quincy Adams, who said: "We must learn the arts of war and independence so that our children can learn architecture and engineering so that their children may learn the fine arts and painting." Resolutions to educate the total human being are not honored in the breach, not when the physics or accounting departments need van de Graaf accelerators or IBM 360s.

Under these conditions, the teacher who can sustain his own creative vitality while inspiring students in a typically hostile or uncaring academic climate is exceptional. Some few have done it—Hans Hoffman, Josef Albers—and maintained their reputations as major influences in the world of art. They are joined by others who are admired and respected, if not venerated. Robert Kaupelis is one of these. Then, as throughout the professoriate, come the mediocrities. They isolate themselves from the major art centers. They settle in Salina, Kansas, and Mobile, Alabama, and accept the plaudits of provincials and snarl about the evils of the trendy art scenes of the Northeast and West Coast, reproducing sufficient numbers of flashy renditions of dated concepts to fill their assigned spaces in the annual faculty art show. Kaupelis is not one of them.

In the elevator after his class, Kaupelis is revved up and loquacious, like most teachers who really enjoy their work. About the nun, he says his ten-year-old daughter has a much better notion of what art is all about.

"And the nun teaches children art! Isn't that sad?"

The elevator groans to a stop, Kaupelis lunges out. He moves like Joe Namath leaving a huddle.

He cuts right when he leaves the building, undismayed by a blast of mid-afternoon heat, then right again at the corner. This is the eastern border of Washington Square, the park that serves as the *de facto* campus of New York University. Catty-corner behind him is the university's new $24 million library, President James Hester's realized vision, Philip Johnson's design, and Elmer Holmes Bobst's gift. It is an awesome monument in red stone dominating the square. On its dedication, a *Times* reporter enthused about "an edifice of Medici magnificance." Representatives of the Greenwich Village community were less enthusiastic. They fought the building for five years, contending, among many things, that it would throw a shadow on the park. It doesn't.

Kaupelis doesn't pause to consider the building or the controversy it raised. He's talking about the people in the class just ended.

"That nun is going to be sick when she goes back and shows the bishop her transcript. I'm going to give her a 'C.' That's the same as flunking her, right? But it's being dishonest. She really should get an 'F.' How the hell can I give a nun, who's worked hard, an 'F'? How?" At the corner of Waverly Place, he tries to hail a cab while he keeps talking. "You know, that one joker, Don, he's doing that drip thing. That's really dumb for him to be doing. But he's thinking! And I like what he's thinking about, even though the imagery is so derivative of everybody in the world. He's done so many good things, and y'know, the guy can draw fantastically well."

A block further, at University Place and Eighth Street, Kaupelis succeeds in flagging down a taxi. He gives directions to his studio uptown on Seventh Avenue and keeps talking.

"The best painter in that class is Ellen. She was the one covered with paint. She has a *feel* in her paint. She knows what it's about. And she's aware of that business about Rothko, but she's not whimsical. A good painter." Ellen had said that Cooper Union had offered her great diversity of facilities—in photography, graphics, sculpture—that she couldn't get here.

"We don't have good equipment," Kaupelis concedes. "But for anyone who really wants to do any sculpting, they can sure as hell go down and weld and use plaster and plastic, just about anything. I've heard a lot of negative comment about schools like Cooper Union and Pratt. They take themselves almost too seriously, there's a competitiveness that's almost unhealthy. A friend, an art teacher, was telling me that he had taught at a couple of professional art schools. *He* thinks NYU is just terrific. He likes the relationships we have with each other in the art department. This is a big institution, but people constantly say that they go to other institutions, but then come back. People complain here, say this is an impersonal paint factory . . . but that class I just had had sixteen students, not sixteen hundred. People say this is a great place, especially after you've been somewhere else."

Finally, the cab lurches to a stop. Kaupelis' studio is an old loft building over a bar. It has a stamped tin ceiling, wooden floors, and plaster walls, all coated with a primeval urban grime. There's a toilet, a telephone, a cot. And space. A non-representational artist, Kaupelis works under artificial light. That "north light" cliché is for painters who work from live models or landscapes. Constant, unchanging illumination is what Kaupelis needs. Anyway, he does most of his work at night. Usually, he stays and paints at the studio from Tuesday through Thursday. The long weekends are spent at his home in semi-rural northern Westchester County. If he didn't maintain the studio, he'd lose his creative time to the Penn Central Railroad. At home, he takes drawing materials and sits before the television set, producing dozens of exploratory color sketches at a sitting. The good ones he takes to his Manhattan studio. Some of them become paintings.

Ten years ago, Kaupelis produced semi-figurative, loose-limbed works, full of juicy splashes of color, arch humor, bits of collage and poetry. Someone interested in pigeon holing his work would most likely have thought of Larry Rivers or Robert Rauschenberg. One piece, now in the NYU collection, featured an impossibly voluptuous and faceless caricature of a Playmate-of-the-Month, with paper Christmas stars for nipples and the legend MOM beneath. Pop Art was in vogue at the time. The administrator who chose the painting for his office had to contend for weeks after with the stony disapproval of his elderly office supervisor whose view of motherhood was more exalted.

The representative elements are gone from his work now. Hard-edge stripes and edges meld with free-wheeling splotches of exquisitely pure and intense hues. Seemingly they are spontaneously rendered, but the exuberant brushwork is controlled, however imperceptibly, and the structure and value relationships are in immaculate balance. His creative process involves long moments of careful contemplation punctuated by frenzied attacks upon the canvas. He talks to the painting. "Come on, why the hell don't you work? What color do you want? What do you need? Why won't you accept this green? Why are you rejecting this red? *Talk to me!*" Painting is a lonely pursuit.

A current work is tacked to the wall, under brilliant light. To the left of the easel, there are ceiling-high racks of stretched paintings and piles of still others, rolled. Boxes of color sketches sit about. Any one of the sketches, with their vibrant color and witty detail, would be a welcome addition to any collection. But for Kaupelis, they are merely half-formed visual thoughts—doodles, almost.

Kaupelis guesses he has produced about three thousand finished works in his career, and he doesn't count the thousands of sketches.

Kaupelis leads a faintly schizoid life. He has his teaching at Washington Square, his painting on Seventh Avenue, his family in Westchester and a summer house on Candlewood Lake in Connecticut. He's given a lot of thought to the conflicts between them, to the contrasting demands of his son's Little League games, departmental meetings, grading, his dealings with patrons and gallery owners. He's written it out on paper:

> When I was in high school I wanted to paint . . . as far as I knew at the time painting meant copying the covers of magazines. My art teacher said, "The way to do that, Bob, is to become an art teacher . . . look how easy it is, nothing to it."
>
> When I went to college I had no idea there was anything like pedagogy . . . terrible word, pedagogy . . . that there was an ART of teaching and that teaching was an honorable profession . . .
>
> > that it was a tough profession and that it needed people with some vim, vigor, and a hell of a lot of *guts*.
>
> So when I left Buffalo I *was* a teacher.
>
> I was transformed, I was no longer a painter . . . oh! I painted! . . . but my whole point in life was to change the state of
>
> art education in the United States.
>
> VERY PRESUMPTUOUS KID!
>
> So I taught for a while in the public schools and eventually I got to NYU.
>
> I had been painting all of this time . . . been doing all kinds of things . . .
>
> > constructions
> > jewelry
> > sculpture
>
> but I wasn't *committed* to any one art.
>
> > At NYU a faculty member has to be a producing artist . . . they expect it and I think that may have been one of my motivations . . . I wasn't hired to be an artist, yet they wouldn't hire me if I wasn't . . .

They hired me because they thought I was a good
teacher . . .

I had an excellent record.
But . . . one was also expected to be involved in his own
thing . . . his own creative work.
I became more and more involved
and finally
I left all of the education
courses that I had been
hired to teach and taught
nothing but studio courses since that
is where my real commitment was and one day . . . I
don't know when . . .

at what point in time . . .
I considered myself a painter.
Nevertheless, to this day I still
think of myself as an art educa-
tor because everything I do in a
studio teaching situation, as far
as I'm concerned, *is*
art education.
I'm wondering . . . *why* paint?
Does an artist have to paint?
Of course not!
An artist may be
a lot of things.
But then, why do I *choose* to paint?
I have only a slight idea.
It's work.
It's pain.
It's torture.
The worst moments of my
life have been
passed in my studio . . . wondering
struggling
thinking
feeling

crying . . . because a thing doesn't work or out of utter frustration because *I don't know*

what to do.

Kaupelis is uncommon in both halves of his professional life. Where many (perhaps most) art professors at other colleges are unproductive most of the year, Kaupelis is actively drawing and painting and thinking every day of his life. And where other painters of lesser talent immerse themselves in the frenetic New York art scene, Kaupelis rarely does. He doesn't have time for socializing.

He doesn't regret missing those fringe pleasures of the life of a New York artist. His son's baseball games arouse more excitement in him. He is enthusiastic about both professional roles, even though he has come to think of himself as a painter first and a teacher second. He experiences no visible discontent of any significance. But . . . no one's *that* happy.

Perhaps, in Kaupelis' case, there is the recurrent desire, however fleeting, to drop the teaching and the schedules and the faculty meetings and devote all his time to his art. After all, his work is represented in the collections of several corporations and colleges and dozens of private patrons. He has exhibited his paintings in nearly a hundred shows he can remember, and that doesn't include sixteen one-man exhibitions. Kaupelis' paintings are good. Everyone says so. Critical reviews are gaudily enthusiastic, even downright hysterical.

But even a person of his talent must recognize the odds against making a living by painting alone. Reality intrudes. And Bob Kaupelis lives the good life, though his wife works too. They have two houses in the country, his studio in the city. They need the money. Even without both houses, paint is expensive, two dollars or more a tube. Canvas, brushes, turpentine, painting knives, drawing paper can run into the hundreds of dollars in even a few months, especially for a prolific artist.

If the thought of cutting loose does intrude, Kaupelis must suppress it. He seems a practical man, and the compromise is a small one.

Art is important to him. It is not irrelevant, as some are saying. A former student, a good one, came by one day. He had stopped painting. Kaupelis asked why.

"Man," he said bitterly, "the whole world is going to hell. Like, people are beating up each other, it's an oppressive society. The blacks hate the whites, the whites hate the blacks. People die of napalm in Vietnam, students get shot on college campuses. So what's the use of it all? How can art have any meaning under the conditions in which we live today?"

Kaupelis thought about that, and wrote:

> I guess painting is not important anymore; yup, he's absolutely right . . .
> painting is not important
> that's true . . . if for instance, the flight of a butterfly is no longer important,
>
> or the song of a bird, or the rustle of leaves, or the sun reflecting on a river . . .
>
>   yeah, then I guess it's not important.
> I just can't agree with that.
> Not in the slightest.
> If this is what humanity is about and if art is irrelevant . . .
>
>   there's not much left.
> I'll throw my cards with the artists, they are the humanists of our day.
> Contrary to some schools of thought at the moment, I believe that abstract art is humanistic. I think Mondrian is one of the most passionate painters to have ever existed and that's because
>   he was committed
>   committed to an idea

                committed to relationships
                            because he created form
                            because he painted with LOVE.

   Bob Kaupelis, artist who teaches, teacher who paints, is
glaring at the painting on the wall. He puts down his glass,
goes to his paint table, swirls a brush in a dollop of red, and
lunges at the picture. It's talking.

CHAPTER 13

A college president is of a singular breed. To succeed—and mere professional survival has become the basic component of success—he or she (but mostly he) must represent the combined skills of diplomat, military tactician, orator, machine politician, scholar, dockworker, captain of industry, priest, raconteur, and chief of protocol. He must summon up the appropriate talents in a dozen quick changes per fourteen-hour day, and it will not hurt if he is suave, handsome, charming, and warm. Which of the attributes will be most critical depends upon circumstance and fashion, but they all must be there. Inevitably, he is the natural enemy of the Ovsiews and Zinns.

Superman and Wonder Woman. And no letup. Douglas Knight, onetime president of Duke University, described the job as comparable to standing at an intersection with five herds of buffalo coming down the roads at once. Whatever he does, it will have been wrong.

The president of the Claremont University Center in California, Louis Benezet, once described the reactions of his constituencies: "The president has been too lax; he has been too firm and unyielding; he has not listened to his faculty; he has waited too long to act; he has called in the police; he hasn't called in the police. Whatever it is he should have done, he didn't do it; whatever he shouldn't have done, he foolishly did."

With the ebbing of student activism and the tight economy of the Seventies, the president's skills as a fundraiser are in greater focus, but the others must still be there, ready. One college board of trustees, seeking a candidate for its presidential vacancy, listed the following qualifications:

A man of integrity who is a distinguished scholar in his field, who is an educational statesman and who is aware of the mission of teaching, research, and science. A man who has had previous executive experience and demonstrated executive ability, and who is not only able to head a million dollar corporation, but who also has the political awareness to be able to work with senators, congressmen, and state legislators. A man who has a sense for public relations combined with social skills and good health and who is between thirty and fifty-five years old.

All this, to deal with the traditional three estates of a college or university—the students, the faculty, the administration—plus those of the alumni, the trustees, the government, and the community. Few such people exist. When they do, they more often enter industry or government, where the rewards are more inviting.

Nevertheless, there are always those willing, even eager, to try.

A gloomy mid-December day in 1972. Across the bay, cars slither along freeways in two inches of unaccustomed snow. Here in the City, the rain fades to clammy mist and back again. The office of the most famous college president in the world is blessedly warm. The ambiance is cluttered, informal. Folksy. The floor is covered in the rust-colored plush carpeting that is *de rigeur* for university presidential suites. A large triptych featuring an orange disk superimposed upon a mushily defined landscape is the dominant decoration.

274

The reception area is presided over by a placid, grand-motherly sort with mounds of silver hair swept loosely back and heaped precariously at the back of her head. Dainty steel-rimmed glasses are perched upon the end of her nose, over a tiny rosebud mouth. When the President opens his office door and leans expectantly against the frame, she sorts through the waiting visitors and selects a young reporter from *The Phoenix.*

Inside, the reporter is seated on a utilitarian leather sofa in one corner of the spacious room. Dr. S. I. Hayakawa takes a facing chair. He doesn't *look* like a college president. Most obviously, he is not Caucasian. He is probably the first Japanese-American to hold the position anywhere in the United States, and that in a state historically inhospitable to Orientals. His clothes are not modish in cut or combination—he wears a lavender shirt and a striped Rooster tie with a narrow-lapeled hounds' tooth jacket and black loafers. His gray-brown hair is brushed straight back from the high forehead and he wears a closely trimmed mustache carefully spaced between his nose and lip. There is an Indian turquoise ring on his third finger, left hand, and he wears large hornrimmed glasses.

His manner is one of controlled dynamism. On the coffee table is a dish full of matchbooks, two autographed baseballs nestled among them. While the younger man arranges his thoughts, the President selects one of the balls, hefts it, squeezes it between both hands, puts it back. He aligns a small pile of books with the edge of the table. Then he settles back. For the moment.

"Okay?" He is resigned to another series of the same questions he has been answering for four years. He wants to get it over with, but he is tolerant. He has been—and is—a journalist himself and he accepts the inevitability of the questions, though he is no longer flattered by the attention.

"Ready?" he prompts again.

"Yes," says the reporter, although he is not. He is, perhaps, a bit awed and determined not to betray that. "What did you see as your first duty when you took office that December?"

The President shifts in his chair. His answer is in phrases.

"I believe that . . . given the situation as it was in 1968 . . . the first and most important task was . . . the restoration of order on the campus and instruction in the classroom. . . . No changes for the better could be effected while the campus was in turmoil. . . . You couldn't get Black Studies going, you couldn't get interdisciplinary studies going . . . you couldn't let in more EOP students . . . you couldn't do a damn thing unless the campus was organized and ready to receive students and conduct instruction. So . . . I did what was necessary to reestablish . . . an academic . . . environment."

His thoughtful manner and measured responses befit a renowned scholar. But in this instance, they are indicative merely of simple courtesy—the pauses give the reporter time to scribble his notes—and of a desire *not* to be misunderstood yet again. After some years of relative calm, this latest siege of journalistic probing into the mind of President Hayakawa is inspired by the announcement of his retirement. He has had time to reflect, to formulate his answers to the inevitable questions.

"Now, since that time . . . the changes that have taken place . . . are only partly a result of my actions. Most are very much due to forces external to the university itself."

"Which changes?"

"Changes in the atmosphere of the campus you see four years later. One is the de-escalation of our participation in the war. Another is the elimination of the draft. The need to demonstrate against the system diminishes."

"Basically, the students don't have anything to demonstrate against anymore?"

"That's one thing. Then another important fact is . . . that economic conditions have changed. A recession has set in and

276

students realize that a college education is no longer a guarantee of gainful employment on graduation. . . . Therefore, there's an awful lot more of serious, career-minded studying going on now than there was. . . . Or let's put it the other way around. Four years ago, a majority of our students were engaged in career-minded studying, but there was a strong minority that were not. That minority has either changed its mind or disappeared."

Images intrude of white-helmeted, visored police, batons at the ready. Bloodied heads. Tear gas. Unintelligible screams rushing at microphones, careening away. Placards. Scuffling feet. Blurred, uncomprehending images on TV sets that turn blood to Day-Glo. It is impossible to be with this gentle man with the soft, modulated voice and not remember. Isla Vista. Jackson State. Orangeburg. It blends now, it's hard to sort out. Which was first? What happened where? Berkeley, Columbia, Stanford. The Harvard yard. The math building at Wisconsin. Kent State.

San Francisco State.

No one died here. A boy blew off his hands when he tried to set a bomb in the Creative Arts building. The bedroom of a professor's daughter was firebombed. Students and teachers were beaten by police, students beat teachers, students beat other students. But no one died here.

At center was Samuel Ichiye Hayakawa. From Berkeley in 1964 to Kent State in 1970, the youth revolution—if that's what it was—produced a bountiful supply of heroes and devil-figures. Which was which depended upon personal and ideological perspective. But the activist leaders, instinctive masters of media manipulation who were largely unencumbered by subsequent accountability, were the most arresting figures in that six-year succession of horrifying incidents tumbling over agonizing confrontations. Mario Savio, Mark Rudd, Tom Hayden captured attention and imagination—or roiled the bile. They were admittedly bright, unconventional, direct, and eminently quotable. They were easy to despise or emulate.

Never trust anyone over thirty.

College and university presidents, the most visible and accessible proxies for the Establishment, were overmatched. Maturity and experience were liabilities. Years of seeing all sides, of balancing the demands and needs of several constituencies, had squeezed dry their psychic viscera and drained their passion. In the face of intolerable insult, they smiled fixedly and walked on. Confronted by unspeakable collective provocation or individual rage, they feigned disinterest or sympathetic understanding. They sputtered, they buckled, they caved in. They were, in the main, juiceless, gray, imperious, and cool to the touch. Robots.

That was not really the way they were, but it was the way they seemed, which suited perfectly the needs of the white middle-class student revolutionaries caught up in their paroxysm of single-minded idealism. Their symbols of filial or institutional authority had to be unloving but loftily avuncular, uncaring but hypocritically tolerant. Most of all, they had to be dryly unidimensional. Investiture of enemies with human complexities created hesitation, muddied purity of purpose. Consistently bland civility, that was the ticket.

S. I. Hayakawa didn't fit. That was the *real* reason he became the object of such intense loathing for the assorted Third World militants, professorial activists, uncertain liberals, and sunshine radicals at San Francisco State in the winter of 1968–1969. When someone yelled at him, he yelled back. Threatened, he retaliated. Stung by words or actions, he struck out, often without thinking, sometimes to his subsequent personal regret. From time to time, he made public jokes, and even needled his opposition.

All this very human behavior was quite startling and unacceptable to would-be revolutionaries accustomed by newsprint and pictures to Clark Kerr of Berkeley, Grayson Kirk of

278

Columbia, James A. Perkins of Cornell, and Nathan Pusey of Harvard. It was, indeed, contrary to their experience at the sprawling Holloway Avenue campus in west San Francisco. In the months before Hayakawa was appointed acting president, one predecessor resigned, and a second was fired. They had followed the accepted pattern.

Hayakawa was different. He got angry. He fought to be heard. His was not an august dignity and it infuriated his opponents.

On December 2, 1968, there was a sound truck at the entrance to the college campus. Demonstrators were urging students, at a highly amplified decibel rate, to close down the campus until the non-negotiable demands of the Black Student Union had been met. In an impulsive action that hit front pages around the world, Dr. Hayakawa mounted the bed of the truck and began tearing out the microphone and speaker wires. Jeered by the demonstrators, he turned and mockingly led them in their chants. Later, as he moved through the crowd, someone snatched his tam-o'-shanter from his head. Instead of walking on, he plunged into the hostile crowd and retrieved the tam.

Allowing for reportorial flourishes, that was the way the incident was seen by most of the Establishment press. Left-wing participants and right-wing observers had different interpretations.

Kay Boyle was a member of the English department at San Francisco State in 1968. She is a prolific writer of fiction and poetry, an essayist, member of the National Institute of Arts and Letters. She is a practicing radical of many years standing and her lifestyle apparently fits well with the communal jeans-backpack-boots-naturalist ethos of the counterculture. In *A Long Walk At San Francisco State*, she waves her credentials frequently: ". . . I had lived on mountain tops, carried my babies in a rucksack on my back when I skied, believed in poets more than any other men, honored French Resistance fighters and Italian partisans, crossed into Spain with letters from the exiled to the brave and the defiant and the imprisoned there, and brought their illicit messages out."

Understandably, she described the sound truck incident from another perspective:

And then the amplified voice abruptly stopped speaking, and students were crowding around the sound truck and crying out in protest. On top of the truck was a whirling, irate little man, wearing a tam-o'-shanter, a plump little figure who was tugging and leaping and close to foaming at the mouth. The acting president of the college was pushing and shoving at those who mounted the truck, including newsmen, and clawing furiously at the sound truck's wires. Once he had jerked them out, he swung around to the crowd, and, like a demented orchestra conductor, with arms and hands savagely beating out the rhythm, in furious mockery he led the students in the chant of "On Strike!" "Shut it down!" [Later, still shaken, he told the press: "I can't stand that mindless chanting!"]

I stood close to the truck, which was student-owned, and the owners were struggling now to keep the amplifier from destruction at Hayakawa's hands. He was flinging out to right and left into the crowd his "loyal to Dr. Hayakawa" scrolls, each tied with a blue ribbon, and every now and then he dodged as a student flung the scroll back at him. He was shouting the protestors down, his voice gone shrill as a banshee's, and I called out to him as loudly as I could: "Hayakawa Eichmann!" He swung around, trembling, and demanded above the uproar to know what I had said. When I repeated the two names, he shook an agitated finger down at me. "Kay Boyle, you're fired!"

This self-serving interpretation of the feelings of others ("close to foaming at the mouth") is as characteristic of the description of events offered by people in conflict as is elaborately disproportionate insult ("Hayakawa Eichmann"). Professor Boyle cannot be faulted for that bit of humanity. (Her choice of the photograph to appear on the dust jacket of her book is more subject to question. Throughout the text, she identifies herself with the aspirations of Third World peoples, and against the oppression and racial slanders of the majority white society. Yet she is pictured leaning against a lifesize caricature of Dr. Hayakawa which features the slanty eyes and buck teeth of a 1942 Hearst cartoon of Hirohito.)

College presidents, however, are not expected to respond in kind to the provocations of the moment. Hayakawa did. Since his life and career had not led him inexorably to this point in history, he did not really know how a college president was supposed to act. He didn't care. He was not trained, through inclination, breeding, or societal insistence, to be an administrator. And no one asked him to solve the problem of youthful turmoil at San Francisco State.

But to him, the victory of the Free Speech Movement at Berkeley was one of the great academic disasters of his lifetime. When he saw the movement spreading, "with its dogmatism, its interference with academic freedom, its irresponsibility," he "thought and thought and thought" what had to be done to stop it.

Unbidden, he had spent the previous Christmas putting his solutions on paper. Eleven months later, he happened to be there when the state Regents were casting frantically about for more presidential cannon-fodder. He was later to say that once he became president, he stopped thinking. He already knew what he was going to do. Naturally, his detractors seized upon the remark, as they did many others reported out of context or without explanation.

Anyone who has not faced a crowd of angry people for whom he is a symbol of the hated oppressor is incapable of imagining the degree of pure animal courage which must be mustered to stand ground. Courage is buttressed by pride, ego, and moral conviction, of course, but they are not always enough. Once exposed to such a situation, one is constantly fearful of responding irrationally, or being caught in a lie or in ignorance . . . or simply being thought a fool. That's the worst of all. For a college president, any one of these lapses can be sufficient to end a career. So most of them do their best to avoid the confrontations. Hayakawa didn't. It was partly calculation ("I wanted them to be more afraid of me than I was of them"), but mostly he considered, acted . . . and responded. That he did not observe the rules of presidential behavior or the precast role assigned to him by his adversaries was not surprising. He was sixty-two, and this was not a new profession. Rather, it was a momentary duty he felt obligated to undertake.

In his office, now near retirement, he sighs inwardly as the earnest *Phoenix* reporter begins to forget who is interviewer and who is subject.

". . . that's what I was talking about mostly," the reporter is saying. "The political revolution was a joke all the way through. But the social revolution was kind of apparent. I mean, there were a lot of changes that came about . . ."

"Like what?" The President betrays some impatience. He's heard this before, and he sniffs a bit as he demands specifics. "Sexual freedom?"

The reporter is taken aback. He tries to regroup.

"Not so much that . . . ah . . . more tolerance for different points of view . . . the fact that . . ."

"No, no! There was less!" The President's voice rises just a bit. "That was the characteristic of the radical movement of '66 to '70. There was *less* tolerance than there ever had been before."

"I mean the *social* part of it," the reporter plunges on. "I'm not talking about the SDS, 'cause they were a different thing altogether, they were falling off the left wing. The mere fact that you can have a lot more diverse lifestyles . . . people don't get upset like they would back in the early Sixties. It used to be everyone was concerned with everyone else's business, and today it seems to me the attitude is more like 'Let him do what he wants' . . . y'know . . . 'I don't care' . . . y'know . . . 'It doesn't affect me . . . as long as he doesn't shoot me or something' . . . and . . . ah . . . I got off the track there. . . ."

The young man stops. He is beginning to come apart. As he spoke, Dr. Hayakawa stood, walked to a table by the window, moved a small ceramic an inch to the right, walked back, leaned against his chair. His expression has been . . . well . . . inscrutable. Now, seeing the reporter's discomfort, he softens. He has been a teacher most of his life, and he uses a teacher's device to help the young man complete his thought.

"In that sense there has been tolerance of new lifestyles?"

The reporter brightens. "Yes! One interesting thing I must admit along with that. Casting off the middle class as everyone did in the middle Sixties . . . it was pretty much a fad, no one really thought about it much. You'd see your old man go off to work from nine to five, and he'd be grumpy all the time and you'd say you weren't going to have any part of that. But a lot of things have been happening to, like, my friends and everything. They meet women they fall in love with and they decide they want to live with just this one woman and they care a lot for them and they think it wouldn't be a bad idea to get some insurance, some security. And they want to live in a nice place and they go out and get a job. . . . I find so many of my friends who were flaming radicals of the late Sixties falling into a middle-class existence. It's very ironic, but it seems like there's a lot of credence to middle-class lifestyles. Responsibilities . . ."

Dr. Hayakawa sighs audibly now. The reporter stops again. The professor-president sums up. The young man knows that the interview is over. Pleasantries are exchanged.

The President must feel he has provided copy for every

journalist in the world, while at the same time having to listen to their personal evaluations of whatever topics were under discussion. One morning in January 1969, he had to give fifteen radio interviews in a single morning. The reporters were from all over the world. The BBC asked him to come to London ("Goodness, I couldn't take time out, though I would have loved to in the middle of all that"). Not long after, he was boomed as a Senatorial candidate. He would have loved to have done that, too, but he couldn't leave the college yet. He was needed there.

He shows the reporter out, pauses, then walks across the room to answer the buzzing intercom. On the top shelf of the bookcase behind his desk is a row of hard hats, gifts from well-wishers. One is from a member of the Cook County police department. On a visit to Chicago, he had cemented the admiration of the cops by beating five of them in a poker game at the back of a precinct station house. On his relationship with the police, he was later to reflect: "What happened so often, police were given no specific orders, they were called in—unwillingly—in insufficient numbers and then were given a bad time. Then they struck out blindly. I decided there was only one thing to do—call in enough police and give them full backing. No withdrawing of charges. The sound truck incident was shown on television. That day I won the hearts of the police. They said, 'Goddammit, there's a man with *guts!*' They respected that. And gee, their discipline and morale improved right down the line."

To the left of the books and the hard hats is a wall of superb African masks of museum quality. To the right, another painting by the artist represented in the anteroom, and a huge sculpture of a winged beast. Margedant Hayakawa carefully selected the salmon-colored paint on the walls to set off the collection.

He riffles distractedly through a magazine, goes to the window. Construction machinery thumps and hums outside.

Two weeks later, he is to be pictured in the newspapers, in one of the hard hats, lofting rocks through the windows of a food-service building to publicize its demolition, making room for a new student union building.

An assistant enters the office to discuss recent fund-raising efforts. He gets ten minutes, and Dr. Hayakawa defers a minor decision. Next is a student government leader soliciting the President's advice and participation in a speakers' series. A strapping, handsome, golden Californian youth, his hair is gathered at the neck by a clip. He is articulate and deferential, but not obsequious. The President suggests several speakers and subjects, with a view toward lively controversy. "You want a person known for his liberalism, but not fierce and dogmatic, don't you? Now who could that be?" Pause. "It isn't Axen, because he's quarrelsome. No, Mr. ———— is so preoccupied with educational finance, salary scales and stuff like that he's just a big bore. . . . Why don't you leave that question with me?" Another name. "No, we'd be too polite with each other, and that wouldn't be much fun." Decision deferred. A chat with his secretary after he shows the boy out.

"Did you hear that young man say he wanted to restore a sense of community?" he says to her with visible pleasure. "The fact he *wants* to means it's already being established." More evidence that his duty is done.

The afternoon continues. Six giggling freshman girls are ushered in. They are being initiated into a sorority.

"Part of their gruesome ritual," he explains, "is to be photographed with the President." Gales of giggles. "A very cruel and unusual punishment."

Then another aide, Homer Dolby, here to discuss the Banker's Club dinner. Is there a firm the President can approach to bankroll the event for $1,000? Yes, says Hayakawa, but he wants to talk it over with members of his advisory board. A professor next, seeking a letter over the President's signature to be sent to foundations requesting support of an endowed chair in Japanese–American relations. They need $200,000 over the next three years for instruction, administrative salaries, publication of monographs. The President asks him to leave the materials to study overnight.

The buzzer again. A student is here again to complain about a professor whose lectures she believes to be incoherent, rambling, and incompetent. Dr. Hayakawa is troubled, for while routine administration is not his milieu, students and teaching are. He feels some element of malice in this student's repeated petitions. Again, the thoughtful moment before opening the door.

She is tall, plain, intense, and holds herself as if afraid of hurt. A friend has come with her—blonde, overweight, her guileless face temporarily fixed in determined support of her friend's allegations. Dr. Hayakawa half-sits on the edge of his desk, arms folded. When his visitors do not speak, he does.

"Professor ——— has learned of your complaints, of course. Has he reacted in the classroom on the subject? Has he done anything or said anything?"

Her voice is reedy, pinched. "Not that I know of."

"Umm. We're dealing here with a professor of seniority and rank, and it's a very delicate matter. I've already had one conference with his dean and I have another meeting on the subject with the dean and others, including the professor himself. You mustn't expect anything drastic. If you're hoping to see him shot at dawn, you might as well give up now. And he himself has some complaints—not about you as a class—but the situation in which he has been placed. There has been a peculiar increase in the number of students enrolled in the department. There are far more students than planned for, and they are far less prepared."

His tone is not one of chastisement. Perhaps he can temper their fierce resolution by explanation of all circumstances. But students are rarely sympathetic to those they feel are guilty of incompetence or wrongdoing. Years of sacrifice and earnest endeavor, family responsibility, the maintenance of a career and the unlikely resumption of it elsewhere at an advanced age—these are matters they are unlikely to comprehend or consider. When the President is interrupted by a phone call, they exchange glances that speak of confirmation of their assumption of ultimate whitewash. The professor is guilty. Off with his head.

The blonde student's hair is cut in bangs that stop at her eyelids. She must raise her jaw to see, which gives her a pugnacious look and makes her blink.

"Will there be a hearing?" she demands when Dr. Hayakawa has finished the telephone conversation.

"There is nothing in the nature of a formal charge to require a hearing."

The chief protestor's lips go thin.

"But you said that a teacher could be let go in two days on a major charge. The charge remains incompetence. The semester is drawing to a close and we're tired of him playing games with our heads. We have grades to worry about and we have to take the class. We're getting nothing out of the class and we see 'D' or 'F' on our papers."

"I understand that," the President replies, "but we're treating it as a complaint, not a formal charge."

"Okay. When you have a complaint, what do you do? Just discuss it?" She is increasingly indignant, but her voice is under control. "You're just going to have a few more meetings? When does a complaint turn into a charge?"

"That's a legal question I don't know the answer to."

"Who would know?" she snaps.

"The dean, I suppose. Have you talked to him?"

She brushes that aside. "What was Professor ———'s response to the charge? Did he take it as a joke? The last time we told him about our complaints before we brought them to you, he laughed! He said, 'Oh, you just think I'm a bastard,' and went on to say that when he was a student that kind of

287

teacher was a good teacher. Which has nothing to do with it."
She is *incredulously* indignant.

The discussion continues, the two students pressing, the President deferring while attempting to resolve his puzzlement with their vindictiveness. Elvis Stahr, once president of Indiana University, said upon his resignation that he had "finally asked himself how much longer he wanted to spend endless hours talking seriously about many demands which were serious only because not wasting time on them might be dangerous."

There is an element of that here, although the danger is of a different variety. Certainly a college president must allow enormous amounts of his time for often fruitless conversation, if only to avoid the accusation of autocratic behavior.

The students eventually are mollified by Dr. Hayakawa's proposal that their final papers be graded by a qualified stranger. But when they leave, it is clear that they will return. He sighs. Outside, the gloom has turned to an early night of cold, persistent rain. He will leave in another hour or so, arriving home with an attaché case full of papers to be sifted by morning. Ten to twelve hours a day in the office, another two or three at home. At least there is no dinner or reception or lecture tonight. Most nights there is.

"Home" is over the Golden Gate Bridge, in Mill Valley. In 1968–1969, a popular placard slogan was "Tojo Is Alive and Well in Marin County." The spacious but unpretentious Hayakawa home is nestled among tangles of cypress at 225 Eldridge Road. It is close to its neighbors, unprotected. Even after two bomb threats, their number and address were listed in the telephone directory. The Hayakawas didn't hide.

The house is cool, dim, calm. The color scheme is neutral to display more examples of the collection of African sculpture and Japanese ceramics. There is no decorator fussiness. Its atmosphere seems a proper extension of the less flamboyant half of the couple who own the house.

Mrs. Hayakawa is taller than her husband. She is dressed neatly, her yellow hair cut short and without contrivance. Her manner when greeting a visitor is shyly tentative. Amplified in her are the gentler traits of her husband—vulnerability, thoughtfulness, courtesy. Trust. She is quick to confirm that those characteristics, as ascribed to Dr. Hayakawa, truly describe him.

"He is a remarkable man, not afraid of the bad opinion of his peers," she says. "But they'll find out one day."

She was afraid for him a lot, as the time he went to the dangerous Fillmore district to meet—at their request—three girlfriends of militant student leaders. He snuck away from his police guards to go, taking only a young female friend from Berkeley. "Anything could have happened, but his conversation with them probably marked the end of the strike."

Mrs. Hayakawa remembers the time without pleasure. She obviously does not have his taste for the limelight. But she knew he had to do it. He had become increasingly concerned about the drift of events. He said that giving in to the more outrageous black student demands was condescension, another form of racism.

That December, he had called her from the campus and said "Guess what? I'm Acting President!" She smiles at the memory of his excitement, and at her determination not to betray her concern for his safety and her unhappiness with the drastic change in their way of life.

Along with the threats and the twenty-four-hour police guard, there was a $400 telephone bill the first month and 25,000 letters—largely supportive of his stand, she says—in the week before he opened the college.

Margedant Peters Hayakawa couldn't believe it was all happening. It was unreal. She had to become used to his long hours, "very strenuous, very tiring, the combination of administrative and ceremonial duties." The uproar was hard on their children, she knows. "They had to confront their peers. But they made it. I'm proud of them."

Their eldest son, Allan, is twenty-seven, married, living on a farm in Oregon. He doubts he will return to the insurance business. Daughter Wynn is training to become a potter at the university in Santa Cruz. Both have traveled to Japan to visit their grandparents. Their second son, Mark, is twenty-three and lives at home. He is severely retarded, the subject of a moving *McCall's* article by Dr. Hayakawa, "Our Son Mark." He spends his days at a workshop in San Rafael. "He's quite well-adjusted, very sweet, but he will always have to live in a sheltered environment. Don is wonderful with him."

Dr. Hayakawa ("Don") and his future wife met when Margedant was an undergraduate at Wisconsin and he was a graduate assistant. He was giving a talk on T. S. Eliot to the campus literary club. It was 1936, and Don was being baited by his colleagues who disapproved of his support of Eliot, who was an Anglo-Catholic (a now murky basis for academic distaste). Margedant admired his pluck, though she tended to agree with his opponents. They saw each other again while working on the literary magazine, and they married in May, 1937. His parents had returned to Japan when Hayakawa was at the University of Manitoba. Her parents were pained by the mixed marriage, primarily because they were afraid for her. She is sorry that her father didn't live to see it "all turn out so well." They didn't encounter too many problems because of their races, but when they settled in the Chicago area, his status in a country at war with his parents' homeland was uncertain in the extreme. He could not become a citizen, and the government kept reclassifying him from "enemy alien" to something else and back again.

Hayakawa was not deterred. He was co-author of an Oliver Wendell Holmes biography published in 1939. *Language in Action* came out in 1941, the book that established his reputation as a semanticist.* The fact that it was a Book-of-the-Month Club selection gave comfort to those of his colleagues who even today denigrate his scholarship as that of a "popularizer." (The academic community chooses to believe that commercial success is proof of intellectual superficiality.) From 1942 to 1947, he wrote a weekly column for the *Chicago Defender*, a black newspaper with a national audience. He was also a member of the NAACP at a time when it was widely assumed to be a Communist front organization. He thus identified himself with the human rights movement long before it was fashionable, when there were now-forgotten race riots on a vicious scale and when Japanese-Americans were being put in internment camps. It was before most of his later opponents at San Francisco were born, and it took perhaps as much courage as facing them. Even Kay Boyle might have approved.

"Don seemed quite as comfortable at the White House [twice during the Johnson administration, twice with the Nixons] as at the Flame Bar on the South Side of Chicago where he'd go whenever he could to listen to jazz. [He was the only jazz disc jockey in Chicago in the Fifties who held a Ph.D.] I, on the other hand, was quite awed at being shown into the Oval Office at one A.M."

Margedant Hayakawa smiles shyly again. "He's the same guy wherever he is. He loves to dance, though he does so in a rather antique way. I imagine it causes others who see him some amusement, but he loves it. It has always been fun to be with him. He was a women's libber long before it was popular and had many friendships with women. He likes them as people.

"Don has always known how to guide other people's

* *Language in Action* was revised and expanded and appeared under a new title, *Language in Thought and Action*, in 1949. This later title is still in print (Harcourt Brace Jovanovich).—Ed.

reactions to him. Especially since he became president at State, people assigned him quite a lot of beliefs that he didn't share."

He was often invited to address patriotic and conservative groups. "He would build a rapport and then tell them things about the racial situation he thought they should know. He would ask them why there were no black faces among them, explain the justice of black grievances. Because they thought he was one of them, and because he has a way of talking to an audience as if it were better than it really was, it always actually came out better.

"He had become very aware of the use of colorful technique. The radicals and militants talked to the people through the media, so he learned to, also. The tam and the hard hats were part of it. He became a 'defender of American institutions' to many people. Anyone who read those letters we received would have a tremendous sense of what was troubling people. Don had that. His first speech as President was full of understanding and sympathy for black students, but the papers only reported 'President Adopts Hard Line.' There seemed to be no way for the truth to . . ."

Her words fade for the moment. She pauses, considers, using the same mannerism as her husband. People together for so many years with such obvious regard for each other grow closer in many ways. Finally, she does not want to be misunderstood, so she drops the uncompleted thought.

"But he has a good, strong ego, and, apart from a few miscues, he used the media well. The mythology grew, and it terrified his enemies and strengthened his hand."

Margedant Hayakawa stares into the fireplace for a long moment. Her voice is very soft.

"I wanted so many times to say 'protect yourself.'" A log crumbles in a shower of sparks. "I'll be glad to get him back."

The demands of the job upon a college president are substantial, and varied. The men and women who seek and hold the position are as young as twenty-two and as old as seventy, but they are typically in their middle forties. They run colleges with faculties and student bodies of under 100 to in excess of 250,000. The operating budgets for which they are ultimately responsible can run as high as $150 million, and their capital budgets even higher. They must deal with problems of labor, fiscal integrity, production, supply, food service, housing, maintenance, and community relations comparable to those of any business executive or government bureau chief or general. Some—those at private institutions—are more concerned with fundraising, others with political relationships, but all do both to some degree.

Dr. Hayakawa, with an annual operating budget of $27,811,385, a physical plant valued at $40,642,751, equipment pegged at $4,091,516, a faculty of 1,273, and a student body of 18,000, draws a salary of about $40,000. Although above the national average, the money is little more than he might receive as a professor, and the job affords him a good deal less freedom. Certainly, it is less by far than what a private businessman might receive for similar responsibilities.

There are compensations. His newspaper column, carried by some ninety newspapers in the United States and Japan, adds substantially to his income. Since the quality of his writing is uneven, especially as his subject matter strays further from his areas of expertise, it must be assumed that his international fame is stimulus for a newspaper exposure for which many better writers would sell their souls. The same ripple effect undoubtedly heightens his appeal as a lecturer. The combination of writing and speaking should easily match his present income and make his official retirement both comfortable and fulfilling. And he does have other plans.

For over a year, he has taken tap dancing lessons.

CHAPTER 14

One of Hayakawa's short-term predecessors, in writing about still another president who had died, spoke of the pressures of the office. "I have known presidential colleagues," wrote Robert Smith, "who wept openly in tense situations, who dissolved their marriages during the campus-confrontation years, and who got quietly drunk and napped away the time during ceremonial duties and official meetings. Another required three months' recuperative leave and resigned shortly thereafter. While president of San Francisco State, I fought with my family, smoked too much, and at times found myself unable to dial a telephone number correctly in less than several tries."

Dr. Smith was president for only six months. That same year, the president of Swarthmore died of a heart attack during a campus conflict. Charles Johnson, president of the University of Oregon, lost his life in an auto accident. It was said that he suffered from periods of amnesia and loss of orientation incurred as a direct result of his official duties. All of these people, and untold others, were the victims of one of the most grueling positions of any enterprise in America. And of their own pride and egos as well.

Boards of trustees' search committees can usually distill their notions of what an ideal president should be into a roster of specific qualities and achievements, no matter how unrealistic that outline inevitably will be. Social scientists have tried to sketch what kind of person a president is, and the face he presents to his constituencies. In *Leadership and Ambiguity: The American College President*, authors James G. March and Michael D. Cohen described their typical president (of the forty-one they interviewed) as socially conservative, white, male, Protestant, middle-aged, native-born, of small-town, middle-class, professional or managerial parents. Descriptive means are rarely illuminating, this one less than most. Certainly it does not allow for S. I. Hayakawa. Nor for the thirty-year-old woman president of Bennington (whose vice-president is her husband), nor Father Hesburgh of Notre Dame, nor Jacqueline Wexler of Hunter College, nor the president of Franconia College, who was barely two years older than his graduating seniors when he assumed his position.

All these exceptions, however, share one experience much less common among college presidents than it was twenty years ago—they were all professors and they probably will be again. The move away from professors as college presidents began about the time Dwight D. Eisenhower was named to the post at Columbia University in the 1950s. The boom in higher education was starting then, fed by returning veterans, and some boards of trustees felt their institutions could no longer be directed in the loose-limbed manner followed by many former academics. The complexities of operation were multiplying, relationships with government and industry intensifying. The ideal president began to be seen in an image indistinguishable from his corporate opposite number, his prior affiliation with higher education increasingly secondary. Admirals and generals and managers were hired rather than former professors who had followed the traditional route of department chairman to dean to vice-president.

Occupied by men who had never taught a class, the office became more distant from the academic community it served. But as long as the colleges thrived financially, no one seemed inclined to reverse the trend. Disillusionment set in with the unrest of the Sixties, when presidents at ease in board rooms and at White House dinners found they didn't speak the same language as their now more vocal students and faculties. Confidence in the infallibility of the model corporate executive was shaken. Private enterprise, which could not make mistakes in 1966, seemed unable to do anything right by 1969. Those who had said of college presidencies that what was needed was someone who knew how to meet a payroll were speaking more softly in the face of such assorted disasters as the Penn Central Railroad, Lockheed, Ling-Temco-Voight, Pan Am, and Con Ed. The ability to communicate with students and faculty became the prerequisite presidential quality. Once again, professors were desirable candidates, but now they were lifted directly from the classroom, frequently without any administrative experience whatsoever. Nuts and bolts could be learned, presumably, but empathy could not.

The new-old-style president is hard-pressed to explain why he or she accepted the crushing pressures of the office, the professorial lifestyle being very nearly idyllic by comparison. One of them, John William Ward of Amherst, said: "There was, humanly enough, a large personal component in my decision. One's ego is involved: the mere fact that an estimable place like Amherst would consider me as president is gratifying . . . which is perhaps to say that I am not sure that anyone fully knows why he chooses to do what he chooses to do. I have a certain skepticism about the rationalizations we give ourselves for our actions." Which is to say, he doesn't exactly know why he took the job, making him merely more honest than most of his fellows who answer with talk of "challenges" and "expansion of my basic role of educator."

Certainly there is challenge, if one is intrigued by situations in which whatever action one takes will be wrong. In a college, let alone a university, there is no such thing as consensus, let alone unanimity. At least one of the president's internal and external constituencies can be expected to demand his dismissal over any of two dozen issues which cross his desk every day. In one four-week period in the Spring of 1974, as a modest example, four college presidents found how fragile their rights to decisive action really were:

1. The faculty of the New York State College at Old Westbury voted 59 to 4 to both censure and demand the resignation of President John Maguire. The faculty accused him and his staff of "mismanagement, vacillation, and incompetence." Dr. Maguire was implementing a new master plan mandated by the State University.

2. The board of trustees upheld the dismissal of one of Georgetown University's vice-presidents by its chief executive officer, but then publicly criticized the "precipitous manner" in which President Robert Henle fired Father Edmund Ryan, at the same time praising the "fine personal qualities and administrative abilities" of Ryan.

3. The ultra-conservative publisher of the Manchester, N.H. *Union Leader* launched a sustained three-year assault on President Thomas Bonner of the University of New Hampshire, which was widely held as the primary cause for Bonner's resignation. Publisher William Loeb, as is his wont, charged viciously and continuously that the university under Bonner's leadership coddled Communists, disseminated pornography, undermined patriotism, and squandered tax money.

4. The acting president of Concordia Seminary, an institution torn by conflict between conservative and progressive factions of the sponsoring Missouri Synod, didn't bother with the usual platitudes of "mounting personal demands" or "new professional challenges." He said he was resigning due to "nervous exhaustion."

So why? There is the money, of course. The average college president draws $32,035 (1973–1974), and about one-fifth make more than $40,000. Usually a rent-free house or apartment is provided, and other fringes include cars with chauffeurs, expense accounts, free maintenance of living quarters, and servants. Few of these are bestowed upon other administrators and faculty, except at the larger universities. When these noncash compensations are added in, forty presidents receive over $65,000 a year in salary and benefits. In 1973–1974, one private university president received $100,685 in total compensation, with place and show positions going for $95,437 and $91,451 respectively. At the other end of the scale, only 5 percent make less than $20,000 in salary.

There is the prestige: rubbing elbows with senators and noted authors and captains of industry and Nobel Prize winners. And the modest fame: journalists think presidents have opinions on everything, even though they were in a better position to express them when they were professors. But power? That's something else again. Tyro presidents commonly think they have the authority to do the things they want, because from the perspective of a faculty member it appears that way, and because their boards of trustees assure them full backing and cooperation.

But the quality of presidential power is ambiguous in the extreme. He daren't dismiss even the most outrageously libelous or incompetent professor, either because of tenure or academic freedom (which cover virtually every conceivable act except ax murders). Even if he can prove moral turpitude, he must tip-toe if the professor is black, female, or gay, and especially if she is all three. Although the trustees are supposed to function as milch cows—kicking off fund-raising campaigns with hefty donations—they must be made to feel respected (if not loved) for their vision and perspicacity alone. Students are downright eager to sue for redress of grievances and alumni feel that their annual $10 contributions entitle them to selection of the new football coach. Students can no longer be suspended by presidential fiat. Grievance proceedings installed during the Sixties and presided over by Jello-spined faculty nearly always absolve students of wrongdoing—witnesses, photographs, and defiant public confessions notwithstanding. Alumni can't be fired, and neither, it increasingly seems, can non-tenured, non-faculty administrators, who have grievance procedures of their own.

With the power of dismissal eroded nearly to ineffectuality, the new president might believe he still has power of the purse. To a degree, he does. But if he announces, for example, that the institution is too far in the red to raise salaries or to meet cost-of-living escalations, then he risks his institution's credit rating and potential donors shy away. And in order to wield control by budget, he must know what is being spent for what. Even in a smallish college, that's not easy to discover. His "civil service" of middle- and junior-level managers, full of resident dragons who were there before he came and will be there after he is gone, is not eager to volunteer the possibility that its ranks are over-populated. Hiring-freezes make them grumble and dig in their heels. Then finding out what is going on in the offices of plant maintenance or the registrar or the bursar is just made more difficult. Bureaucracies protect themselves. As Shana Alexander wrote in another context: "Human bureaucracies never self-destruct. It is not in their nature. Rather they self-perpetuate. They grow, like crystals; they ossify; they become rigid. They creep like fungus, sprout tendrils like tropic vines, throttle and try to bring down the edifice or idea [for which] they were established."

No, the days of presidential autocracy are gone, benevolent or otherwise. March and Cohen found that "the presidency is an illusion. Important aspects of the role . . . disappear on close examination. In particular, decision-making in the university seems to result . . . from a process that decouples problems and choices and makes the president's role more commonly sporadic and symbolic than significant. Compared to the heroic expectations he and others might have, the president has modest control over the events of college life."

The ambiguities of the position render the proudly proclaimed "qualifications" of a new president meaningless. He or
she may be "a person of ideas, of high scholarly achievement,
with broad administrative experience, possessed of integrity
and purpose." But many who possess these virtues have failed
spectacularly under duress, where the seemingly ill-equipped
have triumphed. Among these last, there have been college
presidents who never taught a class, who undertook the job
past retirement age, who were incapable of speaking in public,
who couldn't add a short column of double-digit figures, who
never wrote a memorandum or answered correspondence,
who irritated everyone with whom they came in contact, who
couldn't hold two martinis, who seduced students, and even
some who never went to college themselves. Yet their
institutions not only survived, they flourished.

Vision, compassion, and purpose are all very well, but by no
means essential. All other skills and aspirations aside, the even
temporarily successful president must be a consummate political animal, in the broadest sense of the phrase. By instinct or
premeditation, he must know when to threaten, when to
flatter, to cajole, to listen, to reward, to punish—at all times
acutely aware of the interrelatedness of issues and people.

Asked to reflect on this, Amherst's John William Ward
observed that he strives to forge "an intelligent link between
education and politics, to show that politics is not something
external to the academy but is implicated in its essential tasks."
Tellingly, he credited his interrogator's questions with leading
him to this insight into his methodology.

"Bill" Ward knows. On May 10, 1972, in his first year as
president of patrician Amherst, he said to an assembly at the
college chapel: "Write a letter! To whom? One feels like a
child throwing paper planes against a blank wall. I do not care
to write letters to the world." Instead, the next day he joined
his students in a conscious act of civil disobedience, a
demonstration at the gates of Westover Air Force Base. He

and his wife and 498 others were arrested. It was as dramatic, though opposite, an act as S. I. Hayakawa mounting the sound truck, and received almost as much notice. It will also color his entire tenure as president.

Apart from the fact that both violated the canon of presidential neutrality, it would be difficult to discover two men in the same profession who share so little in background and responsibility. Hayakawa's Western, public, large, coed, urban, proletarian San Francisco State bears not the slightest resemblance to Ward's Eastern, private, small, rural, male, exclusive Amherst. Ward is quintessential Boston Harvard WASC, to Hayakawa's California Asian-American. Hayakawa has more faculty than Ward has students (1,232), and his operating budget for one year would keep Amherst going for four. On the other hand, San Francisco State's significance to the nation is based upon its temporary notoriety, Amherst's for its 151-year production of members of the leadership élite.

Both Hayakawa and Ward, however, insisted upon their rights as individuals to speak and act. This was most unpresidential of them. But while Hayakawa could walk off into retirement, Ward could not. He agonized, before and after. So did his faculty, his students, his trustees, his alumni.

An Amherst English professor wrote, in effect, that Ward had no choice but to join the demonstration. The new president, already labeled a centrist at a time when fence-sitting was the cardinal sin, had to reassert his leadership by taking the step no one believed he would permit himself to take. He had to be seen, said Benjamin DeMott, "as a person possessing the courage of wager, personal wager, a man willing to create his right to lead on his own—and on the spot." In other words, it was an expeditious and calculated gesture to bring the Amherst community to his side.

An Amherst student reporter, manfully attempting to avoid sycophancy, nevertheless enthused: "The . . . President's vision, as it should have been, was perhaps a little beyond us because it asked for a state of being at Amherst that so few ever imagine, though some may on occasion dream it. But President Ward's idealism was pure, and it was sensible, and when he said it, it was visible."

A recent alumnus saw a different Ward: "You are naïve. You say you sat down at Westover because you reserve your right to be Bill Ward. Swell. But you ought to know that any controversial deed performed by the holder of an important office will inevitably be identified with the office. It is patently naïve—or irresponsible—to involve yourself in controversial activity while holding the office of president of Amherst College. Your lack of perspective betrays you, [and all those of] the wealthy white educated, liberal, northeastern Establishment babble belt."

A trustee, after the board had turned down Ward's subsequent recommendation favoring coeducation, a hot issue at Amherst, was quoted as suggesting: "If only Bill Ward hadn't been arrested at Westover, or if he had waited until he had been on the job a little bit longer, we might well have had a different vote."

In an address to a session of a meeting of the American Association of Higher Education some months after the event, Ward tried once again to explain:

"The question before us, 'Should College Presidents Take Stands on Sensitive Public Issues?' is an important one. It does not readily lend itself to answer.

"In a talk to the students and faculty on the campus, I draw a distinction between my office, my role as president, and myself, what I intended to do as a citizen. As President, I insisted that I did not intend to allow anyone or any group to turn the college into a political and social instrument, that as President I would always act to preserve the space for freedom, for difference of opinion, because of my commitment to the principle that education requires a setting free from coercion in any form.

"I then shifted into my voice as a single citizen and gave reasons why I chose to engage in an act of civil disobedience. I tried, in other words, to maintain the distinction between myself and my role. Pragmatically, it worked; that is, faculty and students understood the dilemma in which I found myself and respected, or at least tolerated, the distinction I wished to maintain.

"Of all people, the President should recognize that the essence of his own institution is the dialogue by which the institution transcends its present state and maintains the vitality for growth and change. That process requires the courage to be critical of what is. The President must have that courage and act on it."

In a period of super-heated feelings, some said Ward's was an act of cunning, but as it served their purposes—a highly visible demonstration—they'd accept it at face value. Others called it noble, still others, fatuous. But it worked. The trustees supported the president—publicly. They, too, had little choice.

"Because they are very intelligent men," says Ward in his sun-washed office a year later, "they knew that if they had fired me at that moment, a new president with faculty and student body solidly behind him, they wouldn't have been able to function. So while I realized I might have made my future life very difficult, I knew I had put the board in a position where they could not dismiss me. Afterwards I tried very hard not to let that possibility surface again. Actually I think my relationship with them was better than it ever might have been otherwise. As men in business, accustomed to hierarchical order, they learned from those events that it was possible to disagree with someone without destroying him."

Which is not to say that at least some of the trustees did not nurse a grudge. Ward found that recommendations he made later encountered resistance. That was a risk he had taken knowingly. Ward says board meetings are . . . well . . .

304

"much less inhibited" now that trustees express their opinions more candidly. He says he likes that.

It is July and the campus is empty. Ward is dressed in sport shirt and checked slacks and sandals. No jacket, no tie, no socks. There seems little artifice about him. Asked that question about why on earth a professor would want this job, he says:

"A member of the faculty said it was a classic case of incipient male menopause. I suppose I wasn't even aware of what now seems to have been a growing restlessness. I was on the presidential search committee. At one point in the winnowing process, another member of the committee turned to me and asked if *I* would be interested. I laughed it off. It hadn't even occurred to me. It wasn't within my conception of what I was."

By the time the list was down to the final three, they asked him again. By now, the extensive interviewing of candidates had piqued his interest. He said he'd like to be considered.

Because Amherst is small, he undoubtedly suffers less from the isolation of presidents of larger institutions. There is the sense that he can know every one of his staff and faculty and students, receive feedback, and act with full knowledge of the consequences. Still, it must take a certain personality to seek the job and to persevere. His response to that underscores the assertion that the creative manipulation of contending forces is the base attribute of a successful president.

"A psychoanalyst friend says that if one is lucky he'll find a job in which his potential neuroses become virtues."

What are his potential neuroses?

"I don't get upset over problems, not major ones, anyway. My wife says it makes me pretty hard to live with. When she gets upset about something, I will be very rational, try to determine exactly what the issue is, while she's going up the wall. Perhaps it's that I don't really have deep feelings about other people. But the effect is that a trait which is bad in a private situation is a virtue here. Someone who is sensitive about the way other people perceive him would go mad in this job."

A primary function of any president of a private institution is fund-raising. All colleges and universities try to attract such support. Most have "development" offices to help. But while gift monies collected by public, tax-supported institutions are only a fraction of assets, private colleges cannot survive without them. And when people with money to give have indicated receptivity, they want to be coaxed by the top person, not functionaries. This sets up a common conflict when professors are enlisted as presidents. They often insist, as did Ward at the outset, that they know nothing about money-gathering and don't want to know. Some have it stipulated in their contracts that they will not be expected to raise money.

Considering that its enrollment is smaller than most high schools, Amherst has an admirably secure financial foundation. Its assets in 1972 were worth $92,424,000, its endowment fund had a market value of another $90 million. Naturally enough, it wants to keep things that way, improve, if possible. Ward insists he doesn't mind putting the arm on prospective benefactors, once he'd done it a few times.

"I found that as long as I know that we're talking about giving for something that is educationally worthwhile, something we want to do but can't, there's no embarrassment at all on my part. I find, too, that people who have money actually like to be asked for it. They really do! It's a compliment to them to have a president go out of his way to visit."

How does he broach the subject with a possible donor?

"They know I'm there for a reason. After the pleasantries, I tell them what it is I have on my mind, trying to explain the project's importance to the quality of education at Amherst. Of course, I go into that office or home fully briefed. We have a superb development office. If I'm going out to Chicago or the West Coast, even if it's just to give a speech and return, I get a complete advance rundown on who I might meet by chance and who I can contact on the way out or back. When I call on someone, I have a complete dossier on him, very highly detailed. I must know where he's already given, the nature of the gifts, whether he's more likely to go for a restricted or unrestricted gift, what projects we have in mind that might fit our needs and his interests."

But Bill Ward thinks of himself as an educator first. "It seems to me," he had said in an interview shortly before assuming office, "that the function of the president at Amherst is to set the terms of the discourse that goes forward; that is, that he creates a situation in which students and faculty address themselves responsibly to the problems that higher education faces. I do not like the notion of the president as someone who is passive, who implements what other people do."

He combats passivity well. He arises at 6:30 every morning, often earlier. He is in his office by 7:30. Paperwork and phone calls until lunch, appointments at half-hour intervals the rest of the day. After dinner, he goes over the day's new problems and prepares for the next. He has staff meetings every Monday, faculty and board meetings once a month. Every other Friday, he has dinner parties for ten or twelve faculty and staff, which he keeps up until he's seen all 144 professors and their wives. Then he starts over again. He makes a point of eating in the student cafeteria periodically. Then there are alumni weekends, commencements, visiting firemen, trips to New York to speak with trustees. A sixteen-hour day, a little less on Sunday, with an occasional week off in Paris or Ireland (where he has visited the homes of his "illiterate, bog-trotting, peasant Irish ancestors").

307

Once, in an Irish pub after an excursion with his eldest son, the barman asked Ward what he thought about Bobby Kennedy.

"Did he win in California?" Ward asked, not knowing.

"Oh, no," he said, "he has been assassinated."

All Ward could say was, "Oh, Christ, not again."

The barman served their beers and said to them: "You know, if you Americans are going to go around the world pretending you are the bearers and defenders of freedom, you had better straighten out your own society at home."

Ward's son turned to him and said, "He's right, you know."

Bill Ward told the story in an address to Amherst parents in 1968. Four years later, he was sitting in the road in front of Westover Air Force Base.

CHAPTER 15

The overweening collective arrogance of the professoriate is wondrous to behold. Witness the declaration of a Professor Miro M. Todorovich: "Being *the* developers of new knowledge as well as *the* depository of the old, college and university faculties have been and still are *the only available arbiters in matters of knowledge and of dissemination of knowledge.*" (Emphasis added.) Such patent nonsense might be brushed aside if it did not enjoy the status of an unimpeachable verity for professors, so deeply absorbed as to be no more subject to question than the existence of marrow in our bones.

Apparently Professor Todorovich would exclude, for instance, the Library of Congress, the 19,372 other public libraries, and the 691 museums of the arts and sciences not affiliated with colleges or universities, from his list of "disseminat[ors] of knowledge." He obviously discounts the hundreds of research and study institutes sponsored by every major department of the U.S. government and such private foundations as Rockefeller, Carnegie, and Danforth, although most of them assign greater expenditures to "outside" agencies than to those under the auspices of colleges and universities.

As for individuals, he must also reject any claims as "arbiters" or seekers of knowledge by curators, research librarians, and laboratory scientists not on university payrolls. Presumably he would dismiss as meaningless the results of a compilation sponsored by the National Science Foundation (another organization unblessed by university supervision) which listed the nation's 172 leading intellectuals and noted that only 40 percent were professors. (Oddly, he won't surrender the squabbling thinkers of New Jersey's Institute of Advanced Study to the unwashed ranks of the benighted, although it is part of no university, has no students, and awards no degrees.)

Were such myopic *hubris* restricted to just a few professors, it could be regarded as a harmless curiosity. Many of us still accept the traditional professorial archetype promulgated by Hollywood, that of a mufflered, bespectacled, ineffectual bumbler who forgets it's January and drops books all the time. We cannot deny such an unworldly and impecunious figure his amusing eccentricities. He has little else to comfort him. Let him believe himself the guardian of the flame. We warm ourselves with other pursuits.

But the view reflected in such expressions of intellectual authority as Dr. Todorovich's is *not* confined to an occasional Latin professor. The assumption of innate superiority is endemic, the base from which all academic pronouncements flow. It is there, lurking amid the observations of the usually admirable people described in these pages, and it permeates the literature of educational philosophy. It is shared by those of humane instinct and those notable only for self-aggrandizement, by the grandees of Princeton and the peasants of Grand Rapids.

Setting aside the impact of this conviction of professorial rectitude on the future leaders in their charge and on social, military, and governmental policy, consider its effect on the prospect for change in the profession itself. Remembering that faculties recruit and select themselves, the attitudes implicit in Professor Todorovich's comments are ensuring that needed change in higher education will face barriers affecting children not yet born. Nowhere is this more evident than in the push to desegregate the professoriate.

College teaching is perhaps the most discriminatory field of all, and the pace of rectification is painfully slow. In 1970, 38.1 percent of the United States labor force were women, but only 22.5 percent of all full-time college and university faculties were female. Blacks, Hispanics, and other minorities comprised 14.9 percent of the total force the same year, but only 5.3 percent of the professoriate. The Carnegie Commission on Higher Education predicted in 1973 that the proportions of women and minorities represented on college faculties would not equal their 1970 shares of the national work force until the year 2000! And this assumes stabilization of the national proportions at current levels, an unlikely circumstance.

Once accepted into the academic fraternity, women can expect, on the average, 17 percent lower salaries. On the surface, this might be understandable in light of the only very recent entry of women to the profession in relatively large numbers; they would be at entry levels and therefore naturally make less than the typical male. That argument has been put forth by men who dominate the field. But it is not the case. At every one of the four professorial ranks, women receive smaller salaries. The National Center for Educational Statistics reported in 1973 the following mean salaries: male instructors, $11,005, female, $10,143; male assistant professors, $12,232, female, $11,450; male associate professors, $14,472, female, $13,748; male full professors, $19,127, female, $16,978.

Getting a faculty job in the first place is still not easy for women. The "old boy" method of recruitment and hiring has prevailed too long. Chairmen with job openings call their old graduate professors for recommendations, or acquaintances from academic conventions, or former classmates now teaching at other colleges, or just plain drinking buddies. The names of promising women candidates are rarely tendered, often be-

311

cause they are judged not as serious as men or that they "just up and get married on you."

The result is that potential female professors don't receive the same exposure to job opportunities as men. They have to settle.

Gay Baldinger, the teaching assistant introduced earlier, began her drive to join the club before feminist groups and "affirmative action" programs had begun to dent the status quo. She had to battle it out alone. Her senior advisor says Gay is a fine teacher. Gay says that the surprised tone in his voice is because she is a woman. This attitude, which she sees in all her relationships with the faculty members with whom she has had contact, makes Gay angry. That makes her "cause trouble," and conversations stop when she enters the door of the faculty lounge. Her militant feminism is genuine. But she also has a strong sense of self-preservation and she wants very much to be a professor, so that isn't her name.

"Why shouldn't I be pissed?" The little O of her mouth straightens into a line, the bird-like hands flutter. "I'm Radcliffe *cum laude*, Phi Beta Kappa, two articles published before graduation . . . and I pick up a big two assistantships out of twelve applications. This place was the best of the mediocre two. I get here and find about fifty-eight semi-cre-tins—*male*—from East Overshoe State, all getting 20 percent more money than I am."

Her conviction about her salary in relation to those of her male colleagues is not one she can prove. Her department chairman will neither deny nor corroborate the accusation. Given national means (which however don't include T.A.'s), her guess probably isn't far off. Even if her salary is equal, though, the fact remains that only two of the sixty graduate assistants in her department are women. Since 43 percent of all bachelor's degrees given in her graduating year of 1970 were to women, the odds favor at least *some* highly qualified female applicants for the position being passed over for less remarkable men.

Gay's case is extreme, and her university has been the subject of action by the Department of Health, Education, and Welfare for failing to comply with affirmative action guidelines intended to open opportunities to women and minorities. Individual women and feminist groups have sued for change, but Gay's university is not unique in that regard. In mid-1973, more than four hundred colleges and universities were the defendants in sex-discrimination actions.

Admittedly, the under-representation of women and minorities on college faculties is not a self-contained phenomenon. As with other issues of social justice, colleges are targets of anger and litigation at least partly because of their own pretensions of high moral purpose. They should be better than they are. But if imbalance by sex and race were merely a question of discrimination at the post-graduate level, the problem could be resolved within the decade. For that to be accomplished, there would have to be much larger numbers of women and minorities with appropriate degrees at each level of academic achievement. That is not yet the case.

For although slightly more women graduate from high school than men, and those who go to college get better grades than men, they continue on to higher degrees in smaller and smaller proportions.

Only 36.5 percent of all advanced degrees were awarded to women in 1970, and only 13.4 percent of Ph.D.'s went to them. (It has not always been thus, as might be assumed. A little over 45 percent of present undergraduates are women, but in 1920, 47 percent of college students were female.)

Gay Baldinger has one explanation: "It's reinforced sex roles, the assumption that we're only good for baby-making and housekeeping. And our *acceptance* of that role!"

Apparently this remains largely true, despite years of

313

determined consciousness-raising. The Educational Testing Service asked 21,000 college seniors due to graduate in 1972 about their plans. Although 44.6 percent of the men said they intended to go on to graduate and professional study, only 29.4 percent of the women had the same expectation. The disparate levels of aspirations were so pronounced that nearly as many men in the study with "C+" or lower grade averages planned to pursue advanced degrees as did women with "B+" or better grades. Further, although 3 percent of the women surveyed wanted to go to schools of law or medicine, 12.7 percent of the men did.

In *Saturday Review* magazine, some years ago, Dr. Florence Howe underlined the origins of sexual stereotyping in one of many articles which led to the current re-examination of the ways boys and girls are depicted in children's books. "Children learn about sex roles very early in their lives," wrote Dr. Howe, "probably before they are eighteen months old, certainly long before they enter school. . . . We throw boy babies up in the air and roughhouse with them. We coo over girl babies and handle them delicately. We choose sex-related colors and toys for our children from their earliest days. We encourage the energy and physical activity of our sons, just as we expect girls to be quieter and more docile."

Such observations are no longer as provocative as they were when Professor Howe offered them in 1971, committed as the ideas now are to the consciousness of every young parent deliberately encouraging a daughter to play marbles and a son to sew. But that doesn't mean the absence of visible fatherly twinges over the son who plays with dolls or the daughter who can throw a football forty yards. Under the conditions which have until recently prevailed, it can surprise no one that a young woman entering college in 1975 carries a lot of residual emotional baggage from her childhood in the years before feminism came to mean more than just the distasteful utterances of radical lesbians on talk shows.

In concrete terms, it is a fact that highly capable women are, in effect, screening themselves out of higher education, thereby aiding and abetting those who don't want them anyway. This was the conclusion of a 1972 study of fellowship programs by the Association of American Colleges. It found that of those applying for seventy of the nation's most respected fellowship programs, women represented fewer than 25 percent of the applicants to all but eleven programs. Because of known and suspected obstacles to women in college careers, the writers of the report surmised that "a more rigorous process of self-selection occurs among potential female applicants than among males." An equally strong possibility is the lingering lack of self-esteem even educated and capable women may carry as a by-product of upbringings which reinforced the notion that "brain" work is man's work.

Apart from the likelihood that women have, to a degree, denied themselves professorial careers, there is no question that sex bias of the most blatant sort exists. The first fissure in the formidably masculine wall erected by graduate and professional schools in almost every discipline but education and social work came in 1968, with the termination of draft deferments for graduate study in anything but medicine and the allied health sciences. Law schools, in particular, had to lower barriers to women in order to sustain their enrollments. Prophecies of doom rolled across the campuses. Law schools would die. As Harvard President Nathan Pusey so neatly expressed the trepidation of his male compatriots: "We'll be left with nothing but the lame, the halt, and the women."

The law schools not only did not expire, they flourished, and the biggest jumps in enrollment began that very year. By 1973, 27,756 law degrees were awarded, a 24.2 percent increase over the year before. Although women still comprised only 15.6 percent of total law school registrants, those 16,760 students compared dramatically to the only 1,883 just ten years before. The same thing happened to medical schools, where number of female students doubled between 1970 and 73. By then, first-year women in medical schools had reached 19.7 percent of the total. All of this is a far piece from parity, but it means that by 1980, or soon after, those professors who resist the intrusion of women into their clubby enclaves will have to find other excuses than that "there just don't seem to be any who have the proper background."

Some male academics have seen the future, and they dread it. Professor Todorovich is outraged by the hammerings on the door to the tabernacle of truth and scholarship by "crusaders for vulgar egalitarianism." The chorus of quivering wattles was joined by such academic luminaries as Sidney Hook, Bruno Bettelheim, Seymour Lipset, Nathan Glazer, and Oscar Handlin, members of the "Committee on Academic Non-discrimination and Integrity." Although HEW's affirmative action guidelines specify the opening of faculty openings to *qualified* women and minorities, Professor Emeritus Hook insists that the "effect of the ultimata is to compel them to hire unqualified Negroes and women and to discriminate against qualified non-blacks and men."

Certainly, abuses of the law occur, as do incidents of women and minority group members who choose to explain away their own inadequacies by crying discrimination. A Jewish former dean of admissions at one university delights in recounting the charges of anti-Semitism leveled against him by rejected applicants. His successor has been called a racist by black students turned away because they had not graduated from high school. White men have no doubt been passed over for faculty positions in preference to less-qualified women or blacks, and personal vendettas have been waged under the banner of discrimination when nothing of the sort was involved. It is in no way soothing to advise the victims of such violations of the spirit of the law that life is unfair, nor to invoke the greater good.

Nevertheless, the system of hiring as it now pertains is

unfair, and the professoriate—and not just the white men who dominate it—must accept the blame. They don't seem inclined to alter the tradition. According to the American Council on Education, only 33.6 percent of 53,034 professors polled believed there should be preferential hiring for women and minority faculty at their institutions. Since all this means is that of two *equally qualified* applicants for a position, the black female would be given the job over the white man, hopes for early revision of the racial and sexual composition of the professoriate are naïve.

Simple justice aside, there is good reason to believe that improving the ratio of women faculty members would cause a positive shift away from the pertaining overemphasis on research. In the ACE survey cited, 58 percent of the women professors considered it essential or very important that they help to provide for the emotional development of their students. Only 36.5 percent of their male colleagues agreed. Beyond this, 73 percent of the women faculty members placed high priority on aiding students to deeper levels of self-under-standing, compared to 52.5 percent of the men.

All of which confirms one of the principal fears of male professors who regard themselves as scholars—that universities would be "reduced to mere teaching institutions." This breath-taking prospect is ominously confirmed by the fact that 80.4 percent of all professors want teaching effectiveness, not publications and research, to be the primary criterion for advancement. Those who view such developments with alarm follow a professorial habit: extension of personal experience to all of higher education. That is, a scholar assigned the haven of a theoretical teaching position at a major research institution regards his circumstance as the rule, ignoring the fact that at least three-quarters of the nation's colleges support very little research. They are, in fact, teaching institutions already.

Still another conflict is shaping up which will undoubtedly set conservative white male professors to chortling. While women have begun to make inroads—often by using techniques pre-tested by the civil rights movement—blacks and other minorities are making much slower progress in securing their share of faculty positions. Although female academics hold a share of the professoriate only two-thirds that of their representation in the total work force, blacks and other minorities hold a mere 5.3 percent of the faculty positions, fully two-thirds less than that in the national total.

Many blacks and Hispanics feel that women are less threatening to white men, and that however reluctant the latter might be to open the doors to women they find that preferable to seeking out minority professors. Dr. Kenneth S. Tollet, a professor at predominantly black Howard University, was quoted on this point in *The Chronicle of Higher Education*:

"Minority groups . . . deserve better than hostility or aggressive competition from other segments of society, especially indefatigably persistent and outraged middle-class white women. Yet the groundswell interest in discrimination against women in higher education is deflecting attention and effort away from steps to correct the more virulent form of discrimination, that against blacks, Chicanos, and Indians."

It would appear that many of those in positions to hire faculty prefer black women to black men, thereby adding to their charts of faculty sexual and racial characteristics in not one but two columns. In 1970, 9.0 percent of all female professors working at private colleges were black, but only 3.5 percent of male faculty were. At public institutions, it was 7.1 percent black and female, only 3.8 percent black and male. As one department chairman said over a vodka martini:

"The absolutely ideal candidate these days is a black Jewish lesbian from Harvard whose last name is Rodriguez."

And whose father is a full-blooded Sioux, whose mother is a Sicilian Catholic, and who is a Vietnam veteran confined to a wheelchair, suggested his companions, in one of the more popular, if surreptitious, bar games in these days of affirmative action. Nearly as rare a creature is the black man who has reached the level of full professor. A spokesman at the AAUP guessed that less that 1 percent of all the professors in the country fit that description, and most of them are at largely black institutions. Demographically, that makes Dr. Hobart Jarrett a very special person.

Dr. Jarrett is a full professor at Brooklyn College, the second largest division of the second largest university in the United States. Of some two thousand faculty at the college, he can think of only six other full professors who are also black. This, in the city described as the most liberal in the country, with the largest minority population. But Dr. Jarrett is annoyed when identified as a black professor. He is a teacher of English and classics who happens to be black.

A friend tells of the time at the apex of the black student movement when Dr. Jarrett was approached to head a new Afro-American Institute. At the time, administrators were scrambling to find blacks—*any* blacks—to head up such programs. Militants demanded it. At a neighboring university, a teacher of physical education was named head of the Black Studies program. It was not due to his scholarship in the new field.

When Dr. Jarrett was asked to consider the new post, he replied, truly perplexed: "But my area is Greece!"

Today, he reflects that it is remarkable how many blacks undertook such responsibilities when they had no training in the discipline. A courtly and gentle man, he quickly adds that "it's marvelous how well some of them did, and certainly *someone* had to. But I'm a seventeenth-century person, Shakespeare . . . and the Greeks, of course."

Where would he choose to die?

"Florence. No question, really. That would be my heaven."

Where was he born?

"Tulsa. I grew up there, finished high school there. I'm still very fond of my hometown."

Earliest memories?

319

"The race riot. In 1922, I think. I was seven years old. My family and its various parts and all the other Negro people were obliged to leave our homes in North Tulsa. My father was a grocer. His store was burned down. When we returned from having run, we found our house was not burned, but our things were strewn about in a terrible shamble. On the top of our upright piano I had a bank made of Little Boy Blue. In it I had saved thirteen dollars. My father refused at that time to bank his money, and he had kept it all in a safe in that demolished store. The thirteen dollars was all the capital my father had to start again."

What caused the riot?

"There were many conflicting stories, but it seems that a white man saw a black man kiss a white woman in the elevator of a department store. Nothing more sexual than a kiss. Within twenty four hours, the whites were moving into North Tulsa, burning and looting. My grandfather really made me proud. He refused to leave in the pickup truck with us, along with his wife, my father, my mother, all the uncles and aunts and cousins. My grandfather sat on the front porch with a shotgun. Because of him, neither his house nor ours was burned. He was a great, fine-looking man."

It was a time of race riots, quite different from those of the Sixties. In East St. Louis in 1917, thirty-nine black people and nine whites were killed. In Chicago in 1919, twenty-three blacks and fifteen whites died. North Tulsa was not as bad, but the statistics did not favor black people. They still don't. Dr. Jarrett fears that this is forgotten, often by people who should know better. He remembers teaching at Bennett College in Greensboro, North Carolina, after World War II.

"Jewish friends of mine who had fled Germany told me how terrible things were there. I never got angry but I explained to them that I knew Hitler was terrible, but that they had the run of the city of Greensboro and I didn't. They went to the movies and sat wherever they wanted to sit and I couldn't go because I refused to sit in a segregated place. They ate dinners in nice places, I told them, and there was no place I could eat downtown. So I asked them please not to tell me what a wonderful place the United States was just because they had been persecuted somewhere else. I was still being persecuted."

Dr. Jarrett met his wife at Syracuse University and took her to Langston, Oklahoma, where they obtained their first jobs. "She detested it. The patterns of life in the South were not amenable, to be generous, especially to a girl from New York. So whenever we traveled, we went across the ocean."

By the time he reached Greensboro, he'd had enough. The whole world had changed, but not for blacks.

"One of the great highlights of my life was working with the sit-ins in Greensboro. There were two Negro schools in Greensboro. As a lark one day, some North Carolina A&T boys decided to go to the Five and Dime to eat and they did. The town became very excited, and the boys announced they were going back the next Saturday. Nine men, black men considered prominent in the town, met the next morning. I was named coordinator of the group, the liaison between adults and the students. We contacted others, the thing snowballed, and then I was named president of what we called the 'Greensboro Citizens Association.' Things had to be done in a hurry because we expected there would be bloodshed.

"Black people, people who had been anti-change, came forward, wrote out bail bonds for dozens of kids. When we saw we were winning, I said to a group of our people, 'Why don't we *really* educate all these people? Let them know how important it is that they boycott everything in downtown!' Business came to a standstill, and then the managements of the stores were ready to listen. We met. They said we were ruining everything. We said that was the way it was going to be."

That was the beginning. Yet now it, and everything that followed, seems almost forgotten in the most unlikely places of all, the colleges and universities. Blacks remember, and many want to know if the climate of liberation they created will again benefit someone else. An officer of the AAUP, Ezra Naughton, thinks so:

"There is no doubt that the black movement has been subverted by the women's movement, that the women's movement has been given preference in higher education."

Dr. Jarrett continues. When he moved to Brooklyn, he soon was on a committee to increase the numbers of black and Puerto Rican students on campus. The total percentage of these minorities at the college was less than 4 percent at the time, largely because the free City University was dominated by white middle-class students with better grades from better high schools.

When Jarrett was asked to join the committee, the organizer made the old mistake. He said he wanted Jarrett's experience as a black person and his knowledge of other blacks. Jarrett agreed to serve after making it clear he never wanted to be asked that way again. His blackness was not to be thought of as the totality of his personality.

The committee presented its plan to the faculty meeting as a whole. A white professor wanted to know why they needed these obviously ill-equipped students, "these people," he said. The students came anyway, and two years later the City University opened its doors to all high school graduates. Now "these people" want to become, among other things, college professors. How they realize that wish will be one of the major currents in higher education through the rest of this century and beyond. One hopes they will know the satisfaction Hobart Jarrett knows:

"Literature not only affords the touchstones that intelligent, sensitive, honest, good human beings need, but helps them understand their very life processes. Teaching people those ideas is an honor, a challenge, a joy. I know no one who looks forward with glee to going to work. I do."

CHAPTER 16

Indeed, why should not professors be pleased with their lot? If Dr. Jarrett is unusual in enthusing over the prospect of yet another day of teaching, his fellows must secretly chortle over their wisdom and good fortune in opting for a profession which not only serves up comfortable salaries for minimal return, but heaps on non-cash benefits and perquisites on a scale sufficient to turn all but an occasional electrical trade unionist puce with envy. Quite apart from the three- or four-day weeks and eight-month years, the lifetime security of tenure, and a freedom of speech and thought which borders on license, there is a bountiful menu of other brow-smoothing ancillary comforts.

Consider just one: A full-time professor of any rank at virtually all colleges and universities is entitled to free tuition for his dependents at his own institution, and often at cooperating colleges as well. At *current* rates, tuition for one child for four years at a private college runs between $2,000 and $3,500. For an average family of three, that is a potential saving of from $24,000 to $42,000! No second mortgages or backbreaking loans for them, unless, of course, they accede to their offspring's demands to go to college at the other end of the country. At least they have the option of exercising parental will in behalf of parental solvency. Needless to say, this privilege is granted to no one else. To put this in perspective, that $45,000 represents nearly one-tenth of the average *lifetime* earnings of a typical college graduate.

Or another: Over and above the three-month summer vacations and the four weeks of shorter respites during the academic year, academics are entitled to what are called sabbatical leaves. Normally, a professor is eligible for an up to 12 months' leave every seventh year. He or she is usually paid one-half of current annual salary, but *full* payment is not rare. A sabbatical is intended to provide time for reflection and scholarship. A great many professors find that the likeliest sources of documents critical to their proposed research can be found only in London, Paris, or Marrakesh. When location is carefully selected, an academic on sabbatical can live like a caliph on one-half of an American professor's salary. The publisher's advance for the book intended to result from the leave helps cushion the blow, too.

Medical and life insurance, discount purchase plans, and retirement programs flesh out professorial compensation. In the last area, the customary annuity plan ensures a professor emeritus of monthly payments in his golden years totaling 60 percent of his average salary in his peak earning years. At some universities, the professor makes no contribution whatsoever to this retirement annuity. Even the most parsimonious institutions at least match his contributions.

It is clear that the public continues to swallow whole the image of the professor, in Milton Mayer's words, as a "put-upon man, at least as much to be pitied as to be scorned, [with a] collar-turning slattern of a wife who despised his pretentions, a litter of kids with prematurely weak eyes, and a thin gray line of credit at the shoe store and grog shop." But as must now be evident, today's academic lives (in Mr. Mayer's description) "The Life of Professor Riley."

Very well. Having recognized the myth, it does not follow that the professoriate should be dragged back down to material equity with other workers. National priorities should likely be just the reverse. That question aside, there are other reasons for closer examination of the profession. For openers, most professors are on the public payroll. Some 80 percent of all college students are enrolled in public, i.e., tax-supported, institutions. The rest attend private colleges and universities receiving state and government assistance comprising as much as 50 percent of their total budgets. They are taught, however, by men and women who do not consider themselves public servants accountable to their once-removed employers.

This in itself is not cause for alarm. Professors are notably inept sinners, and in the admittedly raveled tapestry of American life, institutions of higher education maintain a generally high level of conduct in the use of other people's money. From time to time, an administrator diverts financial aid funds to his own use and athletes are granted excessive monetary assistance, but these infrequent disclosures cannot hope to match the rampaging avarice of elements of the corporate and political worlds.

There is, however, a discernible paralysis of ethics seeping through higher education, for which the professoriate must accept a substantial share of responsibility. Consider: Bribe-paying and price-fixing corporations are run by college graduates who were taught by college professors. Lying lawyers, fee-splitting physicians, scheming politicians, and murderous military leaders were taught by professors, and frequently advised by them after graduation.

Although they must be doing *something* wrong, professors understandably turn away from such accusations of complicity. It is the society, they say, environment, heredity, even the lower schools; students are already formed by the time they matriculate as college freshmen. The excuses might be accept-able were it not that professors have pretended to the inculcation of high moral purpose and the transmittal of the loftiest ideals of our culture. Since they do so declaim, they must at the least concede they're failing in what they expect of themselves.

Part of the explanation lies in the academic personality. For a profession in which its practitioners delight in charting the amusing peccadilloes and subcultural quirks of office workers and Amazonian aborigines, there has been remarkably little inclination to turn the microscope around. Few really probing studies of the professoriate are available. Recognizing the frailty of generalization, certain inferences nevertheless can be drawn from the analyses and self-revelations of the individuals and study groups presented in these pages.

To wit: As has already been observed, a concentrated strain of arrogance flows unceasingly through the veins of the body academic. Whether in compensation for deep-seated insecurities, whether masked in mock humility or thundered about the ears of all who will listen, it is the single most pervasive characteristic of the members of the professoriate. In its enveloping air of superior wit and insight, and especially in its conviction of personal and collective probity, any meeting of ten professors will cause a comparable group of Wall Street lawyers to appear as a gaggle of forelock-tugging bumpkins. Were manifestations of these assumptions not muted by the conventions of the scholarly community and bracketed by astounding ignorance of what is happening over the crest of the nearest discipline, professorial self-esteem would be more alarming. The relatively few Dr. Strangeloves who wriggle through to the outside world are at least identifiable oddities.

What is more troubling than arrogance itself is its effect upon students during their passages through the cocoon. There is, in this quality, the mentality of a neighborhood bully. Armed with the tangible club of grade-granting authority, the professor has also the implicit weapon of presumed acuity. For the student who wants to be a doctor, the weight of this authority is awesome. In their classrooms, professors can and do indulge in the suppression of both cherished nettles and bumptious young intellects. A student who chooses to continue chewing gum in the face of professorial reproof does so at risk of a lowered grade. Whether the professor would *actually* drop a grade from "C" to "D" is beside the point—the student knows he *might*. This is not overdrawn. It can become just that petty and just that fearsome. In his classroom, the professor is king, for he can punish any offense with the threat of poorer grades. The power is absolute, and it is wielded against people vulnerable and not yet fully formed.

But as the bully quails before concerted counterattack from those he has tormented, so does the professor retreat before the unexpected challenge of his students. This comes most often from those who learn they are brighter or more adept at rhetoric than their mentors. In the Sixties, it was their sheer numbers, united in their mindless chants of dogma. In either case, professors are found wanting in fiber. They urged acquiescence to "non-negotiable" demands of student demonstrators, whatever their merit, surrendered their classrooms to mini-despots, vacillated over response to the persistent foolishness of students ordering the faculty to stop the war in Vietnam. Often, professors simply swallowed whole the current mode of the youth culture. Gasping with empathy, they grew their hair, smoked grass, and turned from instruction to "rapping." They felt cast adrift when the students went back from revolution to career preparation and frat parties.

With declining enrollments, faculties turned to gimmicks and fads to hold their students. Ill-conceived "experimental" programs bloomed and withered within months. Elimination of course requirements, independent study, credit for "living," and institution of curricular reforms which had no form or consensus for being were created to quiet their charges. Students quietly smirked and accepted the innovations, then

327

began to complain of lack of rigor. Virtue does not reside in the young, and courage has not proven to be a professorial commodity.

There are other charges: Professors solicit job offers from other colleges, using them to blackmail their current employers into raises and other concessions. They look the other way when agencies advertising ghost-written term papers and dissertations solicit customers openly in campus newspapers, and when printed summations of their own lectures are sold in neighboring bookstores. They fill vacancies by way of cronyism more often than by qualifications. They take credit (or do not share it) for the work of assistants. And they joke that "it would be a good job if it weren't for the students."

No, all professors do not do all of these things, nor do they all fit these generalizations. But even the largely admirable people profiled here are guilty in some part, and they exemplify the best of their profession.

Change is happening. The next ten years will be the most momentous of all for the professoriate. The black and other minority group students who entered as undergraduates in the wake of academic guilt over the death of Martin Luther King will be a growing fraction of the doctorates produced in the mid- and late Seventies. Women are continuing through graduate school in greater numbers. In hand with a tightened academic marketplace and the push for equal employment opportunity, competition for available faculty positions will escalate and the galloping salaries of the Sixties will slow to a trot.

Many professors will see unionization as their salvation. By April 1973, the faculties of 286 colleges and universities had elected collective bargaining agents, unthinkable just a few years before. Most were lesser-known two- and four-year colleges, but faculties at more prestigious institutions who have rejected unionization for the moment as professionally unseemly will surely shift their votes as the pressure mounts.

They will want to guard their prerogatives and their jobs, and they will notice that unionized faculties make more money. The chancellor of the University of Wisconsin at Oshkosh set out to prove just the opposite in 1974, but found that professors at 88 institutions with collective bargaining received raises which increased 35 percent in a five-year period compared to a 29 percent increase at 88 similar, but non-union colleges.

Unionization has other dimensions, however. Inevitably, faculties in the adversary labor-management situation will have to surrender at least a share of their traditional role as co-managers of their institutions' destinies and philosophies. Tenure will be modified, for while government now directs college administrators to enforce affirmative action, attention will shift to those faculties organized as separately identifiable bodies. Since the unionized faculties will surely insist upon the retention of tenure, they will with equal certainty be the targets of legal action more frequently than their institutions. Tenure will be regarded by the courts as a seniority system paralleling that of conventional unions. To the degree it continues to discriminate against women and minorities, it will be struck down. The argument that tenure is required to protect academic freedom will be less persuasive, for the unions will be expected to provide the necessary protection. It is entirely possible that outside authorities may mandate the end of tenure as presently constituted, at least on unionized campuses.

Tendering useful recommendations for all this is not unlike shouting in an empty echoing corridor. Little that is new can be said that has not already been said—and ignored—before. However, positive efforts must be undertaken to modify the hypocrisies of the profession.

For example: Most professors are primarily teachers, and reluctant scholars. They say, overwhelmingly, that advancement should be based on assessment of teaching effectiveness. Yet no known method of evaluation is deemed acceptable. It is

329

a ludicrous situation ripe for alteration. Professors reject student evaluations of their skill in the classroom, yet their colleagues are reluctant to judge lest they too be judged. One solution might follow the pattern of greater representation of the college constituencies employed in internal boards of student governance, discipline, and the like. That is, evaluation of teaching by teams of students *and* faculty members, perhaps even of alumni and administrators. To be effective, the visits of the teams would have to be unscheduled—like fire inspections. To be fair, the teams would have to reserve judgement until two or more visits had been made to each professor's class, and the composition of the committee would have to be dominated by professors (from all ranks). All teaching members of every department would have to participate. Certainly, this would be unsettling for the teachers under inspection, and they would need the right to appeal negative evaluations.

Once methods of measurement are established, an end must be sought to the fiction of the teacher-scholar. Professorial positions should be clearly labeled one or the other, with equal pay for both. The doctorate required would then be the one providing that particular training: on the one hand, the conventional Ph.D., which is already a research-oriented degree; on the other, a dissertationless degree with additional apprenticeship in the art of teaching. Such a degree already exists—the Doctor of Arts. But it doesn't necessarily demand proven skill in the classroom and it does not carry the cachet of the Ph.D., so only twenty-two graduate schools offer it, and the pace of adoption is slowing. But if professorial positions were clearly designated as teaching *or* research and the appropriate one of the two degrees is *required* for employment, a long step would be taken toward equalization. Teacher training should also be mandatory for those who hope to gain faculty positions in the professional area. This is not to say that a law or nursing professor should be expected to obtain a

Doctor of Arts, but that some exposure to teaching method be deemed essential.

Heavier investment must be made in investigation of teaching technique, and not just in teacher's colleges, which concern themselves primarily with the lower levels. More must be known about motivating students at the college and post-graduate levels, for they are quite distinct creatures, and elementary and secondary techniques are not only irrelevant but of questionable value even for the levels at which they are intended. Perhaps the investigation should be taken out of the hands of professional pedagogues entirely, in the hopes of fresh insight. Liberal arts and science faculties will never accept the advice of education faculties, anyway.

Colleges and universities must stop propagating doctoral programs simply to assuage ambitious or egocentric faculty members. If external legislative action is necessary to at least freeze doctoral production, so be it. Proliferating doctoral programs of dubious quality and little rationale simply pump up student expectations in a job market which shows only very slow expansion for twenty years or longer. Once the growth of programs is arrested, they must then be thinned, perhaps through existing regional associations of colleges and universities. Present and projected needs for professors must be established, discipline by discipline. Perhaps interlocking agreements could encourage college "Y" to phase out a weak graduate business program if university "Z" would reciprocate by eliminating its flagging undergraduate program in journalism. In any event, the pattern of leap-frogging and duplicating programs simply in the hope of attracting more students and tuition money must be ended. Tax resources should not be expected to support six philosophy departments within a five-mile radius of each other. The world can only use just so many analytical philosophers and linguists and sociologists and accountants, and diversion of funds to support marginal

331

departments weakens whole colleges and dilutes the quality their students have a right to expect. If natural selection cannot do the job—and it hasn't—then it must be forced, and if the colleges are unwilling to cooperate in that direction, they must be encouraged to do so. The "all things to all students" educational declaration of most universities can no longer be supported.

And tenure: There have been so many proposals over the years that any new ones set forth are simply variations on modifications. The "academic freedom" justification is largely pretense. It should be openly acknowledged that tenure is important to professors primarily for the job security it provides. Any revision must give protection to those who most need it, yet ensure that the inclination to retire from productive work behind its shield will be substantially reduced; it must give the colleges some latitude in enforcing productivity by the threat of severance while guaranteeing the professor freedom from capricious or precipitous dismissal.

This is by no means a simple issue. As it is now constituted, tenure has fostered an "up or out" policy. That is, a professor not granted tenure at the end of seven years is automatically dismissed. It is a system easily subject to abuse. Tenured professors, being senior, are expensive. They cannot be made to leave. Non-tenured professors, being younger, cost less. A favored way to keep costs down, therefore, is to award tenure as infrequently as possible. The result is a revolving door through which are propelled promising young teachers to be replaced by still younger and cheaper neophytes.

Conversely, the granting of tenure to large numbers of professors in a short period of time can channel a department into a rigid program direction for thirty or forty years, with new blood shut off by quotas imposed on total tenure appointments.

Some smaller colleges have abolished tenure entirely in recent years. The AAUP estimates that some 15 percent of all institutions have no tenure programs. The trend is clear. What is less certain is the alternative forms which will eventually predominate.

In view of considerations outlined above, here is one possibility. Those who most require protection are those furthest along in their careers. They, as other older citizens, have the fewest number of options should they lose their jobs. On the other hand, they tend to be the least productive and receptive to new ideas and methods. Start, then, by setting age fifty-five as the earliest year tenure may be granted. This removes the temptation of withdrawing into the sinecure tenure now represents for professors in their otherwise most productive years, and instead encourages their continued best efforts.

But even the youngest professor, with his life before him, has legitimate expectation of at least a measure of job security. Construct, then, a structure of rolling overlapping contracts in lieu of tenure, increasing in length with time of service, and subject to annual reevaluation. A new instructor would be hired on a two-year contract. If he received an affirmative evaluation at the end of the first year, a new three-year contract would be awarded at that time. If negative, he would serve out his remaining year with ample notice in which to pursue other opportunities.

Those holding three-year contracts would retain the possibility of renewal at the end of the first two years of each term, continuing on from the point of initial employment until ten years' service had been accumulated. By that time, his value to the institution fully recognized, the contract periods would be extended to five years, with renewal at the end of the third year. If denied, this more mature professor could be expected to require somewhat more time to find a comparable position, and would have two years now in which to search. The rolling five year terms would continue until automatic tenure at age fifty-five. Throughout, the institution would retain a degree of flexibility in releasing a professor grown indolent, but the professor would be assured of ample warning of his college's intentions. All of which ties in, incidentally, with the need for more specific and formalized evaluation methods and the segregation of teaching and scholarly professorships.

The American professor has been tickled and stung and lauded before, as often as not by charter members of the guild. One, Fred B. Millet, saw only virtue: "The college professor lives in the hope that . . . he may have trained his students in the techniques of the ways and means of discovering what is already dependably known about whatever subject the student is interested in, and also in sound logical processes of thought, in orderly and rational methods of work, and in the discrimination between what is and what is not evidence."

H. L. Mencken, speaking to a similar point, observed: "The professor must be an obscurantist or he is nothing; he has a special and unmatchable talent for dullness; his central aim is not to expose the truth clearly, but to exhibit his profundity, his esotericity—in brief, to stagger sophomores and other professors."

Professors preen, when flattered, bluster when pricked. They are only human. They are also not all they should be nor what their protestations insist they are. As the mandarins of our educational system, they hold themselves as something slightly more than human and therefore deserving of their lofty splendor. They are dependent upon us, yet demand inviolate insulation. The best of them are the best of us, but even those few must stand accountable. Perhaps they will soon turn to themselves to discover the means by which they might become what they say they are. But probably not.

AFTERWORD

It is in the nature of things that we change, day to day, year to year. The interviews which provided most of the material presented in this book were conducted during the academic year 1972–73. Quite possibly the subjects would have responded to the author's questions differently on other days, under other circumstances. Certainly many of them have changed their lives since then. Jim Bohan, for one, has left the professoriate to enter the real estate business on a full-time basis. After respecting a plea to stay on "just a few more months" as president of San Francisco State, S. I. Hayakawa took a tentative flyer at elective office. Alexander Bickel, often named a potential candidate for the Supreme Court, died of cancer in November 1974. He was forty-nine years old. Gay Baldinger accepted an assistant professorship at a prestigious university which had rejected her for a teaching fellowship five years before. Martin Duberman has relished the agony of giving birth to another play.

It may be painful to see one's words embalmed in print so many months after they were spoken. Gay Baldinger's and Ted Crandell's requests for anonymity have been respected with those pseudonyms and modest disguise, but their spoken thoughts, and those of their colleagues, have been rendered with precision.

The author expresses his deep gratitude to all the professors profiled in this book—for their time, their wisdom, and their openness. Thanks, also, to Dick Kluger and Carol Rinzler for helping it come together.

INDEX

Danforth Foundation: 309
Data disciplines: 101, 142
Davis, Angela: 28, 33, 237
DeMott, Benjamin: 302
Dental schools: 111
Dick Cavett Show: 110, 219
Disraeli, Benjamin: 221
Doctor of Arts degree: 330–31
Doctorate: 23, 31, 101, 250, 328, 330–32; candidates for, 23, 92–93; compared to M.D., 23; dissertation for, 53, 82, 83; prestige institutions for, 74; requirements for, 75–76. *See also* Graduate schools *and* Graduate students
Dolby, Homer: 285
Dramatic Workshop: 107
Duberman, Martin: 31, 137–71, 238, 335
Duke University: 216, 273

Eastwood, Clint: 100, 109–10
Educational Record: 177–78
Ehrlichman, John: 218
Eisenhower, Dwight D.: 296
Ellison, Ralph: 142
Ellsberg, Daniel: 218, 228, 230, 232, 237
Emerson, Ralph Waldo: 208
Encyclopedia Britannica: 112
Engineers: 23–24
Ervin, Sam: 210
Espionage Act of 1917: 218
Evans, Robert: 108
Evanston Four: 237
Experimental education: 173–206; Bensalem College, 173–74; Friends World College, 177, 187, 189, 191–93; Goddard College, 179–206; Hampshire College, 174–75; SUNY, 175–76

Faculty union movement: 118–36
Fairhaven College: 177
Federal Bureau of Investigation (FBI): 235
Federal grants. *See* Grants
Fellowships: 11, 315
Feminism and Feminists: 143, 184, 312
Fermi, Enrico: 35, 142
Film and Film industry: 99–115, 249; students of, 108–9, 113–14
Fisher, Peter: 156
Ford Foundation: 11, 29, 55, 72

Fordham University: 143, 173–74
Foundation Center, The: 55
Foundations: 55, 64, 309
Franconia College: 296
Frankfurter, Felix: 208, 223–24
Freud, Sigmund: 262
Friedman, Bruce J.: 164
Friends World College: 177, 187, 189, 191–93

Gainesville Eight: 237
Galbraith, John Kenneth: 35, 72, 142
Gardner, Helen: 39
Gay Activist Alliance: 156
Gay Liberation movement: 155–56
Georgetown University: 298
G.I. Bill of Rights: 107
Glazer, Nathan: 316
Goddard College: 179–206
Goodall, Jane van Lawick: 191
Grades: 175, 177–78
Graduate Record Examination: 76
Graduate schools and graduate programs: 11–12, 85, 92, 117, 177, 189, 328; prestigious, 74–75; sex discrimination in, 315
Graduate students: 31–32, 72–97, 252; employment avenues of, 95–97; financial aid for, 11, 23; statistics on, 92–93; teaching assistants, 72–97, 102, 240, 312. *See also* Doctorate
Grants: 53–59, 64, 111; approval process, 56–57; distribution of, 54–56; federal, 10, 54–56

Haldemann, H. R.: 218
Hampshire College: 174–75
Handlin, Oscar: 170, 316
Hart, Henry: 223
Harvard Business School: 176
Harvard Law School: 207, 209, 216, 223
Harvard University: 14, 54, 73, 74, 86, 131, 167, 187–88, 215, 277, 279, 315
Hayakawa, Margedant Peters: 284, 288–90, 291–92
Hayakawa, Samuel Ichiye: 4, 277–93, 295, 296, 302, 335
Hayden, Tom: 277
Hebert, Tom: 174
Hefner, Hugh: 110
Henle, Robert: 298

Modern Languages Association: 96
Morris, Richard: 145
Morse, Samuel: 35
Mount Holyoke College: 174, 190
Moynihan, Daniel: 35, 142
Museum of Modern Art: 106, 107
Museums: 249, 309
My Lai: 249

National Aeronautics and Space Administration (NASA): 81
National Association for the Advancement of Colored People (NAACP): 291
National Association for the Arts and Humanities: 58
National Book Awards: 137
National Center for Educational Statistics: 311
National Education Association: 125, 128
National Institute of Arts and Letters: 279
National Institutes of Health: 57
National Labor Relations Board: 130
National Science Foundation: 64, 111, 310
New Atlantis: 173
New England Association of Schools: 175
New Republic: 208, 209
New School for Social Research: 107
New York Panthers: 237
New York State legislature: 142; Regents grants, 11
New York State College: 298. *See also* State University of New York (SUNY)
New York Times: 27, 177, 219, 249, 265; Pentagon Papers, 208, 216–17, 232
New York University: 31, 54, 56, 74, 88–92, 106, 109, 147, 149, 190–91, 216; art department, 250–66
Nixon, Richard M.: 218
Nobel Prize: 142
Northwestern University: 74, 109, 216
Notre Dame, College of: 296

Oglesby, Carl: 201
Ohio State University: 54, 74, 134
Oppenheimer, J. Robert: 142
Orangeburg: 277

Otten, Cheryl: 65
Oui: 110
Ovsiew, Leon: 117–26, 131–36, 273

Packard, David: 10–11
Pauling, Linus: 142
Pearce, Anna: 194–97, 199, 201
Pearce, Anthony: 180–206
Peckinpah, Sam: 115
Pennsylvania State University: 135
Pentagon Papers: 208, 216–17, 232
Perez, Joe: 186, 188
Perkins, Anthony: 219
Perkins, James A.: 279
Ph.D. *See* Doctorate
Ph.D. glut: 10
Philadelphia Community College: 125
Philosophy: 2–3, 6, 12, 13
Physics and Physicists: 81–88, 111, 142
Pitt, Ellen: 260–61, 265–66
Playboy: 104, 109–10, 112
Police: 284
Politics of History, The: 233, 238–39
Pop Art: 267
Porter, Don: 257–58, 259–60
Pratt Institute: 259, 266
Price Waterhouse Corporation: 244
Princeton University: 31, 74, 145–49, 152–53, 167–68, 310
Professionalism: 236
Professors: artists as, 249–72; compared to other professionals, 4, 22–24; dissatisfactions of, 4–20; in experimental colleges, 180–206; of law, 111, 207–25; leisure time of, 5, 27–28; life styles of, 101–3, 162–63; mobility of, 8–9; move to college presidencies, 296–97; politics and activism of, 207–25, 227–48; salaries and income of, 2, 7, 16–17, 111–12, 114, 120, 131, 137, 143, 146, 193, 311, 323–24; sex lives of, 152–56; student evaluation of, 53; wives of, 62, 67–68, 69, 81, 82, 84, 93–94, 132, 194–97, 199, 201. *See also* Academic profession
Psychoanalysis: 159–61, 262
Psychologists: 111
Publish or perish: 5–6, 26
Pusey, Nathan: 279, 315

Radcliffe College: 312

341

DATE DUE

AUG 1 4 1981		
OCT 1 4 1981		
DEC 1 0 '82		
GAYLORD		PRINTED IN U.S.A